CLASSICAL MUSIC & RECORDINGS

a primer

∞

by
GERALD BRENNAN

v.9 - 11-2024

DreamStreet Press
Ann Arbor, MI USA
www.DreamStreetPress.com

To my brother,
John McInerney
It was his idea.

TABLE OF CONTENTS

PREFACE

This book is intended as an introduction to the species of Western music which bears the misleading appellation of *Classical Music*. It contains brief summaries of the most important creators in the artform over the past millennium, the forms it uses, as well as a recommendation for a core collection, notes on how to collect and where, how to stay current, and other topics associated with experiencing fully the art of what we have come to call Classical Music. It is not an encyclopedia (nor a music dictionary, which I recommend as an adjunct to this book.); it is a *primer*.

There are, I am sure, errors and unintended omissions. Note that I write 'unintended,' for the *intended* omissions are many indeed. The composer list could have been twice as long without even having to dig for the names. I wished to avoid overwhelming the target reader, who is not an expert, with composers of more obscure achievement or (and especially) of the lower tiers. Likewise, with the recording recommendations. The list I present is a core of a good, curated collection, but only one of countless possible short lists.

That said, there are still likely to be *un*-intended omissions—composers and recordings I ought to have given preference to over what I have included. Also, errors in fact, typos, grammar errors, etc. I wish to hear about it all so that I may make the corrections and additions (and fire my proofreaders) if I see fit. If you wish to assist in this process, or just rail at me for being an idiot for whatever reason, please email me at *maladaptor@protonmail.com*.

So, who do I think I am to have written such a book, anyway, and why should anyone buy it? In my professional life, I have been fortunate to have worked with many lettered and highly-placed music professionals in most aspects of the art but have also noted with dismay that, upon deeper acquaintance, many of them were hubris personified and others as obtuse as a bag of hammers. I have also worked with unlettered geniuses who live and toil in unearned obscurity but who have enriched my life in ways I had never could have envisioned. Success in the many areas of Classical Music is rarely a measure of merit. This isn't baseball. Hence, I have learned to take degrees and even reputations with a grain of salt. A brief summary of myself, regardless, is appended at the end of the book, for what it's worth.

Let the buyer beware!

CR

INTRODUCTION

Classical Music—the State of the Art

Classical Music is in essence a dead art. This statement should in no way be considered in a pejorative sense.

Wait! You may object with something along the lines of, *Philip Glass wrote a bunch of cool symphonies! That's classical music!*

Well, no it isn't. Not yet anyway. If these pieces stand the test of time, if they are still being played and appreciated a century or so from now, then yes—then we may consider them part of repertory of Classical Music.

But right now? Right now, those works are simply *contemporary orchestral* music. Classical Music, as it is presented in this book, embraces a *repertory*. It starts with Gregorian Chant and continues through all the household names and ends before our current century began. Works written after this time, pieces by composer's contemporary with us, have presented us with *candidates for inclusion in the repertory*. Nothing more, nothing less. I have included in this book these composers and their works which I deem to be candidates for inclusion in the near-future repertoire of Classical Music. I shall be wrong about some of them, and I shall have overlooked other worthies.

O my God! They're almost all white men! Yep. Pretty much. This is not a Social Justice Workbook. I shall not rewrite history in order to unearth every trace of non-white non-male nonentity whoever spilled ink on manuscript paper. Classical Music as we know it (and this shall change) is almost exclusively a product of Western Civilization.

Well? Where are all the women? Were their efforts repressed? Absolutely! Is that okay? Absolutely not! But the unarguable result of this (and there may be other factors present) is that there are fewer great women composers in the Western classical canon than you can count on your fingers. Unjust? Probably, *but there is no way to prove this*, and I won't go digging about for mediocrities who don't have penises to satisfy the current mania of *inclusiveness*. The scene is changing, and great talents shall become impossible to repress—sex, color, and country of origin notwithstanding. This is an essential development, but it is *recent*.

* * *

For the last 150 years, folks pretty much believed that classical music began with Bach and ended a generation before their own contemporary composers were terrorizing them with strange and unfamiliar noises. Before that, there was no classical music appreciation as we would understand it today. The notion of people in Beethoven's town, for example, getting all jazzed up about hearing a Vivaldi concert that weekend would have been unthinkable. Most Germans had little familiarity with Antonio Vivaldi—he was Italian for one thing, but mainly he was *dead!* Such worship of the music of the past is a fairly recent phenomenon, but one that has inspired a whole arena of human recreation and formed the foundation of an industry.

Try to define classical music, though, and you'll enter a bewildering realm of opposites that includes music ancient and recently-minted, using traditional instruments or pure electronics, lasting less than a minute or raging on for longer than the age of the universe, in an ambience of soothing consonance or agonized cacophony, with a strong steady beat or none at all, deadly serious or simply hilarious, played by a computer, a human soloist or by 800 performers, in a structure meticulously ordered or completely left to chance.

It doesn't help that the term *classical music* also refers to a specific period (ca.1750-1840) *within* the realm of what we call Classical Music; but that duplication in terms gives a hint about the way classical music has expanded in definition during the last century. We know now that there was indeed life before the Classical era, and in abundance. In fact, music of the Medieval and Renaissance eras represents a healthy share of the classical music market and is no longer just the province of music geeks gathering at Church halls to play homemade recorders and harpsichords.

So, we can say that, in one respect, classical music means old music. John Dowland was the Lennon-McCartney of his day, penning one pop hit after another in 16th century London, but we call this classical music today. Why? Because 400 years later, his songs are still played and recorded. (Sting recently recorded an entire album of Dowland songs. (Stay away.)) Does that mean that 400 years from now Lennon-McCartney songs will be widely considered classical music? I think that's a smart bet. But how about, say, Eminem? Much of the most successful popular music shows its greatness in a different way, burning blinding-bright for a few years and then disappearing, but not before it affects millions of people in a glorious burst of enthusiasm. In this regard, much of what we call classical music has never burned as brightly, but the flame has been steady and the best of it, even after almost a millennium, is burning still.

In another way, classical music implies a set of formats, like the symphony, the concerto, the string quartet, and opera, to name a few. But just because these formats are still in use today does not make recent sojourns into these forms 'classical music.' They'll have to prove themselves in the arena of time, of longevity. Instant acceptance into the repertory is very rare.

These traditional formats have been stretched and mutated through time almost beyond recognition, but the ideas they represent are so compelling that their essence persists after many centuries. Consider the symphony—all the tribes gathering to sing together as one; or the concerto—the drama of the individual, by turns singing with and pitted against the group. In mathematics it takes a minimum of four points to define what we perceive as *space*, and this is the quintessence of the oddly compelling 'rightness' and perfect economy of the string quartet. Opera is obvious: an entire fabulous, singing universe that stands in stark contrast to the mundane one we all share. These forms can't die because they are *archetypes*, essential organic expressions of what it means to be human in the realm of sonic expression.

So, if classical music is old music that is still in circulation, then why does this book include some music written in the past century? Because these works consciously connect with the traditions of established classical music and some may prove to be contenders for lasting greatness within this tradition. I'm guessing, see?

The unique thing about the 'classical music' contenders and pretenders of the present day is that it the art has been fractured into so many styles, schools, and techniques that no one of these can be said to define the times. Will one hold sway to define the near-future or is the idea of a 'dominant school' at an end? Anyone can guess, but nobody knows.

The Modern and Contemporary music under discussion can always point backwards through time to established classical traditions, not only to justify itself as 'classical,' but to make its appearance seem inevitable. Even John Cage's infamous *4'33"*, a three-movement piece made of nothing but silence with no intentional sounds at all, can point to the progressively brief and sparse scores of Anton Webern, and even to the five minutes of silence that Gustav Mahler insists upon (but which he never gets) between the first two movements of his *Second Symphony*, as precedent.

Classical music evolves. That's why in this book you'll find establishment favs like Palestrina and Schubert, alongside candidates like Brian Eno and Pete Townsend. Eno, because he pretty much invented the idea of Ambient Music, which, in addition to having become a thriving genre on its own, has had a heavy influence on the Minimalist movement and the Contemporary spiritualists like Arvo Pärt and John Tavener. Pete Townsend is mentioned here because *Tommy* is not only amazing face-melting rock 'n' roll, but a full-fledged opera that changed the way we think about what an opera can be. What an achievement!

Opera is a world within the world of classical music that seems to summon the deepest passions of listeners and collectors. Some people, literally, live for it. In a way, it is the apotheosis of the art because it creates a world of divine singing, beautiful music, intense drama, great literature, seductive lighting, breathtaking dress and scenery, innovative directing, sensitive conducting, and convincing acting. That's the idea, anyway. When it succeeds, it is the stuff of legends; also fistfights, stinging invective, and endless argument. Nothing in the entire world of music has roused more antagonism and rapture than the subject of opera singers. They are the divas; the Western world hails them throughout as goddesses, and their male counterparts as idols of legend. Princes and princesses bow to *them*.

This book is not a book about opera. We will for now consider opera only in passing rather than in detail, as a separate realm of achievement and appreciation. There are many worthy volumes available to feed the curiosity of those who will feel the pull toward that specific planet.

One of the things that has kept classical music (so far) from becoming a stagnant museum, or worse, a morgue, is that each generation re-interprets the classics to suit itself. Fortunately, composers are limited in how much detail of their conversation with the muses they can relate, because in order to preserve and communicate it, they must write it down in a score using a small set of symbols. It's amazing how different two distinct performances of the same work can sound without breaking the letter of the law. A few controversial performers even manage to play fast and loose with the letter but bring forth so much of the genuine spirit of a work that no one gets too upset, not even the composer; some of these scofflaws are highly celebrated.

It's not just the greatest music that has lasted for generations; the greatest performances live on as well. Listen and discover for yourself why Arturo Toscanini's legendary version of Beethoven's *Missa Solemnis* has not been out of print for more than 80 years. Did you know that there are eight different recordings still available of Wilhelm Furtwängler conducting Beethoven's *Ninth Symphony*, and each one is compelling in a different way? Is your favorite pianist doing justice to that Rachmaninov piano concerto? Well, you can always listen to Sergei Rachmaninov play them and then judge for yourself. But are composers the best interpreters of their music? Many debates here. (I'm lookin' at *you*, Stravinsky.) You can hear Béla Bartók, Sergei Prokofiev, and Dmitri Shostakovich play their own pieces, or hear Edward Elgar conduct his symphonies and cello concerto. You won't get state-of-the-art sound quality, but what you do get dwarfs the sonic shortcomings.

Today, we can't even imagine a world without recorded music. But even a century ago, music lovers who wanted to hear great concert music would have had to save up their coins not just for the price of a concert ticket, but for the journey to the big city. The home stereo was the piano, where brother and sister could play four-hand reductions of the newest symphonies. Though the sounds they made were pale in comparison to the concert hall experience, the level of amateur musicianship was much higher in those days, with a larger percentage of people taking part. Until very recently in human evolution, to have music in one's home meant that family members had to be musically creative, or at least re-creative. These days we push a button or click a mouse and believe that we are hearing music. What we have lost in this bargain is incalculable.

It's important to listen to *live music,* lest you run a dire and insidious risk of losing your reference to the real thing. In much popular music, take rock 'n' roll as an example, the album is the *original.* Classical music presents a stark contrast: the written score of the work is the original, the performance is the acoustical realization, and the recording is an electronic *copy.*

The technology that has given us our cherished recordings has also produced the inescapable sea of electronic sounds that saturates our living space, in restaurants, stores, elevators, from television and car radios. Combined with the high ambient noise levels of our environment, the sum of this cacophony has subtly and progressively eroded our sensibilities to the extent that most of us accept automatically the seductive buzzings of a loudspeaker as a perfect proxy for the magical acoustic presence of real instruments and voices.

No one conflates a photo of a landscape with an actual landscape, but virtually everyone in our era thinks of a recording of music as actual music. Listeners should bear in mind that a recording of a terrific performance, deeply satisfying and thrilling as so many are, is just that—an electronic reproduction. There's nothing like being caught up in the spell of a magnificent live musical event. It is, in the most authentic sense, magic.

But without great recordings, we are lost. No one is wealthy, long-lived, or idle enough to hear even a tiny fraction of the world's best music in a live setting, and even such a one would encounter but a few of the geniuses who turn the printed page into music. Illustrious performers of the past would be forever unknown, and most of the repertory one would hear would be whatever pieces are in vogue or easy to play with a minimum of rehearsals. This is clearly not acceptable. Here lies the value of recordings.

Along with the change in perception of what classical music has become, there are periodic changes in the industry, how the music is recorded and distributed. These changes transform the art in ways revolutionary and, sometimes, unforeseen.

About 70 years ago the standard repertory (as it was conceived at the time) had been recorded and re-recorded by conductors and instrumentalists of every imaginable temperament; something for everyone was available on monophonic LP records. Stereophonic sound came along and lent depth and spatial realism to recordings. You could now hear the first violins on the left, the cellos on the right, and pinpoint the brass and winds in the soundscape that was created. This re-energizing the industry, and all the music was re-recorded in the new format with most collectors hopping aboard the stereo bandwagon. But after a few years, a saturation of the market occurred, and the classical record industry began to flag. Then something happened that rocked the world of classical music, the effects of which are still ringing to this day.

Call it the 'original instrument' phenomenon, the 'authenticity movement,' or even 'the attack of the scholar zombies.' Whatever we call it, the phenomenon saved the industry's bacon and drastically changed our approach to classical music. The idea was this: music written before the Romantic era (and this includes Vivaldi, Bach, Haydn, Mozart, even Beethoven) was played on instruments that were of a different design from the ones we use today and were played using different techniques. (The only instrument that has not changed since Beethoven's time is the trombone.)

Also subject to re-examination were issues of tempo, phrasing, ornamentation, improvisation, ensemble size—in a word, *everything* was reassessed in the light of how the *composer* would have expected to hear his (rarely her) music. The result was akin to cleaning the dirty varnish on a Rembrandt painting (that smoky darkness was once considered part of his style) and discovering the dazzling play of colors underneath. This new craze expanded the core repertory to include composers, countries and entire centuries marginalized since the days of the gramophone, like the celebrated masters of the French Baroque, Jean Philippe Rameau and François Couperin, who could finally be heard in the splendor of their true colors. And the French need their true colors more than anyone.

As collectors were replacing their Baroque and Classical records with newer and more authentic performances, along came the CD, and most of us rebuilt our collections (often reluctantly, for CDs were about convenience, not high-fidelity) in the new digital format.

An essential issue rarely raised in the discussion of classical music recordings is that our idea of what comprises 'the standard repertory' largely corresponds to what the major recording companies had offered us over the decades. Though the tide is turning, the major recording companies' play-it-safe approach to the classics has conditioned most listeners to believe that a statistically minuscule collection of compositions is what the classics are all about. The aficionado understands that this is not the case.

I had a unique professional perspective on this subject when I served as Director of Content of Classical Music at the (now defunct) *All Music Guide*, the world's largest repository of recording data and editorial content about composers, their music, and the performers who bring it to life. One of our tasks was to maintain the database of every composer's works and their recordings, and we were shocked by how much first-rate music by the master composers is unrecorded, music that even the most rabid connoisseur has never even had a chance to experience.

Few music lovers can cite a Classical-era composer besides Haydnmozartbeethoven. Is that because there were only three from that era who wrote decent music? Of course not, but that's how we've been conditioned. (Try the recording by Concerto Köln of symphonies by Johann Wilhelm Wilms for a refreshing experience outside the box.) The same tunnel-vision is in evidence for the Medieval, Renaissance, Baroque, Romantic, Modern, and Contemporary era composers—and we're talking about masters of these periods, not duffers. We estimated that fully 30-percent of the music of Joseph Haydn remains unrecorded. Other than J.S. Bach, there are few major Baroque composers whose repertory has been comprehensively recorded.

Consider the masters Francesco Landini and Luciano Berio, composers of high rank born 500 years apart. Not only are almost all the works of both composers unavailable, but many await their first recording. Likewise, with Orlando Lassus, who was among the best of his age—a colossus—yet only a fraction of his output is available to consumers, or ever was, for that matter.

This sort of vocal and chamber music, ancient and modern, doesn't require a unionized 150-piece orchestra and jet-set time-beater under contract to a major record company, to make its point. These projects need good, specialized ensembles and a modest production setup. Add a couple of people with some business sense and website skills, marketing directly to the consumer via digital download, streaming, mail-order or in alliance with a good distributor.

9

On such a small scale it has become possible (admittedly, barely so) to compensate musicians decently and still have enough money left over to pay the low overhead of a small company and make it worth the proprietors' while. This development has ushered forth a fresh age of music appreciation, wider and deeper than anything that has come before. It has also put a major cramp in the domination of the big record labels of the past, and that is a good thing. They had way too much power. Still do.

Now it's all about digital streaming services. Most classical listeners are, at this writing (2024) reluctant to climb aboard that train just yet. Pop music still shapes that industry as far as how these services are designed to work (song-based as opposed to multi-movement works), and classical listeners are not wild about the compression that is applied to most streaming music. Up to 90% of the signal is removed, leaving the most audible 10% to reach your ears. The kids don't care; the grown ups have issues. So classical listeners still buy lots of CDs and LPs.

However the music comes to us, and whatever format it comes in, one thing is for certain—the best of it will abide and the passion to obtain reproductions of it will not subside (which reminds me of an old friend who went without lunches for two weeks, so he could afford Georg Solti's recording of Richard Wagner's *Ring* cycle).

As you become familiar with the art, you'll encounter stories behind-the-scenes that will enrich your experience immensely, pulling the great composers and performers off their pedestals and into real life. (These are not always pleasant discoveries. Many of these people were monsters.)

Listen to Bach's *Well-Tempered Clavier* and see if you can figure why Vladimir Ashkenazy told me that he would never play it publicly, only to change his mind and record it five years later. Christopher Parkening told me that when he was a boy, the guitar teacher at the corner music store rejected him as a student, assuring his mother that he would likely never amount to much but suggesting they visit a Spanish family who had moved into the neighborhood and were looking for students. That family was The Romeros, known eventually through their concerts and many fine recordings as 'the first family of the guitar.' History has been kind to Parkening and The Romeros, but not the music teacher. And speaking of teachers, Artur Schnabel's told him, "You will never be a pianist. You are a *musician*." Listen for yourself and find out what the difference is, for the distinction is essential, even mind-blowing.

There remains music through ages past that is simply too good to disappear and has *proved* it; music that has gone through the fires of time and changing tastes and is still available to experience. There is much fine music that has been unjustly forgotten, but there is no music that has lasted for centuries that has been unjustly remembered. If you're new to this world, come and take your first steps here, and find a path through the weeds and brambles for a journey that may last a lifetime.

Gerald Brennan
2024
Ann Arbor, Michigan. USA

CR

ERAS & INSTRUMENTS

Music in the Western world, as a learned discipline, begins about 750 A.D. Of course, the Greeks and Romans had their music (everyone does) but so little of that survived as to be almost useless, and in any case, what we now recognize as art music in the West has little discernable connection with those earlier eras.

We usually cut the timeline up as below, with variations depending upon the surgeon. The more you know and the closer you examine it the less sense it makes—the overlap is huge, and subdivisions are endless. But from the 30,000 foot view it rather looks like this:

- Gothic (or Middle Ages)—750-1430
- Renaissance—1430-1600
- Baroque—1600-1750
- Classical—1750-1840
- Romantic—1840-1900
- Modern—1900-1950
- Post-Modern—1950-yesterday
- Contemporary—that means 'now'

Here follows a brief description of what these eras were all about.

Gothic (or Middle Ages)

Gregorian Chant is hotly debated as to origin and stages of development, but a good guess is that it was developed around 750 from a synthesis of Roman and Gallican chants. Because the Church required it, a standard for musical notation popped up about 1100 that allowed music to be written out and preserved. (Thank you, **Guido of Arezzo.**) Monks wrote the chants (not Pope/Saint Gregory). The more passionate devotees of the art will claim that they did not so much invent the music as *discover* it, so natural and inevitable is the flow from the words and the meaning.

These monks were anonymous. We forget that the idea of individualization, as precious and fetishized as it is today, is a relatively recent development in human evolution. Back in the day, painters did not sign their work; composers did not credit themselves with what passed through them. It didn't really occur to them. That's almost impossible to imagine today. It wasn't until the 15th century or so that individualization was in common force.

Though many famed traveling poets, singers and musicians roamed the lands, it was not until 1098 that a composer was born who had not only greatness, but many documented works of music signed in her hand. That's right, *her*. The first composer whose written music we possess and who has a name attached is a woman, the great **Hildegard of Bingen**. Read more about her in the composer section.

Chant is a single vocal line with no accompaniment, sung solo but more usually in chorus. Eventually, a second vocal line was added. This is called *organum*. It started very simply, often the second voice simply followed the main voice at a set distance singing the same notes, like a *Row, Row, Row Your Boat* round. This eventually developed into an independent second voice, so we have the beginning of true harmony. Then a third voice was added. The *motet* was born.

Also, in this period we find the development of courtly secular music. Minstrels and troubadours were entertaining royalty (and seducing their girlfriends).

Commonly Used Medieval Instruments:
Strings:
Lute

A lute is any plucked string instrument with a neck and a deep round back enclosing a hollow cavity, usually with a sound hole or opening in the body.

It may be either fretted or unfretted. The lute itself was introduced into Europe by the Moors when they invaded Spain in the 8th-century, and its popularity received a boost when the Crusades began to increase Arabic contact about 1100. The name derives from the Arabic word *ud*. Medieval lutes are shown with four or five courses, or pairs of strings, about half the number of later Renaissance lutes. The main difference from the Renaissance lute, however, is that the Medieval variety was played using a quill plectrum on a single line of music. Not a single lute survives from Medieval Europe, but the instrument is depicted in many illustrations, paintings, drawings and sculptures from the period.

Gittern

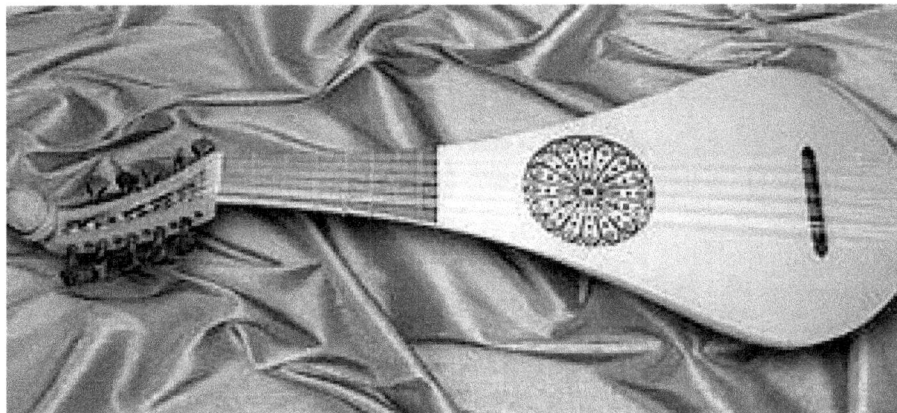

The gittern was one of the most important plucked fingerboard instruments of the late Medieval period. Loved by all levels of society, it was played by royal appointment, in religious service, in taverns, for singing, for dancing, and in duets with the lute. The gittern is a true ancestor of the modern guitar, had four strings and was plucked with a pick. There's only one gittern that has survived, and it has a flat body and the neck and pegbox were carved from one solid block of wood—easier and cheaper to make than a lute. The gittern was smaller and pitch higher than the lute. While they may look quite similar, the gittern and lute are distinguishable in three ways: The backs of lutes are made of several ribs glued together, with a separate neck, whereas the bowl of the whole gittern, including the neck, is carved from a solid piece of wood; The strings on a lute are attached to the bridge, which is glued to the soundboard, whereas gittern strings are usually attached to hitch pins on the edge of the instrument and pass across a bridge that was probably floating instead of glued but kept in place by the pressure of the strings. The pegbox of a lute

15

bends back from the neck at a sharp angle, whereas the gittern pegbox is a curving sickle shape. The gittern was popular into the last third of the 15th century.

Harp

The harp is an ancient instrument dating back to the Sumerian civilization and perhaps long before. In the Middle Ages, it seems to have been strung with gut, except in Ireland where metal strings, likely brass, were used from an early date. The size of the harp as well as the number of strings varied a lot, with a tendency towards increased numbers and size as the centuries wore on. By the 14th-century there were sometimes as many as 25 strings. Around 1400 the harp acquired a more slender shape and also a series of little elbow-shaped pegs called 'bray pins' which touched the strings as they emerged from the sound-box, causing a nasal buzzing sound as the strings were plucked. This was helpful in projecting the sound, since the sound-box of the gothic harp was small and made of hardwood, and thus did not have the natural resonance of larger spruce-bellied instruments.

Vielle, or fidel

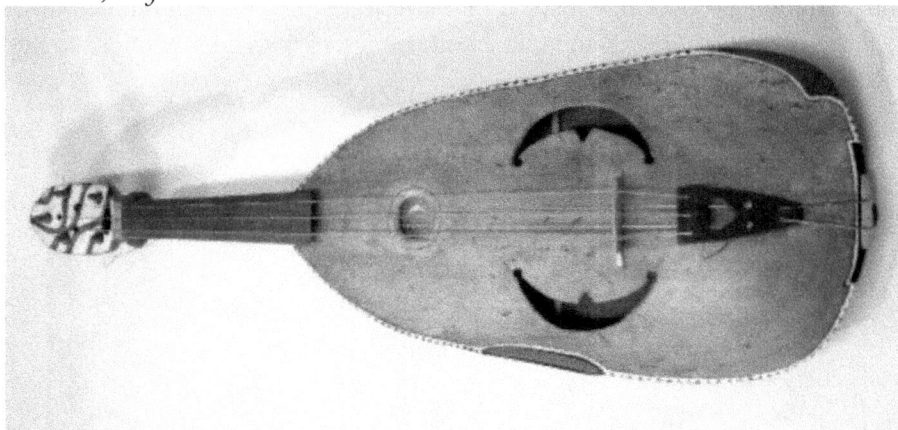

The vielle is a bowed stringed instrument, similar to a violin but with a longer and deeper body, three to five gut strings, and a leaf-shaped pegbox with frontal tuning pegs, sometimes with a figure-8 shaped body. Whatever external form they had, the soundbox consisted of back and belly joined by ribs, which experience has shown to be the construction for bowed instruments. The most common shape given to the earliest vielles in France was an oval, which with its modifications remained in favor until the Italians came up with the familiar violin shape which showed itself superior in playability. It was one of the most popular instruments of the Medieval period and was used by troubadours and jongleurs from the 13th through the 15th centuries.

Citole

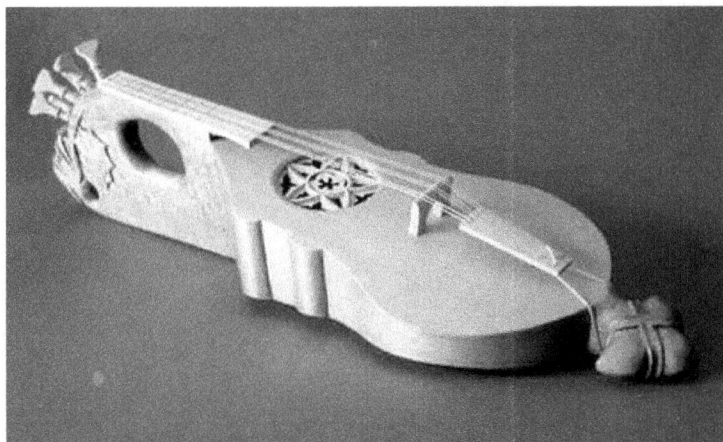

17

The citole was a string instrument, often paired with the vielle and used from around 1200–1350. Like the modern guitar, it was manipulated at the neck to get different notes and picked or strummed with a long, thick, straight pick likely made of ivory or wood.

Rebec

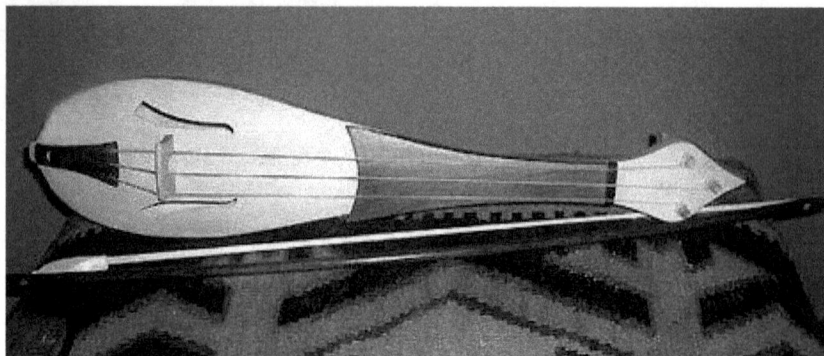

The rebec is a bowed stringed instrument used in the Medieval era through the early Renaissance. In its most common form, it has a narrow boat-shaped body and 1-5 strings. Played on the arm or under the chin, the technique and tuning may have influenced the development of the violin. Popular from the 13th to 16th centuries, the introduction of the rebec into Western Europe coincided with the Arabic conquest of the Iberian Peninsula. In time, the viol came to replace the rebec, and the instrument was little used beyond the Renaissance period.

Hammered Dulcimer

The hammered dulcimer originated in the Middle East about 900 A.D and is related to the much older psaltery (smaller instrument in which the strings are plucked). From there it spread across North Africa and then Europe. The hammered dulcimer is played with small mallets (hammers) made of a hardwood to strike the strings. One side of the hammer is left as exposed wood while the opposite side might be covered in a felt for a softer sound.

Winds:
Medieval Flute

By the 14th century, the flute began to appear all over Europe. These instruments were extremely simple in construction, consisting of a cylindrical tube held horizontally with a cork stopper in one end, a blow hole and six finger holes. Their range was limited, so they were made in a family of different sizes, all very non-standardized at the time.

Recorder

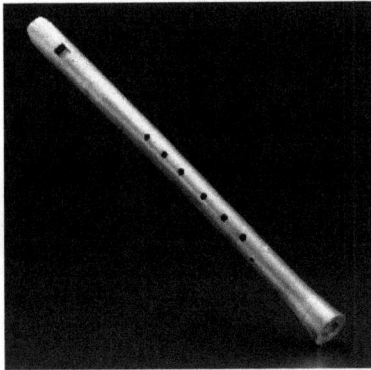

The recorder is popular woodwind instrument with a whistle mouthpiece, held horizontally with a thumb-hole for the upper hand and seven finger-holes: three for the upper hand and four for the lower. Recorders are made in different sizes with names and compasses roughly corresponding to different vocal ranges, soprano, alto, tenor, and bass. They are are traditionally constructed from wood and ivory, while most recorders mass-produced in recent years are constructed from molded plastic. The bore is generally reverse conical (i.e. tapering towards the foot) to cylindrical. The sound is often described as clear and sweet. It is notable for its quick response and its corresponding ability to produce a wide variety of articulations. This ability, coupled with its open finger holes, allow it to produce a many tone colors and special effects.

Shawm

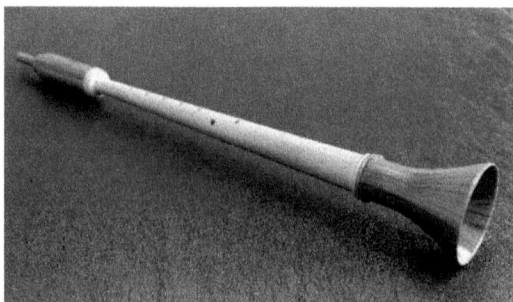

The shawm is a conical bore, double-reed woodwind used from the 12th century to the present day. A conical bore instrument is one in which the bore diameter gradually increases throughout the length of the tubing. It achieved its peak of popularity during the Medieval and Renaissance periods, after which it was gradually eclipsed by the oboe family. The body of the shawm is usually turned from a single piece of wood and terminates in a flared bell somewhat like that of a trumpet.

Bagpipes

Bagpipes are a woodwind instrument using enclosed reeds fed from a reservoir of air from a bag. We know best the Scottish Great Highland bagpipes, but people have played bagpipes for centuries around the globe. A set of bagpipes minimally consists of an air supply (a bag), a chanter on which the notes are fingered, and usually at least one drone. Many bagpipes have more than one drone and chanter,

Brass:
Medieval Trumpet

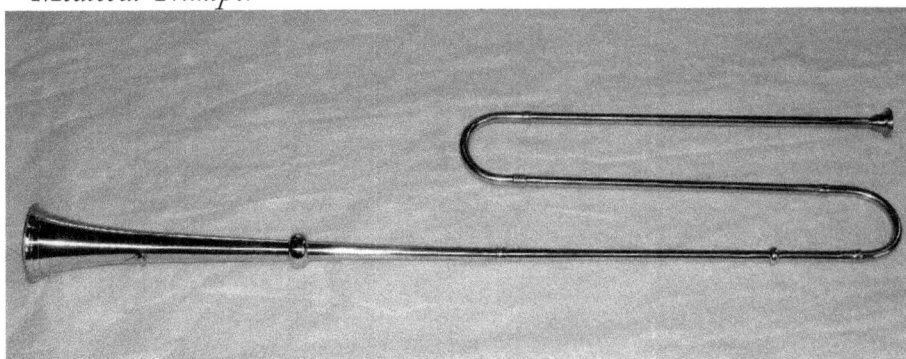

Trumpets were just beginning to be used for music at the end of the Medieval age. Originally used in military signaling, a few structural changes were made to them to make them useful in a musical setting. No Medieval trumpets had valves or keys, giving these instruments a limited ability to change notes. In order to play different notes on this type of instrument, trumpeters would adjust their embouchure, tightening the lips to produce higher notes and loosening them to produce lower ones. Not all notes can be made through the use of embouchure alone so Medieval trumpets were only able to play a series of harmonic overtones rather than the full chromatic scale that modern trumpets are able to play. In their simplest form, Medieval trumpets were shaped like long tubes with a wide end, called a bell, and a mouthpiece that could cover the player's lips. These tubes were made out of metal sheets which were rolled into a cylindrical shape. These simple Medieval trumpets could be anywhere from one foot long to longer than ten feet. Long trumpets needed to be balanced on stands or carried by many people when they were played, so these were less common. Medieval trumpets were also often made into a coil. Coiling the tubing made it possible for longer, and thus lower pitched, trumpets to be easily held by one person. This change in the shape does not affect the sound. Once these instruments were adopted for musical use, it became necessary for the player to be able to change the trumpet's key so that it could be used in different songs. Some Medieval trumpets were made with removable tubing, or crooks, which could be traded with other pieces that were longer or shorter.

Keyboard:
Organ

For a good background, see the section on *Organs*.

Percussion:
Drums and Cymbals of several varieties were played, and the Tambourine was popular.

Renaissance

The Renaissance period was an explosion of learning and of the arts across the board. Throughout Europe there were new schools of thought and less slavery to the Church, though it was still quite influential. What the Church lost the courts gained, and the secular needs of the Royal Courts were as important as those of the Church in sponsoring new composers and musicians. So, alongside the Mass and motets, there were now *madrigals* in many vocal parts, some with instrumental accompaniment, setting secular verse to music, as well as several instrumental dance forms. In this era was born the miraculous printing press which allowed mass production (such as it was) of musical texts and theory books. The earliest example of press-printed music, a set of liturgical chants, dates from about 1465, shortly after the Gutenberg Bible was printed.

The Renaissance saw the arrival of modes similar to the modern major and minor scales that we use today, and an expansion of tonal harmony. The melodies are smoother and more charming, less austere than in the past. The instruments in use during this time included the lute, viol, harp and virginal, organ, recorder, oboe and crumhorn. (See the *Glossary* for definitions.)

Commonly Used Renaissance Instruments:
Strings:
Violin family

The modern four-string violin is generally considered to have originated about 1550 in northern Italy. The earliest violins incorporated features of existing bowed instruments: the rebec, the Renaissance fiddle, and the lira da braccio. The pear-shaped rebec had strings that were tuned in fifths, and this system was adopted for the violin. The shape of the violin was taken from the fiddle and the lira da braccio, as these larger instruments produced a bigger sound, and the hourglass shape made bowing easier. The violin was initially used for vocal and dance accompaniment, while its cousin, the viola da gamba, remained the preferred bowed string instrument for ensembles. The Renaissance viola, a slightly larger instrument also was used, but there was yet little standardization among the sizing. The Renaissance cello was also employed (sometimes called the Bass Violin, or the Violone). This cello was not a descendant of the Viola da Gamba, but simply a larger member of the violin family that needed to be played between the legs due to its necessary size. The Renaissance string bass also existed but the divide between the Cello (Bass Violin) and the Bass was unclear due to so much size variation and almost no standardization.

Viol Family

The other big family of strings that was often employed in this age is the family of Viols.

Viola da gamba ('viol of the leg')

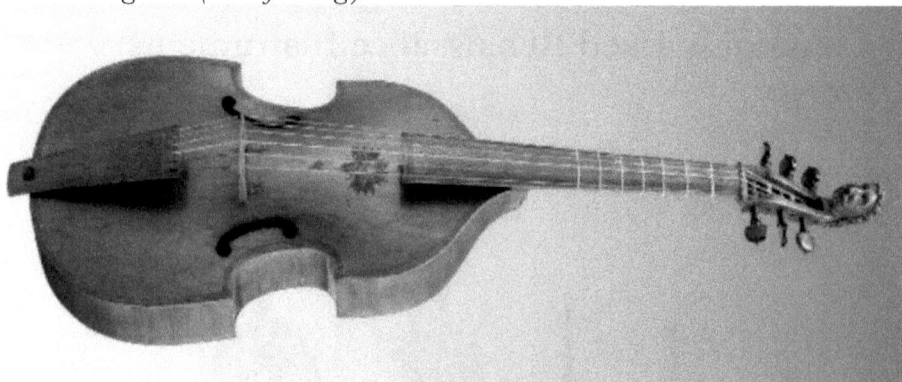

The viola da gamba, which was held and played with a bow vertically, like a cello, and came in several sizes besides the three standard sizes—treble, tenor, and bass. Unlike the cello, the neck is fretted. The viols have a subdued, mellow tone. The blending of harmonies, intricate rhythms and tone quality of a viol ensemble can be most appreciated in a small space.

As the popularity of the violin with a larger sound and the capabilities of being heard in the concert halls, grew throughout the 17th century and the viol could no longer compete. New repertoire, namely the solo concerto, laid the groundwork for the birth of the virtuoso violin soloist.

Lira da braccio (lyre for the arm)

The lira da braccio was also a bowed string instrument. It was used by Italian poet-musicians in court in the 15th and 16th centuries to accompany their improvised recitations of lyric and narrative poetry. Generally, it had seven strings, five of them tuned like a violin with a lower string added to the bottom, with two strings off the fingerboard that served as drones and were usually tuned in octaves. Amongst its exponents at the time were several great painters, notably Leonardo da Vinci, who was widely held to be the leading figure among performers upon the Lira.

Lute

The lute is used in a great variety of instrumental music from the Medieval to the late Baroque eras and became the most important instrument for secular music in the Renaissance. After the Medieval era, lutenists gradually abandoned the quill in favor of plucking the instrument with the fingertips. The number of courses grew to six. This lute design continued to evolve during the Renaissance, during which more strings were added, changes to the width of the neck to accommodate these additional courses were made, and the lute began to be constructed in a wider range of more standardized sizes. The lute was the premier solo instrument of the 16th century but continued to accompany singers as well.

Harp

During the middle of the 14th to 16th century, Gothic harps appeared. This was a relatively tall instrument compared to earlier harps and is the ancestor of the later Renaissance harp. Still small and light by modern standards, the Gothic style Harp was the standard harp throughout Europe through the Renaissance period. They were strung with gut strings at a much lower tension than we are accustomed to today. Earlier models had 19 to 22 strings, later harps known as early Renaissance harps were larger and had 26 to 30 strings. They were tuned diatonically with the soundbox generally hollowed from a plank of hardwood (not as resonant as the later spruce body), giving the harp a distinctive plucked sound to complement the lute. By the late Renaissance, a number of variations on the harp theme were in use, because the single-course Renaissance harp remained only capable of playing seven notes per octave or the diatonic scale (the white notes on a piano). The major composers of the 16th to 18th centuries demanded all 12 chromatic notes of the scale (white and black notes on the piano). One solution was a chromatic harp, a harp with 12 strings per octave. It was a cumbersome design.

Cittern

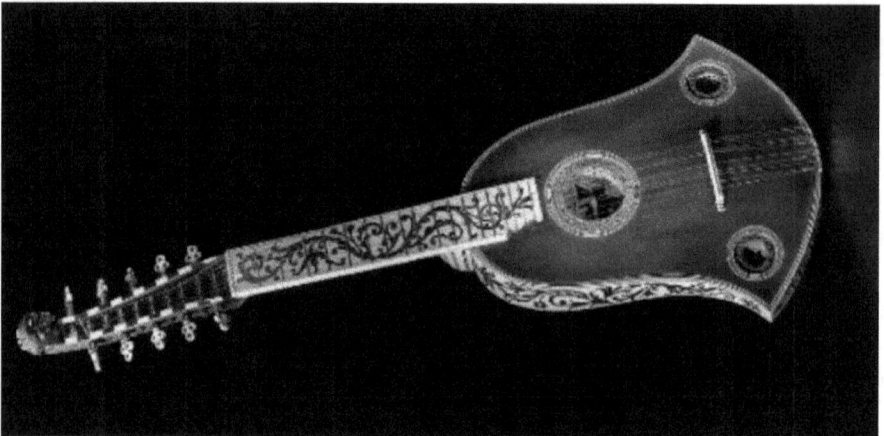

The cittern is one of the few metal-strung instruments known from the Renaissance period. It generally has four courses (single, pairs or threes) of strings, one or more courses being usually tuned in octaves, though instruments with more or fewer courses were made. Its flat-back design was simpler

26

and cheaper to construct than the lute. It was also easier to play, smaller, less delicate and more portable. Played by all classes, the cittern was a premier instrument of casual music-making much as is the guitar today.

Hurdy-gurdy

The Renaissance Hurdy-gurdy developed from the Medieval Organistrum – a larger and more primitive form of the Hurdy Gurdy. In the Hurdy-gurdy the strings are sounded by a wheel which the strings pass over. Its functionality can be compared to that of a mechanical violin, in that its bow (wheel) is turned by a crank. Its distinctive sound is mainly because of its 'drone strings' which provide a constant pitch similar in their sound to that of bagpipes. During the Renaissance, the hurdy-gurdy was very popular, and the characteristic form had a short neck and a boxy body with a curved tail end.

Woodwinds:

Cornamuse

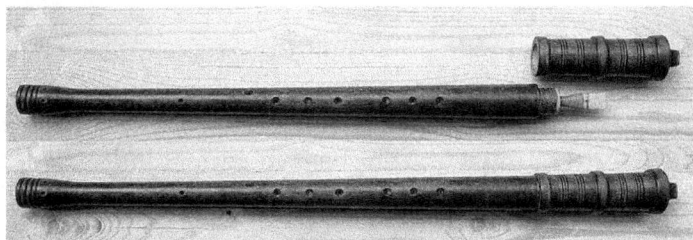

Similarly to most instruments of the 16th century, the cornamuse was produced in a family of several sizes: soprano, alto, tenor, bass, and subbass. It

27

has a characteristic, growling timbre. A double reed is closed in a special mouthpiece so that the reed is not put into the musician's mouth directly. The fingering is similar to the recorder. Cornamusen are made of sycamore wood, keys and rings are made of brass. The instrument was best associated with the royal court, with ceremonial occasions and religious worship.

Crumhorn

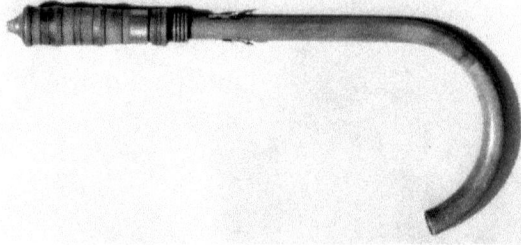

The Crumhorn is also a capped reed instrument. Its construction is similar to that of the chanter of a bagpipe. Like its mates, a double reed is mounted inside a long windcap. Blowing through a slot in the windcap produces a musical note. The pitch of the note can be varied by opening or closing finger holes along the length of the pipe. One unusual feature of the crumhorn is its shape; the end is bent upwards in a curve, which is decorative only and does not influence the sound. Crumhorns make a strong buzzing sound, but quieter than their conical-bore relatives the Rauschpfeife and shawm. They have a limited range, usually a ninth.

Rauschpfeife or Schreierpfeife

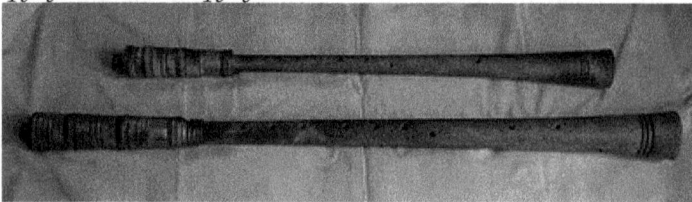

Rauschpfeife is a commonly used term for a specific type of capped conical reed musical instrument of the woodwind family, used in Europe in the 16th and 17th centuries. In common with the crumhorn and cornamuse, it is a wooden double-reed instrument with the reed enclosed in a windcap so that the reed is not put into the musician's mouth directly. The player blows into a slot in the top of the windcap to produce the sound. Rauschpfeifes differ from cornamusen mainly in the shape of the bore, which, like the shawm, is conical. This bore profile combined with the unrestricted vibration of the reed within

28

the windcap produced an instrument that was very unavoidably loud, which made it most useful for outdoor performances.

Shawm family

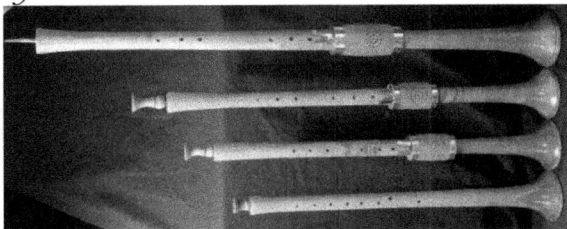

Beginning in the 16th century, shawms were made in several sizes, from sopranino to great bass, and four and five-part music could be played by a consort consisting entirely of shawms. All later shawms (excepting the smallest) have at least one key allowing a downward extension of the compass; the keywork is typically covered by a perforated wooden cover called the fontanelle. The double reed is inserted directly into a socket at the top of the instrument, or in the larger types, on the end of a metal tube called the bocal. The pirouette, a small wooden attachment with a cavity in the center resembling a thimble, surrounds the lower part of the reed—this provides support for the lips and embouchure. Since only a short portion of the reed protrudes past the pirouette, the player has only limited contact with the reed, and therefore limited control of dynamics. The shawm's conical bore and flaring bell, combined with the style of playing dictated by the use of a pirouette, gives the instrument a piercing, trumpet-like sound, well-suited for outdoor performances.

Renaissance Recorder Family

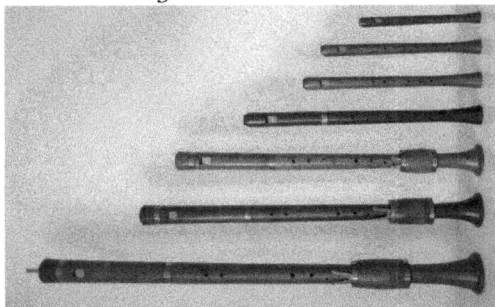

During the Renaissance, the recorder became a mainstream instrument. A quartet comprising bass, tenor and alto recorders was a common ensemble.

Masters such **Byrd** and **Palestrina** produced exquisite consort music, which adapts very well to recorder groups.

Dulcian

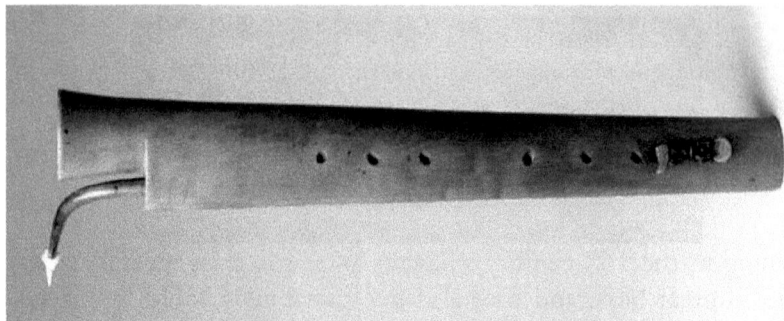

The dulcian is a woodwind instrument, with a double reed and a folded conical bore. The predecessor of the modern bassoon, it flourished between 1550 and 1700. Towards the end of this period it co-existed with, and was then superseded by, the baroque bassoon. It was played in both secular and sacred contexts. The dulcian is generally made from a single piece of maple. The reed is attached to the end of a metal bocal, inserted into the top of the small bore. Unlike the bassoon it normally has a flared bell, sometimes made from a separate piece of timber. This bell can sometimes be muted, the mute being either detachable, or built into the instrument. The outside of the in-strument can also be covered in leather, like the cornett. Although the bass is the most common size, the dulcian comes also came in contrabass, bass, tenor, alto and soprano sizes. The range of each instrument is two and a half octaves. The dulcian is a flexible instrument, capable of being loud enough to play in outdoor bands, quiet enough for chamber music, and expressive enough to join in with the choir.

Brasses:

Trumpet

It wasn't until the end of the Middle Ages that players began thinking of the trumpet as something with which to make music rather than military use in signaling. At the time, trumpeters had a limited vocabulary, because the horns of the age were limited to one primary tone and that tone's related har-monic series. To change keys, the player had to select a different trumpet. More about the natural trumpet in its Baroque heyday in the next section.

Slide trumpet

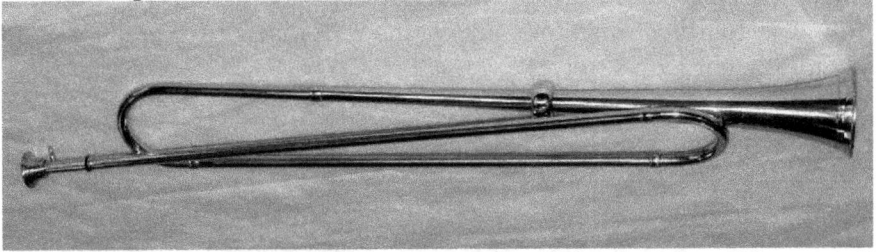

The slide trumpet is a type of trumpet that is fitted with a slide much like a trombone. Eventually, the slide trumpet evolved into the sackbut, which evolved into the modern-day trombone.

Cornett

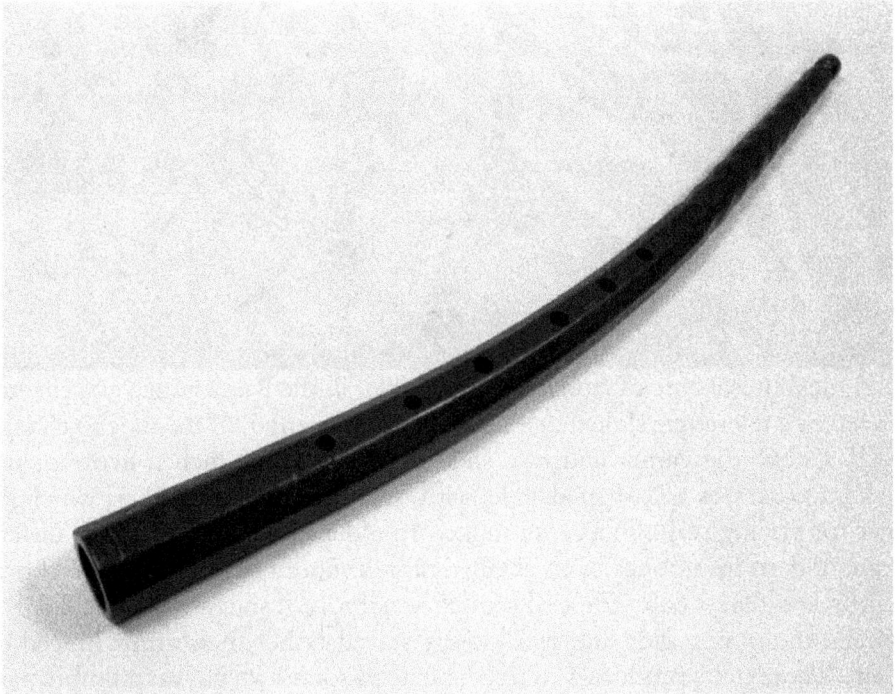

Historically, two cornetts were frequently used in consort with three sackbuts, often to double a church choir. The cornett was, like almost all Renaissance and Baroque instruments, made in a complete family; the different sizes being the high cornettino, the cornett (or curved cornett), the tenor cornett (or lizard) and the rare bass cornett. The serpent largely supplanted the bass cornett in the 17th century. Other versions include the mute cornett, which is a straight narrow-bore instrument with integrated mouthpiece, quiet enough to be used in a consort of viols or even recorders. The cornett was also used as a virtuoso solo instrument, and a relatively large amount of solo music for the cornetto survives.

Sackbut

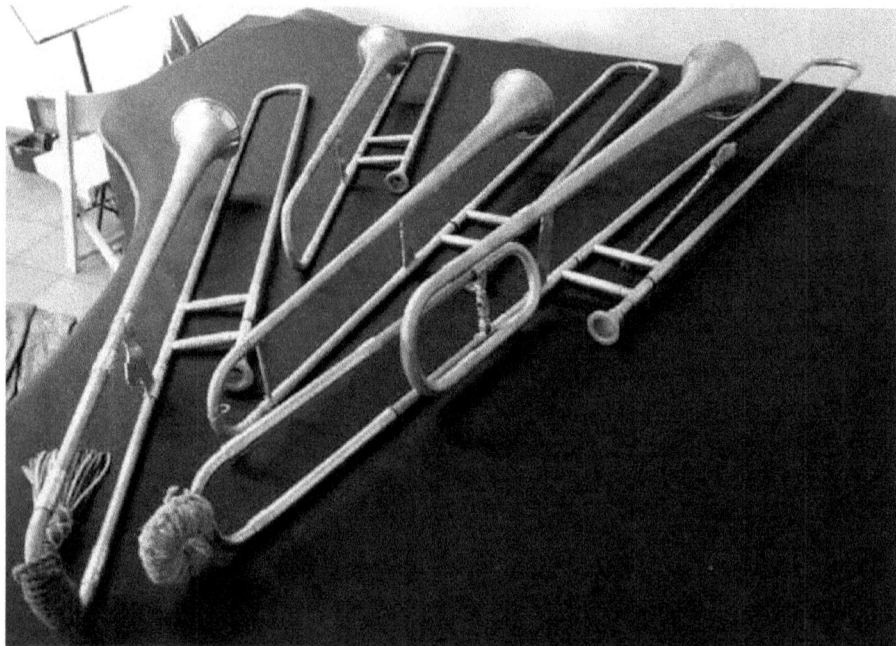

A sackbut is a type of trombone originating in the Renaissance era, characterized by a telescopic slide that is used to vary the length of the tube to change pitch. Unlike the earlier and rare slide trumpet from which it evolved, the sackbut possesses a U-shaped slide, with two parallel sliding tubes, which allows for playing scales in a lower range. An older instrument generally differs from modern trombones by its smaller, more cylindrically-proportioned bore, and its less-flared bell. The bell section was more resonant (since it did not contain the tuning slide and was loosely stayed rather than firmly braced to itself). These traits produce a covered, blended sound which was a timbre particularly effective for working with voices, also crumhorns.

Keyboards:

Clavichord and *Harpsichord* feature large in the Renaissance era. See the section *The Piano & Its Predecessors* for a deeper view.

Virginal

The generic term Virginal was the name under which all keyboard stringed instruments with *jacks* (quilled piece of wood that rose up to pluck a string when the corresponding key is pressed) were known in Renaissance England. 16th century writers are mentioning that the name originated from the fact that the instrument was preferred by the ladies. The true virginal was usually of a parallelogram form, while a trapeze shape was usually associated with the spinet.

Organ

The Medieval organ was growing in size and versatility and had much better playability in the Renaissance era. See the *Organ* section for more info on the organs of this era.

Percussion:

Many and various were the percussion instruments of the Renaissance, including the tambourine and drums of every size.

Baroque

The influence of the Church continued to wane. The modern harmony and relationship of the 12 notes of the octave that we still use today were pretty much established by now. The modern orchestra was taking shape, along with the birth of *opera*, including the *overture, prelude, aria, recitative* and *chorus*, the *concerto, sonata* and modern *cantata*. The rather soft-sounding viol string family of the Renaissance was gradually replaced by the bolder violin, viola and cello. The harpsichord was invented and brought to perfection, and important advances were made in all instrumental groups.

Choral music no longer dominated, as composers turned more and more to writing instrumental works for ensembles of increasing color and variety. Instrumental suites were popular, made up of several movements based on dances. The concerto was developed, pitting solo instruments, or groups of instruments against larger forces. Polyphony or counterpoint reached its highest level of development (with Bach at the pinnacle), and the rise of opera married song and story-telling into a new and abiding art form.

Commonly Used Baroque Instruments:
Strings:
As in the preceding era, the strings available in the Baroque era comprised a far more colorful array than the simple family of Violin, Viola, Cello and Double Bass that we have today. There was the Violino Piccolo, a smaller, higher-pitched violin and there was likewise a smaller, higher-pitched cello, the Violoncello Piccolo that fit between the cello and the viola. Bach's Sixth Cello Suite is written for it. The other strings used in the Renaissance era persisted in ensemble use in the Baroque including the Lute, Theorbo, Mandolin, Guitar and Harp.

The viol family, especially the viola da gamba, still played a large role in the ensemble but the subtle tone of this class of instrument would lose out to the more robust quartet of strings used from the Classical era and after.

Viola d'Amore

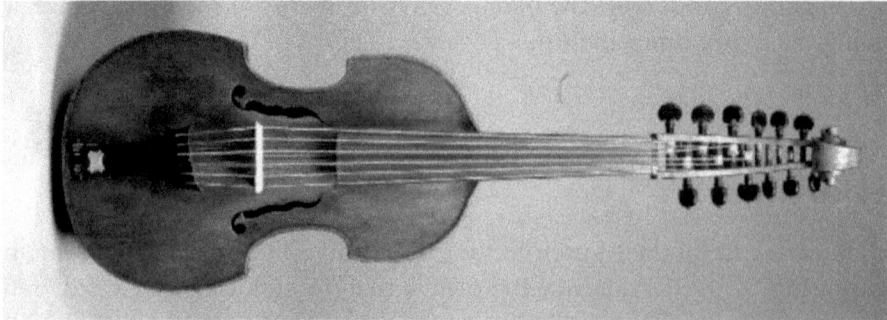

The viola d'amore is a 7- or 6-stringed musical instrument with sympathetic strings used chiefly in the Baroque period. It is played under the chin in the same manner as the violin. Largely thanks to the sympathetic strings, the viola d'amore (like all the viols) has a particularly sweet and warm sound.

Theorbo

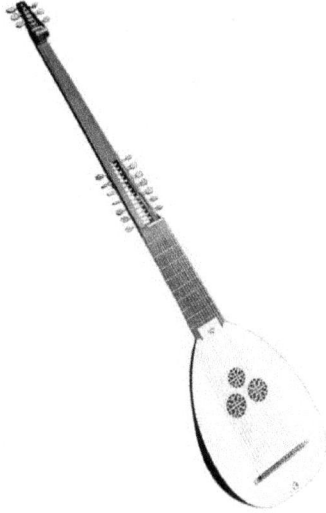

The theorbo is a very large instrument of the lute family. It was developed in Florence during the 1580s. The theorbo retained the double strings of the lute, and almost all surviving theorbos are fitted for double strings on the fingerboard. The theorbo was fitted with a long neck extension carrying additional bass strings, which were single. These are plucked with the right hand only, are tuned to a diatonic scale, and function like the bottom octave of a harp. The very large size of the theorbo, coupled with its very long neck, make it one of the most visually distinctive instruments ever made. The resultant instrument was superbly suited to the accompaniment of the new song style, used in the earliest operas. Double stringing on the fingerboard meant that the theorbo retained much of the color and subtlety of the lute. The long single bass strings give a very powerful bass register, providing superb support for even large ensembles of voices and instruments. The theorbo remained a fixture for opera accompaniment for decades. Many Italian operas of the mid-17th century are essentially continuo operas, and were performed with two keyboard instruments, two theorbos, and a pair of violins to supply instrumental ritornelli.

The theorbo spread widely outside Italy, but it rarely remained unaltered. Different countries had their way with the design and only in England did it not achieve real popularity.

Archlute

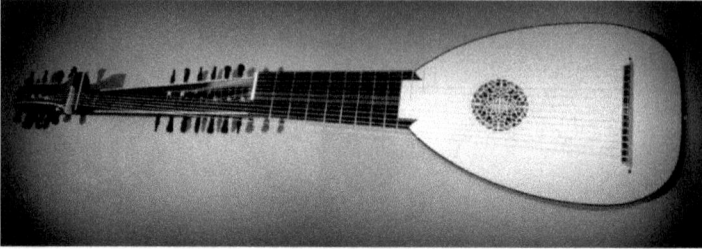

The archlute is thought to be a synonym for the theorbo. This is not the case. The archlute is a plucked string instrument developed around 1600 as a compromise between the very large theorbo, the size of which made for difficulties in the performance of solo music, and the Renaissance tenor lute, which lacked the bass range of the theorbo. Essentially a tenor lute with the theorbo's neck-extension, the archlute lacks the power in the tenor and the bass that the theorbo's large body and typically greater string length provide.

Woodwind:
Baroque flute

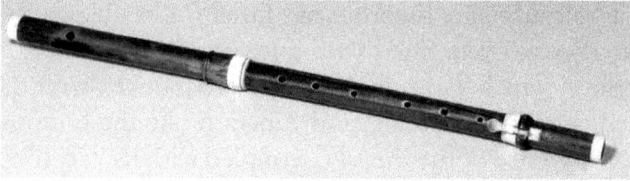

A revolution in flute making took place in the second half of the 17th century. The instrument emerged as the 'baroque flute' with significant modifications from the Renaissance-era model including a conical bore, the addition of a key for the right hand little finger, and a more ornate body made in several pieces. It was now fully chromatic (could play all the notes in its range, in large part because of the key), but more significantly, it was better suited tonally for a role as a soloist (primarily because of the bore change). The bore change made a big difference in sound—improving the intonation and increasing the volume in the lowest notes, in particular. By 1730, the Baroque Flute was taking the recorder's place. This was partly due to the greater dynamic range of the flute (the recorder pitch changes if played softy or very loudly).

Baroque oboe

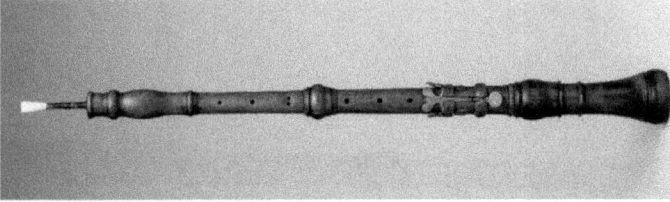

The baroque oboe seems to have developed from the Renaissance shawm starting around the 1650s in Paris. Earlier instruments were loud double reeds intended for use outdoors, while the new, more refined oboe (and its larger cousins) began to find a place in the orchestra starting in the 1670s. Its early orchestral use was in doubling the first violin part, but gradually it began to be used independently for its own color and expressive capability. The baroque oboe's sound is less compact and more plaintive than that of the modern oboe and has been described as more like the human voice than any other instrument. There are only three keys on a baroque oboe.

Baroque Recorder Family

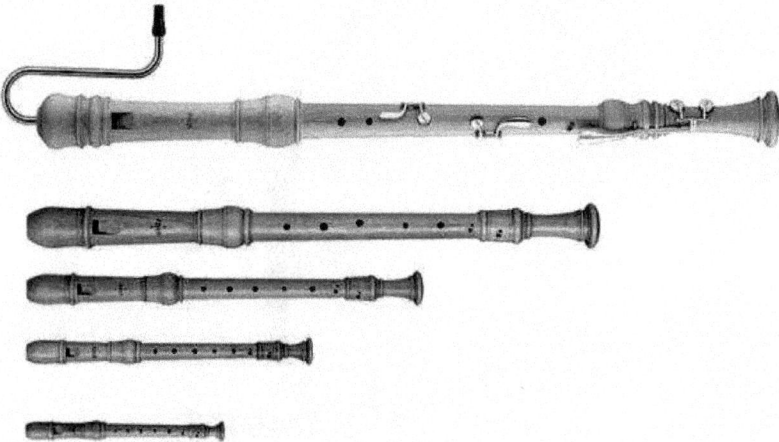

The baroque recorder had three sections as opposed to two for the Renaissance instruments. A thinner and more penetrating tone and wider note range were major characteristics of the baroque recorders. The early years of the 18th century were the golden age for the solo recorder. Handel wrote great recorder masterpieces, likewise Vivaldi with his concerti. Bach wrote many wonderful recorder parts in his cantatas, as well as the incomparable twin recorder parts in the *4th Brandenburg Concerto*.

Oboe d'amore

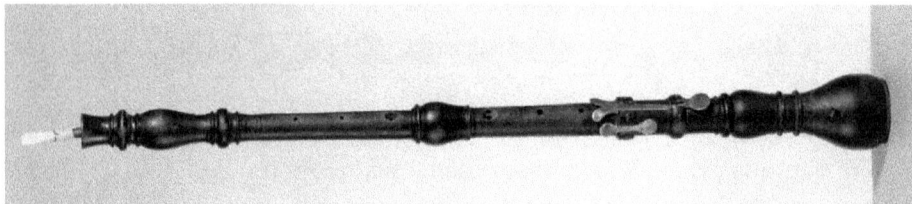

The oboe d'amore, Italian for 'oboe of love,' is a double reed woodwind instrument in the oboe family invented in the 18th century. Slightly larger than the oboe, it has a less assertive and a more tranquil and serene tone, and is considered the alto of the oboe family, between the oboe (soprano) and the English horn. Bach wrote many pieces—a concerto, many of his cantatas, and the *Et in Spiritum sanctum* movement of his *Mass in B minor*—for the instrument. Georg Philipp Telemann also frequently employed the oboe d'amore.

Oboe da caccia

The oboe da caccia, Italian for 'hunting oboe,' is a double reed woodwind instrument in the oboe family, pitched a fifth below the oboe. It has a curved tube, and a brass bell, unusual for an oboe. Its range is close to that of the

English Horn. Bach tended to favor the middle and lowest registers and they are the most characteristic for this instrument. The oboe da caccia was used only in the late Baroque period, after which it fell out of use until interest in authentic performance in the 20th century caused it to be revived.

Brasses:

Baroque trumpet, or Natural Trumpet

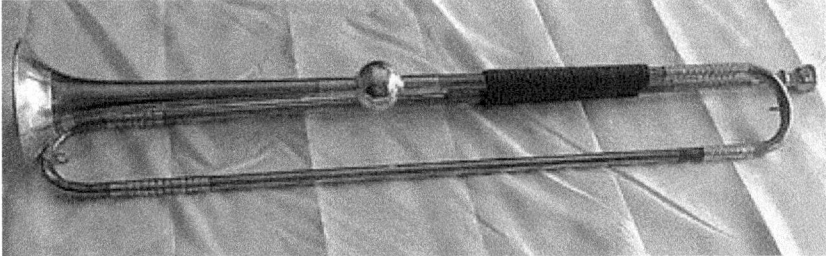

A Natural Trumpet is a valveless brass instrument that is able to play only the notes of the harmonic series. Baroque composers – such as Antonio Vivaldi, Georg Philipp Telemann, George Frideric Handel and Johann Sebastian Bach—made frequent use of trumpets in sacred, orchestral, and even solo works. Many of these trumpet parts are technically quite difficult to play on a natural instrument and were often written with a specific virtuoso performer in mind.

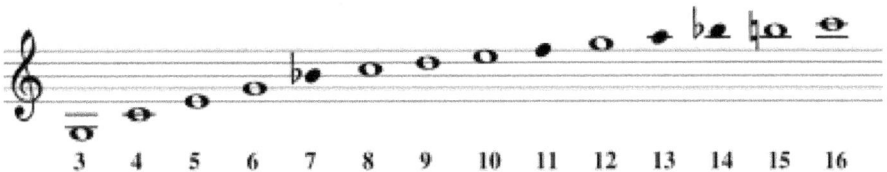

The useable range (from the 3rd to the 16th harmonic) of the harmonic series for a natural trumpet pitched in C. In practice, lower harmonics were never used, and intervals above the 16th harmonic only occasionally called for. Notes that are filled-in are inherently flat and must be lipped up, with the exception of the 11th harmonic, which is lipped down to produce an F and up to produce an F♯. Chromatic notes not in the natural series are produced by lipping the upper adjacent harmonic down a semitone.

Serpent

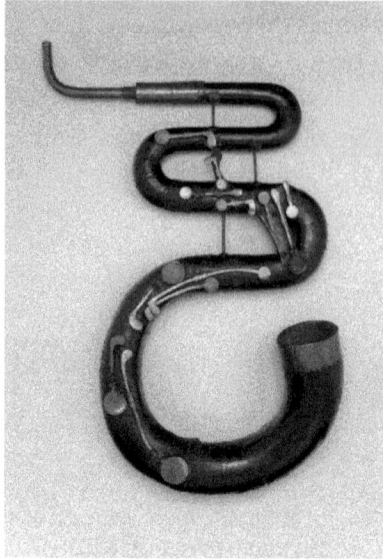

The serpent is a spectacular bass wind instrument, descended from the cornett, and a distant ancestor of the tuba, with a mouthpiece like a brass instrument but side holes like a woodwind. It is usually a long cone bent into a snakelike shape, hence the name. The serpent is closely related to the cornett, but it is not part of the cornett family due to the absence of a thumb hole. It is generally made out of wood, with walnut being a particularly popular choice. The outside is covered with dark brown or black leather. Despite wooden construction and the fact that it has finger holes rather than valves, it is usually classed as a brass. The serpent's range typically covers one from two octaves below middle C to at least half an octave above middle C.

Natural Horn

40

The natural horn is the predecessor to the modern-day French horn (differentiated by its lack of valves). Throughout the 17th and 18th century the natural horn evolved as a separation from the trumpet by widening the bell and lengthening the tubes. It consists of a mouthpiece, long coiled tubing, and a large, flared bell. This instrument was used extensively until the emergence of the valved horn in the early 19th century. Like the Baroque Trumpet, the Natural Horn has several gaps in its harmonic range. To play chromatically, in addition to crooking the instrument into the right key, two additional techniques are required: bending and hand-stopping. Bending a note is achieved by modifying the embouchure (the mouth contact with the mouthpiece) to raise or lower the pitch fractionally and compensates for the slightly out-of-pitch 'wolf tones' which all brass instruments have. Hand-stopping is a technique whereby the player can modify the pitch of a note by up to a semitone (or sometimes slightly more) by inserting a cupped hand into the bell. Both techniques change the timbre as well as the pitch.

Baroque Trombone

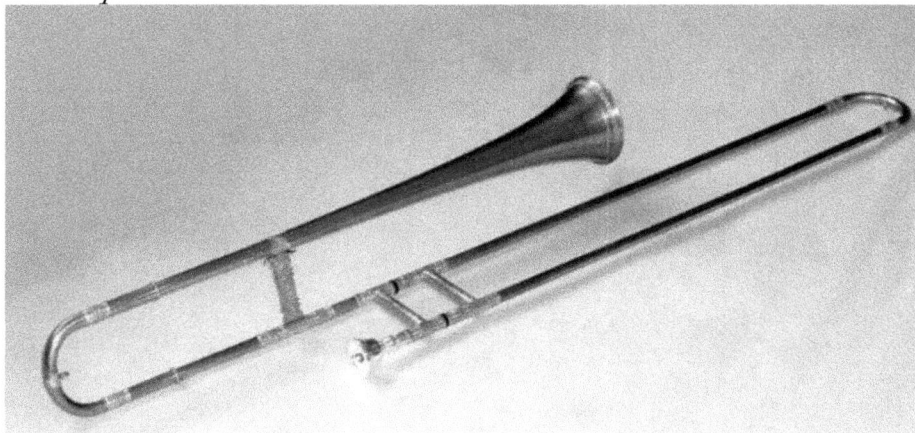

Unlike most other brass instruments trombones have a telescoping slide mechanism that varies the length of the instrument to change the pitch. The trombone simply means 'big trumpet.' It was also referred to as 'sackbut' to distinguish it from its modern counterpart and it has changed very little from baroque times to today. Perhaps the most obvious difference is an increase in the flare of the bell, creating a louder, brighter tone on today's instruments. Like the cornetto, the trombone possesses an Italian chamber repertoire from the early baroque era. The trombone doubled voice parts in sacred works, but there are also solo pieces written for trombone in the early 17th century.

41

Cornett

The use of the instrument had declined by 1700, although the instrument was still common in Europe until the late 18th century. Johann Sebastian Bach, Georg Philipp Telemann and their German contemporaries used both the cornett and cornettino in cantatas to play in unison with the soprano voices of the choir.

Keyboards:

The clavichord, harpsichord, and organ all had their heyday in the Baroque era. For a fuller exploration, see the section *The Piano & Its Predecessors*, and *The Organ*.

Percussion:

Cymbals, Bass drum and Snare drum were also used in the Baroque.

Timpani

Timpani are a type of drum categorized as a hemispherical drum, they consist of a membrane called a head stretched over a large bowl traditionally made of copper. Most modern timpani are pedal timpani and can be tuned quickly and accurately to specific pitches by skilled players through the use of a movable foot-pedal. They are played by striking the head with a specialized drumstick called a timpani stick or timpani mallet. Timpani evolved from military drums to become useful in the baroque orchestra and a staple of the Classical orchestra by the last third of the 18th century.

Classical

Towards the end of the Baroque period, some composers were already setting off in a new direction: away from the complex counterpoint of the high Baroque (perfected by **Bach**) and into a more melody-centered style with a chord-based accompaniment of these melodies. This era opened with the *rococo* or *gallant* style. Some found it a relief from the tangle of contrapuntal webbing of the Baroque, others found it absurdly trite. The sons of **Bach** (**CPE** and **JC**) for example were already seeking new avenues away from the styles of their father, and a freer movement of artists and musicians between European countries helped to give them inspiration. During this Classical period, the forms instigated by the Church were still there, but for the most part the major composers of the day worked for the royalty or nobility of the time. Nevertheless, public concerts were becoming more popular during this time, and concert halls and opera houses were constructed in all major cities.

Instrumental music continued to be even more popular than vocal forms. The concept of a *theme and variations* was popular in this period. *Sonata-Allegro Form* became the foundation of *symphonies, concertos* and *string quartets* as well as *sonatas*. (These forms are defined in the *Glossary* section.)

Classical era musicians continued to use many of instruments from the Baroque era, such as the cello, contrabass, recorder, trombone, timpani, forte-piano (straight-strung, wooden-frame precursor to the modern piano) and organ. The *string quartet* became a standard form. While the harpsichord was still used in ensemble accompaniment, it fell out of use with the rise of the forte-piano as a solo instrument. Because the keyboard instruments are so important in the realm of art music, see the section on *The Piano and its Predecessors* for a more thorough study.

Commonly Used Classical Instruments:

Strings:

The violin, viola, cello and double bass had by now become the standard string section, the violins usually divided into two groups—first and second.

The guitar, and less often, the mandolin would see some use as accompanying instruments. Guitar continued to be featured in concertos with orchestra.

Pedal Harp

A pedal harp is a harp in which pedals control a mechanism raising the pitch of given strings by a semitone (single action) or by both a semitone and a whole tone (double action). The modern double-action pedal harp is the standard orchestral harp. It covers six and a half octaves (three below and three and a half above middle C). Along the neck, or harmonic curve, are two sets of rotating brass disks; concealed inside the forepillar and in the deep metal plates running along both sides of the neck is a mechanism operated by seven pedals, one for each group of strings of a given pitch name. Depression of the pedal to the first notch shortens the appropriate strings by a semitone, to the second notch, by a whole tone. The shortening is affected by the rotating disks, which grip the string at the proper point. The harp is normally tuned diatonically (to a seven-note octave) in Cb; depressing all pedals to the first notch puts it into C, to the second notch, into C#. Playing the pedal harp demands skilled coordination between the hands, which pluck the strings with the fleshy part of the fingertips, and the feet, which, with the pedals, select the necessary pitch changes for the strings.

Woodwinds:

Flute, clarinet, oboe, and bassoon had by now become the standard woodwind component for the orchestra. The contrabassoon, though it saw some use in the baroque had a weak tone and poor intonation and was not terribly popular and never really caught on big until the Romantic era when it was perfected.

Bassett Horn

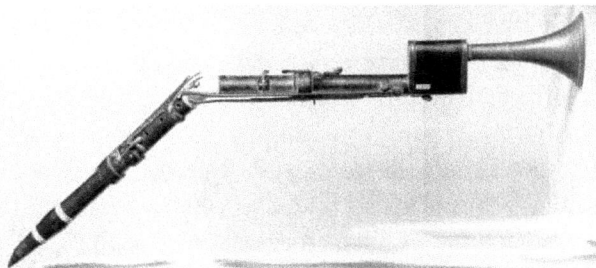

The basset horn has, like the clarinet, a single reed and a cylindrical bore but is larger and has a bend usually between the mouthpiece and the upper joint. It has additional keys for an extended range downward. Its sound is similar to the clarinet's, but darker. It saw occasional use but was never considered 'standard' to an orchestra.

Brass:

Trumpet and trombone constituted the standard Classical-era brass section, along with the natural horn.

Percussion:

Timpani, bass drum, cymbals and snare drum made up the standard orchestra battery. Rarely members of the bell family.

Keyboards:

Clavichord and harpsichord and their variants were losing steam in this era, as the Fortepiano came bursting onto the scene. See the section on *The Piano & Its Predecessors*. The Organ also took a dive in these years. The greatest organ master of all time, **JS Bach**, was dead and a real organ revival had to wait till the Romantic era when a whole new tradition would come into being.

Romantic

The Romantic era saw the birth of the performer as rock-star. Violinist **Paganini** and pianist **Liszt** are the standouts here. Much drama and heart-on-the-sleeve and little restraint. This kind of power needed new techniques and audiences heard ever more complex harmonies and rhythms. Many composers sought new horizons, and diverse schools of thought branched out in different directions. Examples of this being the later Impressionists who used notes to paint musical pictures or impressions, and the nationalists who embraced the folk tunes and styles of their own countries. Classical forms were also modified so that, for some composers, the symphony became a *tone poem* which might tell a story or seek to paint a picture in sound. This is called *program music*, as opposed to the abstract music of earlier eras. Chamber music for smaller forces was also very common, and musical miniatures for solo instruments or singers could be heard professionally in smaller venues or played by amateurs in the home.

In the Romantic era, the modern piano, with its iron frame and extended range became more powerful and sustained in tone with a wider range of dynamics. This spelled the end (until its modern resurrection) of the more delicate fortepiano which, for all its virtues, could not project beyond the footlights of the concert hall.

In the orchestra, the existing Classical instruments and sections were retained (string section, woodwinds, brass and percussion), but these sections were typically expanded to make a fuller, bigger sound. Toward the end of the era an orchestra of 100 players was not uncommon. New woodwind instruments were added to extend the range of existing instruments, such as the contrabassoon, bass clarinet and piccolo, and new percussion instruments were added, including xylophones, snare drums, celestas, bells, and triangles, large orchestral harps, and even wind machines for sound effects. Saxophones appear in some scores from the late 19th century onwards.

With the most notable exceptions of **Brahms** and **Bruckner**, composers of this period shared a general tendency towards allowing their natural inspiration free rein, often pacing their compositions more in terms of their emotional content and dramatic continuity rather than organic structural growth. The operatic supremacy of **Verdi** and **Wagner** rose up, wildly popular.

Commonly Used Romantic-Era Instruments:

The iron-framed piano joined the instrumental lineup outlined in the Classical section, but there were a few additions and changes to note.

French Horn

The transition from the valveless 'natural horn' to the complex tubing of the French horn was a rough ride. Valves were initially intended to overcome problems associated with changing crooks during a performance—a royal pain. (Remember, the crooks' varied lengths would allow a horn to play in whatever key a piece required. But even then, the notes available were only those of the fundamental tone and the overtone series associated with the fundamental tone. Many notes were simply unavailable.) But valves' unrelia-

47

bility, and the musical taste of the performer slowed the adoption of the new horn. Many conservatories and players refused to use them, claiming that the natural horn was a better instrument. **Brahms**, even the Modern-era **Benjamin Britten** preferred the natural horn. Today, a good career can be had by musicians who specialize in period instruments who use a natural horn to play in original performance styles. But he use of valves unquestionably opened up a great deal more flexibility in playing in different keys; in effect, the horn became an entirely different instrument, fully chromatic for the first time, able to play any note in the gamut without physical alterations on-the-fly.

Trombone

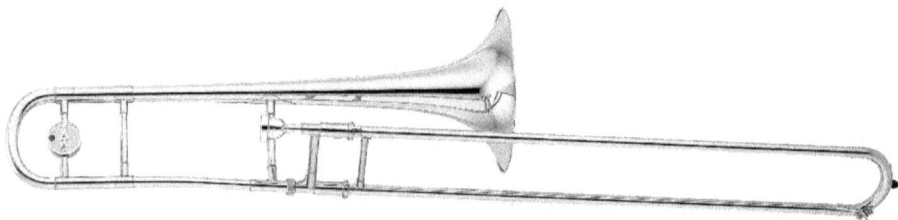

The Romantic era saw improvements, introducing a significant widening of the bore and the wide bell flare. Also the addition of 'stockings' at the end of the inner slide to reduce friction, and the development of the water key to expel condensation from the horn. Later modifications saw increases in mouthpiece, bore, and bell dimensions, and in types of mutes and valves.

Flute & Piccolo

In the mid-1800s, **Theobald Boehm** worked on redesigning the flute in order to improve the instrument's range, volume, and intonation. **Boehm** changed the position of keyholes, increased the size of the finger holes and designed keys to be normally open rather than closed. He also designed flutes with a cylindrical bore to produce a clearer tone and lower register. Most modern flutes today are designed using the **Boehm** system of a keyword. The little piccolo was also employed as a way to extend upward the range of the flute.

Oboe

Inspired by **Boehm's** designs, **Guillaume Triébert** and his two sons did like modifications to the oboe's keying system.

Cor anglaise (English Horn)

Neither English nor a horn, it was invented during the Classical era but not until about 1850 did it start to come into its own in the orchestral environment. It's a double-reed affair (like the oboe and sax) has a range like the oboe but is not very useful in its upper register. In the lower notes of the range of the English horn you get a rich and beautiful tone, with a strong and expressive carrying power. Not terribly useful, but when you need it you need it.

Contrabassoon

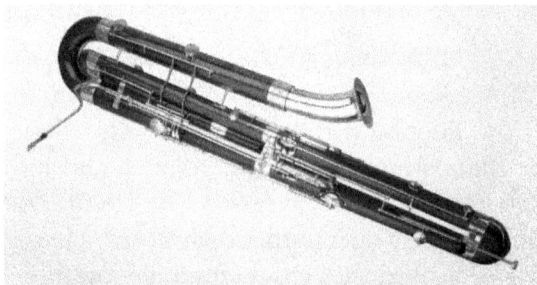

The contrabassoon, also known as the double bassoon, is a larger version of the bassoon, sounding an octave lower. Its technique is similar to its smaller cousin, with a few notable differences. The instrument is twice as long as the bassoon, curves around on itself twice and, due to its weight and shape, is supported by an endpin rather than a seat strap. Additional support is sometimes provided by a strap around the player's neck. The contrabassoon is a very deep-sounding woodwind instrument that plays in the same sub-bass register as the tuba and the contrabass versions of the clarinet and saxophone.

Saxophone Family

In 1846, the saxophone was patented by the Belgian instrument maker and musician, **Adolphe Sax. Sax** sought to combine the elements of instruments from the woodwind and brass family. When his patent expired in 1866 (a paltry 20 years) other instrument makers made their own versions of the saxophones and some of their innovations were real and lasting improvements on the original. The way that the Romantics used the sax will not remind you much of the instrument as it is played today. It's all bluesy and sexy now, but it began life in quite a straightlaced fashion.

Ophicleide

This it was the bass brass from the very late-Classical through much of the Romantic era until the Tuba took over. The Ophicleide is difficult to play, and the relative ease of the Tuba was welcome. Its long tubing bends back on itself, and it is played with a cupped mouthpiece similar to modern trombone mouthpiece. It originally had nine keys, later expanded to as many as twelve keys. It has a color of its own and modern substitutions by the Tuba when an Ophicleide is called for often fall flat.

Tuba

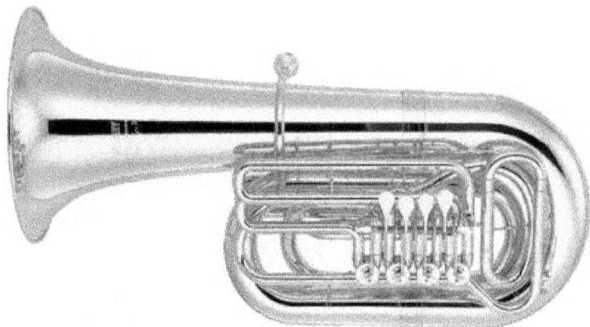

Johann Gottfried Moritz and his son, **Carl Wilhelm**, invented the tuba in 1835. The tuba took the place of the ophicleide. The tuba is now the standard bass of bands and orchestras and it blends perfectly with the other members.

Modern

If the Romantic period saw the start of some fragmentation into different schools, this trend continued and accelerated into what we call the Modern era. There were those who continued to develop older traditions: the neo-classicists, the late Romantics and the Impressionist schools still prevailed, and others took a new path with *Atonal Music*. Some composers created thematic material which were not so much 'melodies' as they were plastic motifs to manipulate intellectually, introducing dissonant intervals and different scales, and unusual rhythms and cross-rhythms were explored.

Film music blossomed and required boatloads of original music. The industry recruited composers educated in the classical music traditions. Jazz became an influence on 'serious' composers. It's safe to say that no single music genre ever assumed a dominant position.

The period since WWII is undoubtedly the most bewildering of all, as composers have pulled in various apparently contradictory and opposing directions. So diverse are the styles adopted throughout the greater part of the last century that only by experimentation can listeners discover for themselves whether certain styles are to their taste.

The close of the Romantic era was marked by the presence of a wall that music was about to hit. We might call it *The Dissolution of Tonality*. This is so crucial to the history of the art that it requires the following attempt at a cogent explanation. So here goes…

Music up to this point was written in a *key*, usually any one of 12 (corresponding to the 12 black & white keys in each octave on the piano), and each key has two main modes, major and minor. So that yields 24 major and minor keys that composers have been playing with, merrily switching in and out among them as the logic and mood of the piece's development would dictate. This movement from one key to another is called *modulation*.

Each key—let's take C major and B minor as examples—consists of a scale of notes that are used in that particular key. For C major, that scale is c-d-e-f-g-a-b—the white keys of the piano—then starts over with c again. If you are playing in B minor, the notes available to you are b-c#-d-e-f#-g-a then start over with b again. The root note (in our case, C for the first example) is the home note (called the *tonic*). The next most important note is the fifth up from that (called the *dominant*), in our case, G. This interval of a fifth, C and G sounding together, is a gentle, consonant interval. The ear deems some intervals, the third (C-E), the sixth (C-A), for example, to also feel consonant, though less so. The ear gets alarmed and uncomfortable over some of these intervals, such as the minor second (C-Db) or the augmented fourth (C-F#). This is an organic sound world, with each interval producing different colors and feelings in our soul. *We did not invent this.* Nature invented it. We *discovered* it. This has been the basis of our music for a thousand years.

Modulation, or going from one key to another, is done by flattening (taking a note in the scale and taking it down a step) or sharpening (raising a note in the scale up a step). This changes the key. It may happen only in passing, a quick color change, and then back to the original key again. Or it may change the key and remain in the new key for an entire section. If we are in our key of C (c-d-e-f-g-a-b) and change the F in the scale of C to an F# then, as long as that change is in effect, we have *modulated* to the key of G (g-a-b-c-d-e-f#).

This modulation, this coloring outside the lines, was done gradually and carefully by the likes of Renaissance and Baroque composers and even Haydn in the Classical era, but as composers got more expressive and emotional, this modulation was going on constantly. Eventually it was hard to know what key a piece was in at any moment, so many sharps and flats and key changes happening so urgently. Eventually, tonality—the sensation that there was an actual feeling of an emotional center somewhere to be felt in the music as it unfolded—became so uncertain that… it simply broke down.

This was *The Wall* that composers hit at the end of the Romantic era. There were, of course, composers who just whistled through the graveyard, pretending that The Wall wasn't there. But they were about to be left behind in the great march of progress that had driven the arts for so many centuries. There needed to be a *system*.

At first, many composers responded to the crisis by ignoring the idea of keys and scales completely. Such pieces, in which no one tonal center exists and in which any harmonic or melodic combination of tones may be sounded without restrictions of any kind, are usually called *atonal*, sometimes *pantonal*. Many composers jumped on this wagon, but the wheels fell off after a few miles. It was, quite simply, *chaos*. Composers longed for a systematic approach to writing music. And boy howdy, did they get it!

Many systems were proposed but one of them dominated. We have now to briefly discuss *serial*, or *12-tone music*.

Its effect on what we call classical music was, in the view of most listeners, debilitating in the extreme. It was a failed experiment full of hubris and divorced from nature, that was adopted by the academy across the Western world and turned music aficionados, record buyers and concert goers away in droves.

It's a hard topic for the layperson so I'll try my best to give you an idea of what happened to music after WWI, when **Arnold Schoenberg** formulated his "method of composition with 12 tones related only to one another." Here are the 'rules'…

In the 12-tone method, each composition is formed from a unique 'tone-row' or arrangement of the 12 different tones. That row may be played in its original form (rectus), played upside down (inverted), played backward (retrograde), or played backward and upside down (retrograde inversion). It may also be transposed up or down to any pitch level. All of it, or any part of it, may be sounded successively as a melody or simultaneously as a harmony. In fact, *all harmonies and melodies in the piece must be drawn from that row and in proper order.* All this provides a unifying basis for a composition's melody, harmony, structural progressions, and variations.

This was an interesting basis for a *personal* style, but it became much more than that. It was adopted by a critical mass of composers and seen as the only way out for the future of music, the only way through The Wall. This completely synthetic, non-organic and unrelated-to-nature 'solution' to the problem was adopted by the academy. This is what was taught in universities and conservatories for decades and still is. Does it matter that few people enjoy it? Of course not.

This may be a controversial viewpoint, but it is time, after a century of unlistenable dreck, to put it all to bed. *It was a failure.* Nobody liked it, except academicians who supported one another's careers while browbeating the great unwashed who were too stupid to understand their brilliance. Classical music has not recovered from this, and partly because of the influence that universities and conservatories have in the orchestra world, it is one of the reasons that the orchestra may not survive as we have come to know it.

Commonly Used Modern-Era Instruments:
Not much new on that scene. Mainly refinements of the standard instruments.

Post-Modern

The generation after Schoenberg took serialism a step further. 'Why just serialize pitches?' some asked. 'What about dynamics, or how loud and soft? Why not have 12 degrees of dynamics and serialize that? Why stop there? How about duration, the length that a note sounds? Let's serialize that with 12 degrees of how long a note can sound! We can even serialize what octave the note will appear in!'

"What fun!" said no listeners, anywhere, ever.

This was a good development, however, as it reduced the 'serial' concept to absurdity and with such clarity that maybe the average academic might finally start to come around. You'd think so, wouldn't you? But no.

For my benefit and yours I am going to stop talking about Serialism now. You're welcome.

Composers found other ways to deal with The Wall, mostly by acknowledging it but deeming it unimportant and going around it. There were composers, considered extreme by some audiences, who used traditional instruments in unconventional ways, overturned principles previously considered fundamental, and questioned the roles of composer, musician and listener. Experimental composers used randomization techniques or gave unusual instructions which might not include any conventional musical notation at all.

Here follows a brief (I promise) overview of each of the main impulses that drove the music of the latter half of the last century and the recent past. They include *neo-ism, indeterminism, microtonality, musique concrète, electronics, minimalism, the new complexity,* and *cultural cross-pollination.*

- **Neo-ism**—let's do this first as it's easy to dismiss. These are composers who write in 'the <*fill in blank with past musical era*> style but with a modern sensibility!' In other words, they hit The Wall and ran the other way, screaming in terror like their pants were on fire. **Penderecki** is a good example. He was one of the very foremost rank of composers when young, fiery and bristling with vigor and ideas. When he got older, he hit The Wall hard and fled in horror to the safe-space of neo-Romanticism. He is no longer influential.

- **Indeterminism** (also *Aleatory music,* also *Chance music)*—music in which chance or indeterminate elements are left for the performer to realize. The term is a loose one, describing compositions from strictly demarcated areas for improvisation according to specific directions, to unstructured pieces consisting of vague directives, such as "play for five minutes." The performers may be told to arrange the structure of the piece by reordering its sections or by playing sections simultaneously as they wish. The musical score may also indicate points where performers are to improvise or even to include quasi-theatrical gestures. Composers themselves may use aleatory processes while writing the pieces, such as having a computer randomize certain parameters of the score—pitches, durations, dynamics, even instrumentation. **John Cage** is the man most responsible for the influence of indeterminacy. Performers with good improvisatory skills can make these pieces into a gratifying experience.

- **Microtonality**—You know the notes on the piano, the black and white keys? There are 12 per octave and each note is equidistant in frequency from the one above it and below it. Well, why does it have to be 12? Why not fewer? Why not a huge amount more, like 100 divisions of the octave instead of 12? Why do the steps between have to be equidistant? You see where this is headed, right? Among the well-known Western composers to incorporate microtonal material into some of their music were **Charles Ives, Harry Partch, Henry Cowell, John Cage, Benjamin Johnston, Karlheinz Stockhausen**, and **Krzysztof Penderecki.** It didn't catch on.

- **Musique concrète**—before there was electronic music there was musique concrète. This is a technique of composition using recorded sounds as raw material. The technique was developed about 1948. The fundamental principle of musique concrète lies in the assemblage of various natural and industrial sounds recorded on tape to produce a collage of sound. During the preparation of such a composition, the sounds selected and recorded may be modified in any way desired—played backward, cut short or extended, subjected to echo-chamber effects, varied in pitch and intensity, and so on. Once the composer had all his or her sounds on tape, they could whip out the ol' razor blade and commence to editing the tape to their liking. The finished composition thus represents the combination of varied auditory experiences into an artistic unity. With the advent of electronic synthesis and, especially, digital production, this technique had a rather short heyday.

- **Electronic music**—Music produced solely from electronic generators was first produced in Germany in 1953. Electronic music was also created in Japan and the United States beginning in the 1950s. A more recent and very important development was the advent of computers to compose music. Electronic music is produced from a wide variety of sound resources—from sounds picked up by microphones to those produced by electronic oscillators (generating basic acoustical waveforms such as sine waves, square waves and sawtooth waves), simple or complex computer installations and microprocessors—that were recorded on tape (now disc or solid-state storage) and then edited into a permanent form. Electronic music is played back through loudspeakers either alone or in combination with ordinary musical instruments. In the pop music arena, electronic music, especially of the dance variety, is a hot scene. In the classical arena it hasn't, yet, really caught fire with listeners. I propose, however, at least one sure-enough masterpiece in the genre: *Gesang der Jünglinge* by **Stockhausen**. Likely there shall be many more. It's an area that shows promise, as the acoustic non-electronic world seems to hit yet another wall. What more can be done with acoustic instruments? Electronics may be the future.

- **New simplicity: Minimalism**—This has been the most important development in music since Serialism. Minimalism arose in the 1960s as a reaction to the complexity, structure and perception of 12-tone Serialism as it developed at the hands of **Schoenberg** and his minions, and all who compose in this style are striving for greater simplicity in the music. Minimalism has a large audience and many of the best-known composers write in this style. They include **Glass, Riley, Reich, Pärt** and **John Adams**. If I had to designate a founder for the movement, I would nominate **La Monte Young**. Minimalism was initially viewed as a form of experimental music called the *New York Hypnotic School.* That ought to provide a good hint as to its nature. Many works in this genre evolve very slowly with very small changes throughout and some will have overlapping textures with different length looping phrases on different instruments. It is often characterized by a strong and relentless pulse, the insistent repetition of short melodic fragments, and harmonies that change over long periods of time. It is often programmed because orchestral rehearsal time, which costs mucho $$$, is, ummm... minimized.

- **New complexity**—This is the opposite of Minimalism. These folks like it difficult and intricate. It sprung up in the 1980s. Though often atonal, highly abstract and dissonant, New Complexity music is most readily characterized using techniques which require complex musical notation. This includes extended techniques, intricate and often unstable textures, microtonality, compound layered rhythms, abrupt changes in texture, and so on. It is also characterized, in contrast to the music of the immediate post-World War II serialists, by the frequent reliance of its composers on poetic conceptions, very often implied in the titles of the works. **Brian Ferneyhough** is the best example of the school, also **Michael Finnissy** and several younger composers, many of them British. **James Dillon** is hot right now. Well, as hot as it gets in the contemporary orchestral world.

- **Cultural cross-pollination**—The world is smaller than ever and the cross-pollination going on among the genres and the nations of the world has had deep influence on all the arts of the West. In classical music of this century, we may cite the Indonesian gamelan, the *raga* system of India, the philosophy and instruments of the orient, and the advanced percussion systems of African nations as all having an invigorating influence on the art. This, along with electronics, shall change the face of what we call classical music.

Commonly Used Post-Modern Instruments:

Electronics in the form of analogue and digital synthesis is the big story here, also instruments from different parts of the world make more frequent appearances.

Contemporary

This means *right now*. At present there is no main school of thought which rules, and that in itself points the way to the future.

I quote here from the closing chapter, *The Future of Classical Music:*

"In music, what has not been done? From Gregorian Chant to electronic noises and chance music, what have we not tried? The era of Minimalism, a form nearly half a century old, is passing and being replaced by an anything-goes aesthetic that uses any method, tool and philosophy ever conjured throughout the centuries in any combination in order to create a compelling concert experience. We have gathered 1000 years of arrows for the quiver, to be used *ad libitum*. In the right hands, interesting music is starting to be created again. And these new artists seem to share a common trait: *To hell with schools and systems and shalls and shall-nots*. For that is the poison that has made so much of new music unlistenable for almost a century."

Commonly Used Contemporary Instruments:

Anything that makes a sound is permissible. Traditional instruments continue to be refined, but the big story is electronics. Any explanation of the development and history of analog and digital synthesis necessitates a deep technical study. For a good primer, see this:

https://en.wikipedia.org/wiki/Synthesizer

ℭℛ

OVERVIEW OF MAJOR COMPOSERS & THEIR WORKS

Introduction

In the following pages I will introduce to you more than 150 composers whose influence upon the development of Western art music is incontestable. A brief sketch outlining the reasons for their importance, as well as a list of a few of their key compositions will be included.

The next section of this book is called 'Contenders.' There are a few living composers whose works get played a *lot* more than others. The reasons for this may be sound, or they may be suspect. But I have included this list so that you may see and investigate those who have bobbled to the surface as candidates for inclusion into the canon of classical music.

Elsewhere I do have a list of recommended recordings of some of the core repertory that will likely never be unavailable, so universal is their acclaim. You will not find *The Twenty Most Indispensable Classical Recordings of the Grrrrreat Mahsters* or any such late-night-TV nonsense on that list. There's no such thing.

I do not recommend the purchase of 'greatest hits' albums. These items, often, are 'Classical Music for people who don't like Classical Music.' They often feature bleeding chunks torn from complete works by popular great composers, and if you care enough about an art music collection to read this book, you'll not want any of these hodge-podge items around. Another caution against this type of buying is that it encourages unwanted duplication and is the natural enemy of buying with an eye toward reasonable curation. Don't get the *Air on a G String* from **Bach's** *Third Orchestral Suite* on some hackneyed *Greatest Hits of the Baroque*. Buy the *Four Orchestral Suites*. You won't regret it, I guarantee.

When starting your collection, I recommend beginning at whatever period or style of art music interests you most. If you develop a liking for art music, you are bound to move backward and forward in time as your developing aesthetic dictates.

Remember also that the greatest music and the music which will hold your admiration and attention over the decades will often not be of the immediately appealing genre. There is something lofty and impersonal about the greatest music. It does not cry "look at me!" nor does it appeal to us as party music. The greatest music does not often reveal its secrets easily. One must *listen* to it. If that phrase seems strange, observe how many people put on a record only to eat a sandwich, talk, read a book, leave the room—anything to avoid the cosmic introspection into which the greatest music propels us, and which is its sole aim.

This is not to disparage 'party music' (such as **Haydn** or **Mozart** divertimentos, or **Led Zeppelin**), sandwich music (such as **Telemann's** *Musique de Table*), etc.; it is only a reminder to *use music effectively*. The oratorios of **Carissimi** are awful at a party but meltingly lovely and edifying in the solitary evening. Conversely, **Vivaldi** concertos might seem obtrusive and vapid in meditative moods but prove an exhilarating and ingratiating accompaniment to friends and a few drinks.

Using music effectively also applies personally. *Listen to music that matches your mood.* If you're feeling blue don't listen to happy music; it will make you feel worse. If you're sad, listen to sad music; it will make you feel better. That is the secret to the success of the music genre known as 'the Blues.' A big chunk of Country-Western is also good at snapping a person out of a depression. So you say your wife left you and you just accidentally ran over your best huntin' dog with your pickup truck after getting drunk because you lost your job? Have I got some music for you!

Be assured that I have not compiled here a list of my favorite composers and works. Indeed, I do not care for a good deal of what I have listed below and have withheld some things because they are likely more reflective of my idiosyncrasies than 'objective' worth. However, it is not necessary to like something in order to acknowledge its historical importance and influence.

I have also included, after each composer's name, the suggested pronunciation of that name, both for your information and to avoid embarrassment when speaking with pain-in-the-ass know-it-alls.

Finally, though I have appended a glossary of essential terms, I recommend the acquisition of a good music dictionary as an adjunct to this book. You may wish to delve deeper into some of the terms I must confront you with in this section, and the proper place for help is a comprehensive music dictionary. There are many adequate ones available online for free or as a book.

Overview

What music people played and sang in their own homes and outside the Churches in the Early Middle Ages we do not know, because there is no record. We do, however, possess the great body of...

GREGORIAN CHANT (ca.600–ca.800)

This is the sacred music of the Church from the early Middle Ages. **Pope Saint Gregory** is credited with organizing the codification of all Church music about 600 A.D., but that's just an old nun's tale. The Church is of singular importance during the Middle Ages as it eventually took some control even of secular music and musical practices. The Church music and probably all the music in the Early Middle Ages was monophonic, that is, of a single melody. (Unless you went to the barbaric island of Ireland. There, when people sang, there were as many lines of music going as there were people singing. Pretty glorious sounds from a bunch of savages!) A few recordings of this deathly calm and meditative chant music are essential to any standard collection. Check out also the recordings of the Solesmes monks which have appeared on several labels. The Solesmes monastery has been charged with the research and restoration of the early chants and has recorded extensively. Their approach is not above controversy, but it remains as close to a definitive approach as we may ever get.

- Try the Solesmes monks on any of several collections

In the 11th and 12th centuries, the first reported examples of secular songs appear. They are usually found with Latin texts, though that doesn't mean that people didn't have songs to sing in their own languages, of course. It is just that folk traditions such as this are rarely preserved in 'hard copy.' We simply have no record of these songs preserved in any form. Later, songs in the vernacular show up in early documents all over Europe. For examples of this music look for recordings of songs and dances of the goliards, jongleurs, troubadours, trouveres, or minnesingers, essentially the same bunch of folks from different parts of Europe. These are the travelling secular entertainers from all over the Western world and represent a time frame from about 900 to 1300. The composer —

ADAM DE LA HALLE (ah-DAHM della ALL-ah; 1237–1288)

is a notable among these people, and some of the entertainments which he devised are almost operatic.

- *The Play of Robin and Marion* on Naxos

Most of the composers of this period, both sacred and secular, are anonymous. Therefore, there is little in the way of well-known composers to look for. It's interesting to note that the first composer for whom we have a name, someone who asserted individuality and made damn sure we knew who wrote these things, was a woman -

HILDEGARD OF BINGEN (1098–1179)

She is also known as Saint Hildegard. A German Benedictine abbess, she was a writer, composer, philosopher, Christian mystic, visionary, ambassador and polymath of many disciplines. She scared the bejesus out of most men in power. She is also considered to be the founder of scientific natural history in Germany. There are dozens of good recordings of her works, and the realizations of her scores are incredibly various.

- Album *11,000 Virgins* performed by Anonymous 4
- Album *Origin of Fire* performed by Anonymous 4

Around 1300, we have the first treatise on musical instruments. We know, of course, that instruments were in use before this date (mainly for vocal accompaniment), but we don't know to what extent.

Now we come to note a great moment in Western music history. Somewhere along the line it was suggested that two voices sing different notes at the same time. We take this for granted today, but it had to be invented. Though this development probably occurred in the 5th or 6th century, only in the 11th century was this practice common all over Europe. The aforementioned Irish seem to have been the forerunners of this practice. They seemed to have practiced a peculiar form of this art, sometimes 20 men and women singing different parts at once, all impromptu. This was regarded as somewhat confused and barbaric by the learned continentals, and it was not this tradition which was developed by the mainstream in 'civilized' Europe.

In its early form, the new two-voice part-singing was called 'organum.' In organum the second voice usually sings parallel with the first voice either in the octave, the fourth or the fifth. By the 12th century, organum became more florid and daring. The two parts move with

64

more independence. The two greatest composers of this period, working in the organum form, are:

LEONIN (1125?–1175?) and PEROTIN (1160?–1225?)

Little Leo and Little Pierre. These are the first composers of polyphonic music, probably French, whose names (such as they are) are known to us. Perotin managed to take the intense complexities of the (by then) three and four-part organum texture and thin it out, shortening the phrases and regularizing the rhythms.

- *Perotin* - Hilliard Ensemble on ECM

By 1250 the organum and related forms had disappeared and yielded to the motet. These are more refined and sophisticated examples of multi-voice composition that had, by this time, spread all over Europe. Most motet composers of the 12th and 13th centuries are Anonymous. Their works are found in large collections, hand printed and beautifully ornamented.

The 14th century saw the expansion of the range of voices using more uncommon intervals such as thirds and sixths, (once held to be discordant) and the practice of combining sacred and secular texts and ideals in a single work.

This era ushered in new forms such as the rondeau, ballade and caccia. The best way to find out what these new forms were all about and what their impact was is to procure a set such as:

- *The David Munrow Edition–The Art of Courtly Love*
- Or anything with David Munrow. He had a way with this sort of thing and made several good albums of this kind of material.

GUILLAUME DE MACHAUT (Ma-SHOW; 1330?–1377)

Greatest composer of the 14th century. He was a musician and a poet. Most of his output was secular with some important exceptions. It's amazing how much care was taken in such an early era to preserve his works, about 200 poems and 145 music works at last count. He wrote in the established forms like isorhythmic motet and even the monophonic *trouvère* songs. His big Mass is the first extant complete Mass setting by a single composer.

- *Mass of Norte Dame*

- *Ma fin est mon commencement*

FRANCESCO LANDINI (Lan-DEE-nee; 1325–1397)

Italian organist-composer blinded as a child from smallpox. Also had renown as a philosopher and astrologer. Though a celebrated organist and choir director, all his 150 or so compositions are secular, mainly two and three-part *ballate*, which was a current song form.

- Offerings on the Bongiovanni label, also Anonymous 4 on Harmonic Mundi, are easy to recommend.

POWER, LEONEL (?–1445)

Wrote a good deal more than the 50 Masses and 15 motets which have come down to us. Represents, along with Dunstable, the most important early English composers. Power was notable in shying away from the abstract intellectualism of the earlier age and developing a style full of personal devotion.

- Masses & motets; (Hilliard Ens. on Reflexe)

DUNSTABLE, JOHN (DUN-sta-bull; 1385–1453)

Leading English composer of the early 15th century. We only have about 70 of his compositions, but they show us a genius who wrote in all available forms. It isn't that he was so superior to his colleagues, but that he united the disparate trends of his time and became The Famous Englishman on the continent. He was also a noted astrologer and mathematician. Influenced greatly the next two giants on our list. Try the recording by The Hilliard Ensemble on Angel (EMI), or the recording on German Harmonia Mundi.

- Motets; (Hilliard Ens. on Virgin Veritas; also many recordings on Naxos)

DUFAY, GUILLAUME (du-FIE; 1400?–1474)

Celebrated even in his own day as the greatest composer alive. From his youth he was sought after all over Europe and freely traveled in service from one court to another. Indeed, the first sixty years of the 15th century can be considered 'The Age of Dufay.' He naturally assimilated the style of every court and country he visited and left behind disciples and admiring throngs. Constantly in search of a new point of view, he sounds ever-fresh. Nowhere, even to the unpracticed ear, is there the stench of routine or dry craft. Admired as much for his all-around genius and literacy as for his musicianship.

- selection of Masses and motets (Veritas, Hyperion and Glossa labels)

BINCHOIS, GILLES (bahn-CHOY, zheel; 1400?–1460)

Composer and musician in service to Phillip the Good. Also, a masterful soldier by all reports. We should remember that the world was smaller back then and a genius could make his mark wearing many different hats. Is most noted for his chansons. These are multi-voiced song settings of French secular poetry. In this form, and at his best, he is unmatched.

- Masses & motets (Binchois Consort on Hyperion)

OCKEGHEM, JEAN DE (OAK-ig-em; 1420?–1495)

When Ockeghem died he was lamented in all the world of music, and tributes poured in from north and south in poem and song, commemorating one of the most influential composers who has ever lived. Not very prolific, but in his handful of Masses, motets and chansons, the Renaissance can be said to have officially begun. He delighted in the mathematical intricacies of composition, turning voices backwards, upside-down and inside-out, but with such skill and inspiration that one would never suspect such activity. Incredible intellect though he was, like Bach after him, he never sacrificed beauty for technical display.

- Masses, motets and chansons
- *Requiem*

BUSNOIS, ANTOINE (boos-NOY; ?–1492)

Priest, poet and musician. Poles apart from the philosophy of Ockeghem. His output is strictly secular entertainment with a few sacred works for good measure. Deliberately sought out the strange and bizarre to hold listener's attention. Many nice effects.

- Masses & motets (The Binchois Consort on Helios)

DESPREZ, JOSQUIN (deh-PRAY, often referred by first name alone: zhos-KAN; 1440–1521)

This master must be counted as one of the four or five greatest composers of all time. Martin Luther said, "He is the master of the notes. They must do as he wills. Other composers, they have to do as the notes will." Very prolific. Colorfully imaginative and emotional. Bridged the gulf between early strict contrapuntal style and a looser, more expressive melodic style. Was the centerpiece of a new generation as Ockeghem was before him.

- Masses, motets and chansons (many recordings available; try the motet *Inviolata*, conducted by Higgenbottom, if you can find it. If you don't like that piece, move on from Renaissance choral music because you will never find a more perfect piece of music in that style, or any other.)

ISAAC, HENRICUS (EE-sahk; ca.1450–1517)

Absorbed more national styles than any other composer of his generation. Wrote in all forms, and in his later works may have indicated parts for a written instrumental accompaniment.

- Masses, motets, songs (the Christophorus label has at least two dedicated discs)

OBRECHT, JACOB (OH-brekt; 1451?–1505)

A daring experimenter in the old forms, imaginative and sometimes shocking (relatively speaking). Wrote 24 Masses and about 30 motets. A very facile composer, he could pen a Mass in a single night, but this is not the sign of a great composer. Rather it is his frank and pious sensibility that earns him that distinction.

- Masses, motets, and chansons (a dozen or so good, dedicated discs available)

WILLAERT, ADRIAAN (VIL-ayrt; 1490–1562)

In addition to his very large output of Church music as choirmaster at St. Mark's in Venice (a nice gig and hard to get), he was one of the first composers of *madrigals*. Paid great attention to the careful way he would set the text of his pieces, striving for clarity and sense—not always the case in others.

- Masses, motets, madrigals and magnificats (two dedicated discs available on Ricercar)

TAVERNER, JOHN (TA-ver-nerr; c.1495–1545)

English composer and organist who is credited with taking English music over the threshold from the Medieval to the Renaissance. Wrote eight Masses and many motets. Imprisoned for heresy in 1528 but freed soon after.

- *Western Wynde Mass*. (Based upon a song popular at the time. Taverner strings together beautifully some 36 variations on the song's melody (nine in each of four movements). It was a very common practice for composers to use popular secular (sometimes downright obscene) tunes as material for the most sacred of compositions. They got away with it for a long time before the Pope got mad. Palestrina was charged with 'fixing' this.)
- other Masses, motets and Magnificats (Hyperion and Gimell)

TALLIS, THOMAS (rhymes with 'palace'; 1505–1585)

English composer and organist and one of the very greats. Queen Elizabeth granted Tallis, along with the younger William Byrd, a monopoly on all music paper and publishing for more than 20 years. Great composer of Church music, known too for his viol and keyboard works. Sublime melodist.

- *Spem in Alium*–motet in 40 (!!!) parts
- *Lamentations*
- other motets

- viol works

PALESTRINA, GIOVANNI PIERLUIGI DA (pa-lay-STREE-na; 1525?–1594)

In his later life he "blushed and grieved" for having set secular love poems in his youth. Pinnacle of the Church composer. His music is of utmost calm and purity and never jarring, but in his deliberately narrow framework he can create psychedelic effects. Like Bach in this way. His Mass *Thou art Peter* on German Harmonia Mundi is magnificent.

- *Pope Marcellus Mass*
- a selection of Masses, motets and Magnificats

LASSUS, ROLAND DE (LOSS-us, often referred to by the Italian version of his name: Orlando di Lasso; 1532–1594)

Enormously prolific. Ranks with Palestrina as the best of the age. Incredibly versatile, he embraced all styles and manners in his motets. He enjoyed a fiery, impulsive youth which shows in his early music, and which is becoming to a young man. In older age he mellowed out into one of the greatest writers of sacred counterpoint.

- *Tears of St. Peter* (avoid the wretchedly poor early digital recording on L'oiseaux Lyre; try Harmonia Mundi, Naxos or Sony)
- motets
- *Penitential Psalms*

BYRD, WILLIAM (Bird; 1543?–1623)

Pupil of Tallis. His three Mass settings are possibly the finest ever by an Englishman, but due to the deadly religious oddities in England at the time, had a limited popularity. Absorbed to perfection the current developments on the continent. Has given us, in addition to great motets, beautiful madrigals and music for keyboard and viols. Byrd was a colossal genius, and the finest English composer before Purcell.

- Masses (3); for three, four and five voices
- selection of motets and madrigals

- the *Great Service*
- keyboard music
- viol music

VICTORIA, TOMAS LUIS DE (1548?–1611)

Pupil of Palestrina. Composed only sacred music. Infused the Roman style of Palestrina with a Spanish intensity and mystic vibration. Under-rated and under-recorded, yet never fails to impress.

- *Requiem*
- motets and Masses

GABRIELLI, GIOVANNI (gob-ree-EL-ee; 1554–1612)

Had the St. Mark's in Venice gig for 27 years. His great genius was in motet composition with instrumental accompaniment. Since St. Mark's was so large, he used the *antiphonal* style to great effect. All over the cathedral he could place choirs, brass instruments, and viols in various sizes and mixtures, and combined these with the organ(s) there. He spun works of unprecedented color and force.

- *Sacrae symphoniae*
- polychoral motets
- music for brass choir

This is a good place to insert a note regarding lute music. It is important to realize the high place that the lute held in homes of all nations during the Renaissance. You couldn't be considered a gentleman or lady unless you could play it to some degree. (Its place in history was taken by the virginal and harpsichord, then the piano, and in the Modern age by the stereo system.) Rather than hunting up specific lute composers, try procuring an album or two of lute music from different countries during the Renaissance. Try the many offerings on the Astree label. Make sure to include the French in your selections. Their style is unique, and so different from the German style that they might as well be from different planets.

MORLEY, THOMAS (1557–1602)

One of the greatest songwriters who ever lived. Excelled in the arena of the madrigal. Good pal of Shakespeare. Morley is also well known and respected as a fine editor and author of musical treatises.

- *The Triumphs of Oriana* (I Fagiolini on Chandos)

GESUALDO, DON CARLO (jezh-WALL-doe; 1560?–1613)

Distinguished Italian madrigalist. Far more harmonically advanced than his contemporaries. Well, 'advanced' is one way to look at it. Many just thought him unhinged, undisciplined and contrary. His music is strange and melancholy. He is also known as a jealous husband who killed his wife and lover, and then his child because he thought he noted a resemblance to his rival. We may wonder how a radical, morose and isolated writer such as he ever even got into print. Easy. He was Prince of Venosa and he made them an offer they couldn't refuse. His music is unrivalled for those rare moods we all have, when we would rather wallow in a hopeless sorrow than try to pull ourselves out of it.

- madrigals and motets, many available

SWEELINCK, JAN PIETERSZOON (SVAY-link; 1562–1621)

Renowned mainly for his keyboard music, he was the first composer to work out and write down *fugues*. This is one of the greatest developments in musical history. Fantastic organist and harpsichordist as well as influential teacher.

- harpsichord and organ works (he can be found here and there on almost 200 discs, but the complete keyboard pieces on six discs is to be had on the Glossa label.)

DOWLAND, JOHN (1563–1626)

A sort of Lennon-McCartney of the early 17th century. His lute songs are still played today, and his solo lute pieces are often transcribed to other instrumental combinations so that they too, may share in these beautiful works. A perfect marriage of the tuneful with good form and noble, sincere sentiment.

- lute songs (avoid Sting's attempt. Noble effort but almost unlistenable.)

MONTEVERDI, CLAUDIO (mon-te-VAIR-dee; 1567–1643)

One of the handful of consummate geniuses the music world has produced. He concluded the Renaissance era and ushered in the Baroque. A great melodic mastermind. His operas are unsurpassed even today, and his madrigals (nine books) represent the full spectrum of human feelings. One of the greatest tragedies in musicology is the loss of perhaps six of his operas; his great dramatic reputation rests on only *three* which are his legacy.

- *Orfeo*
- *Return of Ulysses*
- *Marriage of Poppea*
- madrigals
- motets (Try Parrott on Angel (EMI))
- *Vespers of 1610*

PRAETORIUS, MICHAEL (pry-TOR-eeyus; ca.1571-1621)

Greatest musical scholar and writer of his age. German organist and chapel-master to royalty. Wrote mostly sacred music, masses, motets in the chorale style. Very prolific, with more than 1200 songs and chorale arrangements. His *Terpsichore* is a compendium of more than 300 instrumental dances, which is both his most widely known work, and his sole surviving secular work.

- *Es ist ein Ros entsprungen*—(try Gardiner on London)
- *Terpsichore*

FRESCOBALDI, GIROLAMO (fres-co-BALL-dee; 1583–1643)

It's said that 30,000 people (a lot in any era) attended his first organ concert as organist of St. Peter's in Rome. Frescobaldi was different from his contemporaries in that he emphasized a subjective mysticism over mere grandiose virtuosity. Composed in many forms but is to be noted primarily for his keyboard works.

- organ and harpsichord works

GIBBONS, ORLANDO (1583–1625)

English composer and fantastic keyboard player. Wrote in all available forms but excelled in the 'consort song.' These are solos or duets accompanied by viols or sometimes viols and a chorus.

- vocal music
- keyboard music
- viol music

This is a good place to consider the madrigal of early England, also France, but the language and sensibility of the English is more appealing to English-speaking people today. Several composers excelled in this delightful genre and though a few stand out (Thomas Weelkes, 1575–1623; Thomas Morley, 1557–1603; John Wilby, 1574–1638), consider purchasing a collection of madrigals at first for a nice cross-section. It is some of the most delightful music you are ever likely to hear. Avoid over-scholastic, precious or sanctimonious renderings. Early mono recordings can be like that. The King's Singers on Angel (EMI) excel at this repertory but have a strong flavor (and no women singers), so get some variety.

SCHUTZ, HENRICH (rhymes with 'puts'; 1585–1672)

Studied with Gabrielli. His achievement lies in combining Italian vocal style with German polyphonic tradition. His output is almost entirely vocal and in German.

- passions or oratorios
- *Symphoniae sacrae*
- psalms
- *Swan Song*

CARISSIMI, GIACOMO (car-EES-e-mee; 1605–1674)

One of the superlative oratorio composers. Sweet, florid, serene, or austere, the music becomes the text perfectly. His *Jeptha* is the model for the oratorio form itself.

- *Jephtha* (Try Gardiner on Erato)
- other oratorios

LULLY, JEAN-BAPTISTE (loo-LEE; 1632–1687)

'Music Master to the Royal Family' of Louis the XIV. Obtained exclusive rights to opera production in Paris. A rather dodgy court intriguer and wheeler-dealer. Created the French opera and wrote comic opera-ballets with Moliere. He was also noted as a great actor and dancer. A one man show. The account of his unique death is strange. It seems that some conductors in the Baroque era used a big wooden staff in their conducting, pounding on the floor for the beat. A bit carried away one performance, he smashed the stick into his foot. Got infected. He refused to have his foot amputated and died.

- operas
- motets

CHARPENTIER, MARC-ANTOINE (char-PAHN-tee-ay; 1634–1704)

Pupil of Carissimi. Fine composer of opera, oratorio and sacred choral works. A leading figure in the overthrow of the despotic Lully. Baroque music lovers are forever indebted to French Harmonia Mundi for their magnificent series of Charpentier recordings. They are *all* good ones. If you want more, stay far away from modern instrument realizations. Charpentier *cries out* for the proper colors, balances and intensities. Perhaps these can be achieved on modern instruments, but I have never heard them come close.

- operas
- oratorios
- motets
- *Lecons de tenebres*

BUXTEHUDE, DIETRICH (boox-te-HOO-da; don't say BUX-te-hyude or the music goons will getcha; 1637–1707)

World famous in his day as an organist and composer. A great influence on and forerunner of J.S. Bach. Wrote charming chamber music and fine oratorios which work best on original instruments. Bach liked him so much he walked and hitch-hiked 200 miles to see and hear the great man, study and stay with him awhile. Bux liked Bach so much that he offered him his own job. Normally a great gig, but Bach declined. (Bux's daughter was part of the deal.)

- organ works
- trio sonatas
- oratorios

BIBER, HENRICH IGNAZ FRANZ VON (BEE-bear; 1644–1704)

German virtuoso violinist-composer. Wrote in most genres. His use of *scordatura* (de-tuning strings to unorthodox pitches) gives his string works an unusual coloring. His *Missa Salisburgensis* uses 53 voice parts and is perhaps the largest-scale piece of extant sacred Baroque music.

- *Rosary Sonatas*
- chamber and orchestral works
- cantatas
- *Missa Salisburgensis*

CORELLI, ARCHANGELO (cor-AY-lee; 1653–1713)

Italian violinist-composer. Possibly the most lyrical violin compositions ever written flowed from his pen. The violin, in a sense, becomes for Corelli a sort of supervoice, doing things a human voice could never do, but keeping in close affinity. Influenced Vivaldi and Handel.

- trio sonatas
- solo sonatas
- concerto grossi

PACHELBEL, JOHANN (POCKL-bell; 1653–1706)

German organist and composer. Bach admired him greatly. Too bad he's only known for the overplayed *Kanon in D major*. He's not a one-trick pony, but a true master of the art of the keyboard.

- *The Harp of Apollo*
- *Kanon in D* (We know this piece today primarily in its Romantic arrangement for full string orchestra. It is very sweet and lovely. You must be from Mars not to have heard it. Ever been to a wedding? It is, along with Vivaldi's *Four Seasons*, probably responsible for attracting uninitiated persons to classical music more than any other work. Stay away from the 'original instrument' versions unless you are prepared to hear the work at twice the speed and scored only for three violins, cello and harpsichord. It's still nice, but unrecognizable if you are used to the souped-up version which has so captured the imagination of the public. It's a great arrangement.

MARAIS, MARIN (ma-RAY; 1656–1728)

To be noted mainly as a composer and player of the viola de gamba. This instrument, long in disuse, is being resurrected today. You'll see why. Studied with Lully.

- works for viola da gamba

TORELLI, GIUSEPPE (tor-ELL-ee; 1658–1709)

Italian composer of string music. A key figure in the development of the concerto format.

- concerto grossi
- violin concerti

PURCELL, HENRY (PER-sull; 1659–1695)

England's greatest composer. Composed, in his short life, music of astonishing range and beauty. Wrote the first English opera. A genius of Mozartian stature.

- *Dido and Aeneas*
- viol fantasies
- anthems and odes
- keyboard music

- music for the theatre

SCARLATTI, ALESSANDRO (scar-LA-tee; 1660–1725)

Pupil of Carissimi and father of Dominico. Wrote 115 operas, and a good 600 cantatas.

- cantatas
- operas

FROBERGER, JOHANN JACOB (FRO-bear-ger – hard 'g'; 1616–1667)

Early keyboard players love this guy. Like Handel a lifetime later, he was born and raised in Germany, went to Italy (to study with Frescobaldi) and then to England where, unlike Handel, he almost starved to death. In London he finally landed a job pumping the bellows (no electricity, remember) for some second-rate organist. Eventually, his great gifts pulled him up to the station of composer and court organist.

- keyboard works

COUPERIN, FRANCOIS (KOO-pran; 1668–1733)

The greatest writer of French harpsichord music. Also, to be noted for the chamber music he composed *while 'ordinaire de al musique de la chambre du Roi'* under Louis XIV.

- harpsichord works
- chamber music
- sacred vocal works

ALBINONI, TOMMASO (all-bee-NO-nee; 1671–1750)

His 80 operas have yet to see their resurrection, but his concertos are still with us. Fine, light listening. He wasn't an oboist (he was a virtuoso violinist) but he loved the thing and wrote many fine concertos for the instrument. His rep grew to the point where Bach himself used Albinoni's music to teach students. So, we might see a resurgence. Incidentally, the popular *Albinoni*

Adagio isn't by Albinoni at all. A 20th century musicologist uncovered a manuscript fragment possibly by Albinoni; altered, extended, and arranged it, got a copyright on it, and cleaned up.

- concertos

VIVALDI, ANTONIO (vee-VALL-dee; 1678–1741)

He once wrote a five-hour opera in five days. He could compose faster than a copyist could copy. This fiery Roman Catholic priest (who refused to say Mass) is famous today for his *Four Seasons* and other string music, but his sacred choral music and solo cantatas give testimony to the amazing versatility and inventive power of the man. The joke is that Vivaldi wrote the same concerto 600 times, but boy, what a concerto! Taught music to, and conducted an orchestra of, orphaned schoolgirls. Tony Vivaldi and his All-Girl Band.

- *Four Seasons*
- *Mandolin Concerto*
- other concertos and sonatas, zillions from which to choose and none are bad
- *Gloria*

ZELENKA, JAN DISMAS (zay-LAYNK-ah; 1679–1745)

Court composer born in Bohemia and served at Dresden. His unpredictable turns of phrase and instrumentation will keep you on your toes. Not the typical 'sewing-machine Baroque' style. Bach and Telemann both admired him. He has only recently been given his due. I suspect more to come.

- trio sonatas
- *Requiem*

TELEMANN, GEORG PHILLIP (TAY-lay-mahn; 1681–1767)

Has the dubious distinction of being the most prolific composer that ever lived. Wrote in all genres. Catered not only to the professional but gave fine music to the amateur performer as well. Finely crafted and delightful works. The Germans are not as reliant on color as the French, but a good Telemann performance by an authentic-instrument group is almost always to be pre-ferred over a modern one.

- overtures
- operas
- cantatas
- *Tafelmusik* (literally, ambient music to eat, drink and party by)

RAMEAU, JEAN-PHILIPPE (rah-MOE; 1683–1764)

Wrote 20-plus operas and not one before he was 50. The greatest composer of 18th century France. He is possibly the most neglected of composers. Only recently, with the restoration of the original rich colors and textures provided by the best original-instrument ensembles, is his consummate greatness being resurrected. His output is almost exclusively opera and opera-ballet.

- operas
- harpsichord music
- ballets

BACH, JOHANN SEBASTIAN (Bahk; if you want to impress the music dweebs, make a noise like you're choking on a Brillo pad at the end of his name. The geeks will give you the password to their treehouse; 1685–1750)

No greater artist of any discipline ever lived. He flourished at a time when he could be the point of culmination of all that had gone before him, and so lived in an age where such greatness was possible. He wrote the most perfect examples of every genre he attempted. He never wrote an opera, though some of his secular cantatas come close. All of his music was dedicated to "the glory of God" and he inscribed each work at its beginning with "Jesus help me." He saw no difference between secular and sacred music. All music was, to him, for "the recreation of the soul and the glorification of the Lord." Lest we paint too pious a picture, let us note that he enjoyed his wine, food (quite fat), tobacco (actually used to write poems about how great it was to smoke pipes), and sex (two wives, nineteen children). To art music lovers, I strongly suggest picking up a copy of *The Bach Reader* by Hans David and Arthur Mendel or any other of the many volumes of Bach biographies. Though an in-depth description of this miracle of art called Bach is beyond the scope of this book, I feel that to know him better is to love and respect his art even more. Mystic, numerologist, geometrist and philosopher, all contentedly hidden behind the calm guise of the local chapelmaster.

- The *Passions*
- *Mass in B Minor*—the best Catholic Mass ever written was composed by a Lutheran.
- any of the 200-plus cantatas. (More than one-hundred are *lost*.)
- works for solo violin and solo cello
- *Brandenburg Concertos*
- organ works
- *Art of Fugue*
- *Well-Tempered Clavier* (This is the Old Testament of keyboard music and is regarded as such by all professional classical pianists.)
- *Goldberg Variations* (Authenticity is swell, but to hear Glen Gould play Bach on the piano—an instrument that post-dates Bach—is magical.)

HANDEL, GEORGE FRIDERIC (HAN-dul; 1685–1759)

Handel's mastery was to be found primarily where Bach's was not: in the great field of opera and oratorio. This most cosmopolitan of composers (born in Germany, educated in Italy, settling in England) was the culmination of the Baroque opera and oratorio. Lifelong bachelor, he was vain, and playful with the ladies. When old he was so fat he could hardly reach the keyboard. Like Bach, he died blind due to botched surgery by the same quack.

- *Messiah*
- *Theodora* (his favorite of all his works)
- other oratorios
- Any of the 30 or so of his operas are fine investments. His opera and oratorios have been surging big in the past few decades. Handel, for all his fine reputation, is still one of the most under-recorded of composers when one considers his output. His other achievements in the fields of keyboard, cantatas or instrumental areas must not be overlooked. He has been placed too long in the shadow of Bach. Comparisons are inevitable but not valid. Handel's genius is more lyrical and less complex. He has a different style than Bach and must be appreciated on his own plane.

81

- harpsichord suites
- organ concertos
- *Concerto Grossi* (Opus 6, at least)
- Italian cantatas
- flute/violin sonatas

SCARLATTI, DOMENICO (scar-LAH-tee; 1685–1757)

1685 was a good year. Throughout the Western world the newspapers announced: "Bach, Handel and Scarlatti Newborns Arrive to Conquer Music World." Son of the great Alessandro, Domenico is known today almost exclusively as composer of his 600 or so keyboard sonatas. Short works of one movement, they display an astonishing variety of style and mood from virtuoso toccata-like sonatas to lovely pastoral movements, surely reflecting the quieter side of the Portuguese and Spanish countryside where he spent the last 35 years of his life in the service of the queen.

- any of the keyboard sonatas

BOYCE, WILLIAM (1710–1779)

English organist and composer. In the shadow of Handel, his works have never really received full attention. Increasing deafness caused him to resign post after post in older age. His melodies are most engaging, and he is a superb craftsman to boot. Never less than delightful.

- symphonies
- overtures
- concerti grossi

PERGOLESI, GIOVANNI (pair-go-LAY-see; 1710–1736)

Catch the dates. He died at 26. Primarily known as a comic opera composer, his *La serva padrona* is a masterpiece of lyric wit. Watch out for false attributions. Fully half the works attributed to him are by others. He was good business for publishers.

- *La serva padrona*
- *Stabat Mater*

82

BACH, CARL PHILIPP EMANUEL (referred to usually as: C.P.E Bach; 1714–1788)

Son of the fabulous J.S. He can rightly be called the father of the early Classical style. Succeeded Telemann (his godfather) as Church music director at Hamburg. His great achievement was in the development of sonata-allegro form. A fine theorist and composer in all forms except opera. More famous in his day than dad. Inexplicably.

- keyboard sonatas
- keyboard concertos
- oratorios

GLUCK, CHRISTOPH WILLIBALD VON (sounds like 'glook,' doesn't rhyme with 'duck'; 1714–1787)

German opera composer. His works are somewhat neglected at present. His aim in opera was to establish a noble, sensitive, natural style of music irrespective of nationalisms. "I believe that my greatest efforts should be directed to seeking a beautiful simplicity."

- *Orfeo ed Euridice* (The version on Astree is a beautiful realization and conveys the composer's intentions.)
- good performances of any of his other operas on authentic instruments as they become available; or at least a version that shows some consideration to the composer's wishes. This is not Wagner. This is the gentle Gluck.

HAYDN, FRANZ JOSEPH (HI-den; 1732–1809)

One of the most essential artists on the list. Born before and died later than Mozart, he expressed the most perfect and prolific classicism. From 1761 to 1790 he served Prince Esterhazy as his court composer and conductor. Here he built his own orchestra in relative seclusion. "There was no one near to confuse me, so I was forced to become original." His work in every genre is prolific (105 symphonies, 52 piano sonatas, 83 string quartets, we're just skimming the surface) and usually of highest quality. Unlike Mozart, a true appreciation of Haydn is usually enhanced upon hearing his music as he heard it. The best way to maintain the balance and integrity of the textures and colors of his chamber pieces is to hear these works performed on authentic instruments in an authentic manner. The late symphonies do not require this treatment so much. The early ones do. They are chamber pieces. More intellectual than Mozart, he would often sacrifice lyricism for plasticity of workmanship. A calm, pleasant, untroubled genius.

- symphonies (a diverse few from the 104 or so)
- string quartets (try Op. 76)
- piano sonatas (Stick to the original forte-pianos for the earlier items. Also, avoid any hint of pedantics in the very early sonatas. They present only a skeleton structure for the performer to elaborate upon. If the pianist is not up to it—and they usually aren't—they will sound juvenile. Move on.)
- cello concertos (2)

BACH, JOHANN CHRISTIAN (usually referred to as J.C. Bach; 1735–1782)

18th child of old Bach. Known as the 'English Bach' after his London residence about 1760. His 13 operas and numerous instrumental works are characterized by uninhibited scoring and melodic charm which influenced Haydn, Mozart and Beethoven.

- piano concertos
- instrumental sonatas

BOCCHERINI, LUIGI (bo-care-EE-nee; 1743–1805)

Italian cellist and composer. If there could have been an Italian Haydn, Boccherini would have gotten the job. Sometimes called "the wife of Haydn" due to his gentle lyricism while writing in the same forms as Haydn. Wrote 20 symphonies, 91 string quartets, 154 quintets, etc. Went to Spain, which was a mistake, because no one there knew or cared about what a great composer he was. Died there in poverty.

- chamber works for strings

MOZART, WOLFGANG AMADEUS (MOAT-zart. Classical music snobs will snigger at you if you say MOE-zart; 1756–1791)

Perhaps the most natural musical talent who has ever lived. Keyboard virtuoso, extraordinary violinist, and first-rate composer, all by the age of 12. He excelled in every genre. His crowning achievements were the piano concertos and the operas, which permit the unbounded use of his innate and unmatched dramatic sense. Some claim him to be the greatest genius that music has ever known. You must decide for yourself. He is superior to Haydn in concertos and operas, which are dramatic and conflictive in nature. But when it comes to string quartets and piano sonatas, many prefer Haydn.

- *Magic Flute*
- *Don Giovanni*
- *Marriage of Figaro*
- *Mass in C minor*
- symphonies (most, but numbers 29, 35, 39, 40 and 41 are universally acclaimed. Note that #37 is rarely mentioned. This is because it is by Michael Haydn.)
- piano concertos (again, most, but numbers 9, 14, 15 and 17-27 are sure to please you.)
- violin concertos 4 and 5 at least
- *A Little Night Music* (Whatever version you buy, remember that Mozart scored the work for four strings. Not the Berlin Philharmonic. Nor the Fill-in-the-blank Bassoon Octet. Arrangements are nice sometimes, but always try to check out the original intention first. You'll usually be happy you did.)
- string quintets
- piano sonatas and other music for solo piano
- serenades and divertimentos

BEETHOVEN, LUDWIG VAN (BAY-toe-ven; 1770–1827)

The last great classicist, the first great Romantic, and to many the finest composer of all. He radically transformed the spirit and letter of the music of his predecessors. The first composer writing not to fill the orders of patrons, but on account of a great inner need. Treated royalty as equals. As a young man, deafness soon turned this great titan into an increasingly paranoid and self-obsessed creator. The stone deafness of his later life turned him inward, where he translated this great loneliness of spirit into what may be the profoundest expression man has ever made in sound.

- symphonies (all nine)
- piano concertos (all five)
- piano sonatas (all 32)
- *Violin Concerto*
- string quartets (all 16)
- *Missa Solemnis*
- overtures
- *Fidelio* - his only opera

WEBER, CARL MARIA VON (VAY-bear; 1779–1839)

His opera *Der Freischutz* made him, in his lifetime, the most popular composer in Germany. He made German music truly Germanic by shaving away the obvious foreign influences. He wrote in most genres but is to be noted mainly for his operas and clarinet works. He spoke badly of Beethoven, and after hearing a premier of the *Seventh Symphony* wrote in the press: "Beethoven is now truly ready for the madhouse." He's a better composer than he was a critic.

- *Der Freischutz*
- clarinet works

PAGANINI, NICCOLO (pah-gah-NEE-nee; 1782–1840)

The first rock 'n roll-type superstar. No hyperbole there. He didn't make his concert producers throw out all the brown M&Ms in the bowl, but in all other respects, he was a Rockstar. The greatest technician on the violin that has ever lived. Spellbound audiences constantly with little tricks like breaking three strings while playing and finishing a concert on a single string. Pioneered the use of violin harmonics. He was thought by the less astute to be in league with the devil, thus the only way to explain his super-virtuosity and his frail, emaciated, corpselike visage.

- *24 Caprices for Solo Violin*
- violin concertos
- chamber music with guitar

ROSSINI, GIOACCHINO (row-SEE-nee; 1792–1868)

Composer of almost exclusive operatic fame. His operas, both comic and serious, are noted for their grace and wit. He threw away melodies that most composers would kill for. He quit writing almost entirely with 40 more years to live. Became a massive party-thrower. Entertaining famous men in the grand manner became his new occupation, but his fame has never dimmed, and he was as popular with audiences a century ago as he is today.

- *Barber of Seville*
- *William Tell*

DONIZETTI, GAETANO (doe-nee-TZET-tee; 1797–1848)

Revered master of the *bel canto* (long, sustained vocal lines intended to show off the beauty of the voice) opera. Some 70 of them, serious and comic. Stands stylistically between Rossini and Verdi. Deeply rooted in Italian life and folk tradition.

- *Lucia di Lammermoor*
- other operas

SCHUBERT, FRANZ (SHOO-bayrt; 1797–1828)

Ranks as one of the greatest of all composers in most areas (except opera and concerto) and unequalled in the song form, known as *lieder*, but it's an acquired taste for most. His melodic sense was unfailing, but this did not stop him from a fine understanding of form, which he always fancied himself deficient in. His instrumental works are no less imbued with melodic richness and subtlety than are his songs. See especially the works for strings, and the piano sonatas, which are dreamier in form and content than Beethoven's.

- string quartets
- symphonies #5, 8 and 9
- piano sonatas
- lieder

BELLINI, VINCENZO (bay-LEE-nee; 1801–1835)

None of your comic nonsense with old Vince. Master of opera and all 11 of them serious as a heart attack. His style is one of ultimate refinement and elegance of harmony and melodic contour.

- *Norma*
- *I Puritani*

BERLIOZ, HECTOR (BEAR-lee-ohz; 1803–1869)

Often described as the arch-Romantic. He brought orchestral instrumentation and technique into the Modern era. Superbly colorful and dramatic, he was a fine opera composer on the grand scale as well as a facile composer for large orchestra. *Monstrously* large orchestra. The Romantics did not always go in for small-scale chamber works and Berlioz is no exception. If I tell you that, for instance, Berlioz once conducted a performance of one of his works with a sword and finished the piece weeping hysterically while slumped over the kettle drums, you may think that he was missing a few important brain parts. But we must understand the age in which these great Romantics lived. Such behavior was very genuine in its way and understood and shared by the great artists of his day as well as his audience. There was a different spirit animating those times, and we would not seriously disparage it if we understood it. Fortunately, there is more to Berlioz than hysterics and when this fact is truly appreciated the reasons for his formidable reputation will become clear.

- *Roman Carnival Overture*
- *The Damnation of Faust*
- *Requiem*
- *Symphonie fantastique*
- *Te Deum*
- *L'Enfance du Christ*

MENDELSSOHN, FELIX (MAYN-del-zone; 1809–1847)

Though he only lived 38 years, his genius manifested itself mostly in his youth. A conservative Christian convert from a wealthy Jewish family (his banker dad *bought* Felix an orchestra when he was a kid), he had little patience with the passion of the Romantics. Lived with Goethe for a spell. The wild side of the Romantics (people like Liszt) freaked him out, but oddly, he and Berlioz were close buddies. Clear-cut, restrained, and excellently crafted music flowed with ease from his pen. At best he is inspiring and joyous.

- symphonies #3, 4 and 5
- *Piano Concerto #1* (comparing the freewheeling #1 with the 'mature' #2 is a good example of why some prefer the earlier music)
- *Elijah*
- symphonies for strings (also youthful pieces that are staggeringly fun and inventive; he was never so joyful or un-self-conscious as here)

SCHUMANN, ROBERT (SHOO-mahn; 1810–1856)

This troubled genius, lifelong battler of the artistic philistines, was a great composer for the piano and of the song. Died in an asylum. His wife, Clara, was a good composer and even more excellent piano virtuoso. His chamber music is infused with a lyric and deeply felt poetry which is unmistakably his alone. His instrumentation is often criticized, but this criticism is often the result of a lack of understanding of Schumann's purpose.

- piano works
- Symphony #4
- Lieder (German art songs)

CHOPIN, FREDERIC (show-PAN; 1810–1849)

The Poet of the Piano. Composed almost exclusively for the instrument. No one has ever matched the delicate subtlety nor the heroic powerful heights which he could ascend with equal ease. The apotheosis of Romantic-era piano music.

- nocturnes, etudes, waltzes, polonaises and impromptus
- *Preludes*

LISZT, FRANZ (Leest; 1811–1886)

A more fiery sort than Chopin, he stressed virtuosity and vitality over subtlety, and for some people is more attractive than Chopin for this reason. For others a non-stop vulgarity. Clara Schumann, ultra-refined wife of Robert, disliked him intensely. A youthful admirer of Paganini, he set out to be the "Paganini of the Piano." He succeeded. He was likely the greatest pianist that ever lived. The first stage performer documented to have women's underpants flung at him. Chopin once said that he wished he could play his own etudes like Liszt played them. Also, unlike Chopin, Liszt was an accomplished orchestral composer and his two symphonies and tone poems are proof of this. Liszt and Chopin were best buds for years, but their spiteful female companions pretty much ruined their relationship. Toward his old age he abandoned the Rockstar gig, took minor orders from the Church and became Abbé Liszt. Rolling in money, he drank cheap wine, ate little and taught piano. His music changed to a sacred sort and his piano music became sparse in texture.

- *Sonata in B Minor* (the greatest piano sonata of the entire era)
- *St. Francis Legends*
- *Ballade in B minor*
- piano concertos
- an album of late piano works (These display an entirely different side of Liszt. In the last years of his life he became a sort of priest-hermit and his piano music is a vivid analogue of this. It is the beginning of Modern music.)
- *Faust Symphony*

VERDI, GIUSEPPE (VAIR-dee; 'Joe Green' in English; 1813–1883)

Along with Monteverdi, Mozart, Handel, and Wagner, he must be considered in the race for the best opera composer of all time. His main strength was his honesty and realistic portrayal of his characters. Opera was, for Verdi, 'human' drama.

- *Aida*
- *Rigoletto*
- *La traviata*
- *Requiem*

WAGNER, RICHARD (VOGG-nair. You will be chortled at by snotty music dweebs if you say WAG-nerr; 1813–1883)

Wagner was a cruel, selfish, scheming, second-rate human being in many ways. (When obliged to conduct "the Jew" Mendelssohn, he would wear gloves to hold his baton.) He was also the most influential and greatest dramatist since Monteverdi. He consummated German opera and brought 19th century tonality to its inevitable conclusion, meaning, if it got any more chromatic, the tonal center would have disappeared. His pioneering use of symbolism was profound and brilliant and his monstrous influence in music-drama is still felt today.

- *Tristan and Isolde*
- *The Ring*

FRANCK, CESAR (Frahnk. First name SAY-zar; 1822–1890)

Creator of fine organ and choral music which restored a Romantic-Classical idiom to French music.

- *Symphony in D*
- organ and piano works
- *Sonata for Violin and Piano*

BRUCKNER, ANTON (BREWK-nerr; 1824–1896)

Composer of 11 symphonies, (the early '0' and '00' usually not included in his mature catalogue) and most over an hour in length. Also, fine Masses and motets. Devout and humble to a fault. His open fawning worship of Wagner disgusted and embarrassed Wagner, but Bruckner (opposite of Wagner) had no guile. He didn't know how to dissemble. This is all the stranger considering that much of Bruckner's music is superior to a good deal of Wagner's. One critic said of him "It's not the heat, it's the humility." Bruckner was intensely religious. His childlike faith in God lies at the root of these enormous, complex and melodically stunning works. Once, as guest lecturer in a Vienna university, the Church bells rang. Bruckner put down his chalk, turned and fell to his knees in prayer and there remained until the tolling ceased. He then rose, picked up his chalk and continued the lesson. This was not (never has been) acceptable Viennese behavior, but no one ever questioned or doubted his right or reason. He was Bruckner. Once answered the door stark naked to a gaggle of church ladies because he was preoccupied with a musical problem while taking a bath. Probably died a virgin.

- all nine numbered symphonies
- motets

SMETANA, BEDRICH (SMEH-tah-nah; 1824–1884)

Second only to Dvorak as the most important Czech composer of the 19th century. Very nationalistic, this trait is noticed to great effect in the operas. Was prodigious, played in a string quartet at five, composed at eight. Close friend of Liszt. Also known as a great pianist and toured Europe widely. Suffered the tragedy of deafness, and in the *String Quartet #1*, the finale contains a high pitch drone (an 'e') which represents the ringing sound he heard in his head from his tinnitus affliction.

- *Ma Vlast*
- the two string quartets
- *The Bartered Bride*

BORODIN, ALEXANDER (BOR-oh-deen; 1833–1887)

Russian composer who was also skilled as physician and surgeon. Early compositions met with failure until Liszt arranged a performance of the *First Symphony* outside Russia. That did it. His growing fame as a scientist made composing time rarer as he grew older. Failed to finish his masterpiece *Prince Igor*. A very gentle man, his house was constantly littered with 'artistic' types eating up his food and sleeping on the floors.

- *Prince Igor*
- symphonies
- string quartets (2)

BRAHMS, JOHANNES (rhymes with 'proms,' not 'hams'; 1833–1897)

A master in all forms of music except opera, in which he never showed interest. His brand of Romanticism fits well into Classical forms and when it doesn't, he classicizes Romantic methods. A master of piano, chamber music, song, and symphony. His music is unmistakable in its unique mellowness and burnished wood quality. Sometimes I smell fine cigar smoke when I listen to him. Though Liszt befriended him, he showed open disdain for Liszt and his school, and once fell asleep while Liszt played to him. Was also ideologically opposed, and quite openly, to Wagner and his ilk. Though a bachelor, he loved women, especially Clara Schumann, wife of Robert. He loved her, and she loved him very dearly, and Brahms took care of her during Robert Schumann's long hospitalizations when she was not allowed to see him. He even helped with the seven kids. Back in the day, Brahms was slim and handsome and dashing, not the fat old greybeard seen in all the pictures. Brahms liked to buy sex at the sex store, and Clara was a *very* respectable lady. So, did they do the wild monkey-dance? Nobody knows.

- symphonies
- *Violin Concerto in D*
- the two piano concertos
- solo piano music
- *German Requiem*
- chamber music for strings
- *Double Concerto*

SAINT-SAENS, CAMILLE (san-SAHNS; 1835–1921)

French composer, pianist and organist. Extreme child prodigy on the level of Mendelssohn and Mozart. Played all the Beethoven sonatas from memory in public when he was 12. Emotion is not a highlight of his work. Rather, he excelled in music of great formal elegance and richness of harmony. Very protective of his reputation. He would not allow *Carnival of the Animals* to be published during his lifetime lest his peers think he was frivolous.

- *Samson and Dalila*
- tone poems
- works for violin and orchestra
- *Danse macabre*
- piano concertos (#2, 4)
- *Organ Symphony*

BIZET, GEORGES (bee-ZAY; 1838–1875)

French composer and pianist. Most famous for his operas, but also a fine writer of church music and piano works. Another one of those dead-in-his-

30s composers, no one could listen to his *Carmen* (the world's most famous opera?) and not wish he stayed around a while longer.

- *Carmen*
- *The Pearl Fishers*
- *Symphony in C*

MUSSORGSKY, MODEST (MOOSE-org-skee; 1839–1881)

Even lack of training and intense alcoholism could not obscure the natural genius of this composer. Not very prolific but his single opera, many lovely solo songs, and the well-known pieces such as *Night on Bald Mountain* and *Pictures at an Exhibition* testify to the facility of his invention. It has become, thank the music gods, much less fashionable these days to prefer the orchestrations of others over Mussorgsky's original scoring.

- *Pictures at an Exhibition* (original piano version)
- *Boris Gudounov* (not to be conflated with *Boris Badanov* from the *Rocky & Bullwinkle* cartoons; no relation. Try the original version on Philips.)

TCHAIKOVSKY, PIOTR ILYICH (chy-KOFF-skee; 1840–1893)

In 19th century Russian music Tchaikovsky has no close peer. Extremely tuneful, lushly scored, and emotionally fervent. Unequalled in ballet music. His ballets and symphonies are probably the most characteristic manifestation of his genius.

- Symphonies #4, 6
- *Sleeping Beauty*
- *Swan Lake*
- *Nutcracker*
- *Violin Concerto in D*
- *Serenade for Strings*
- *Andante Cantabile*

DVORAK, ANTONIN (DVOR-zhak; if you say DIV-or-ack the music dweebs will shun you and tell all their friends; 1841–1904)

This great Czech composer had a runaway melodic gift combined with outstanding technical facility. Influenced by Brahms, Wagner, and the folk music of his native Bohemia. His fine orchestral works have long been acknowledged as masterpieces and his piano and choral works are only now being reevaluated outside of central Europe. His opera *Rusalka* is universally esteemed.

- symphonies #7, 8 and 9
- *Rusalka*
- late string quartets
- *Cello Concerto in B Minor*
- Serenades (2)
- *Bagatelles for Two Violins, Cellos and Harmonium* (not big or profound, but ultimately charming.)

GRIEG, EDVARD (Greeg; 1843–1907)

Norwegian composer, conductor and pianist. Given more to the miniature than the massive. His songs are famous in Scandinavia, but his best works are for the piano. Liszt championed him. Young Grieg took his concerto to Liszt, who accepted him warmly, sat down at the piano, opened the score and played the concerto at speed, adding orchestral parts if an idle finger could fit them in, all while making comments on the score. Liszt was a piano monster, but Grieg's concerto is considered a masterpiece of the genre while Liszt's concertos are generally less highly regarded.

- *Piano Concerto in A*
- solo piano pieces
- *Peer Gynt*

RIMSKY-KORSAKOV, NICOLAY (rim-skee-KOR-seh-koff; 1844–1908)

Was such a natural that he was appointed professor of practical composition and instrumentation at St. Petersburg at 27, almost totally unlearned in counterpoint and harmony. He was just obviously great. He taught himself harmony and counterpoint in secret, got so good at it that he wrote a wonderful textbook on orchestration that is still read today. Teacher of Stravinsky. Very highly regarded in Russia; less so outside it.

- *Scheherazade*
- *Capriccio espangnol*
- other orchestral works

FAURE, GABRIEL (fah-RAY; 1845–1924)

French composer and organist. Regarded as a master of the choral idiom. His piano and chamber works are also to be noted for their delicate poetic appeal and subtle emotional charm.

- *Requiem*
- piano music

JANACEK, LEOS (ya-NAH-chek; 1854—1928)

Czech composer, conductor, organist, and teacher. Of a nationalistic bent, he consciously rejected mainstream Western developments. Mature works characterized by speech-like bursts of rhythmic melodies, sudden changes of tonality and mood, raw but strikingly effective orchestration. He enjoyed a very late and sustained burst of creativity possibly due to an unconsummated longing for a young married woman who admired him.

- *Sinfonietta*
- *Taras Bulba*
- *Jenufa*
- *Glagolitic Mass*

ELGAR, EDWARD (EL-gar; 1857–1934)

The British have had a few great composers (but almost all of the great rock bands—*why is this?!?!*) and Elgar along with Vaughn Williams and Britten share the honors in the early and mid-20th century. Dignity, virtuosity, and spiritualism are qualities that abound in his writings, but humor finds its place as well. He resurrected the English oratorio and his *Dream of Gerontius* is a masterpiece in this idiom.

- *Dream of Gerontius*

- *Enigma Variations*
- Symphonies

PUCCINI, GIACOMO (poo-CHEE-nee; 1858–1924)

Italian opera composer generally considered the best after Verdi. His early work was rooted in traditional late-19th century Romantic Italian opera. Later, he successfully developed his work in the realistic *verismo* style, which emphasized true life in its gritty realism, of which he became one of the leading exponents. His works are strongly melodic, and he had little interest in cutting-edge developments.

- *La bohème*
- *Tosca*
- *Madama Butterfly*
- *Turandot*

MAHLER, GUSTAV (MAH-ler; 1860–1911)

Some would claim that he is the greatest symphonist after Beethoven. Mahler took the symphony to the hidden recesses of the soul. He can terrify you as well as make you feel like a child. His output is almost entirely limited to symphony and song-cycle, but in that narrow scope he can show us a part of ourselves that other composers don't really want to know about. He was standing outside the rehearsal hall one day, conversing with another gent. Mahler shushed him, and they listened. They could hear the orchestra rehearsing in the hall, and a poor busker playing his violin on the corner for a few pennies. Down the street at the same time comes a marching band. Mahler looks at his friend and says, "Now, that's counterpoint!" If you listen to his symphonies you will discover that he was only half-kidding.

- symphonies (all nine)
- *The Song of the Earth*
- *The Tenth Symphony—first movement.* Do not miss out on this, nor look askance upon it in its unfinished form. A good deal of it was completed, the big first movement is considered finished by some, and that which was not stands before us as an essential and undiluted torso—almost unbearable to look upon in its una-

dorned nakedness. Some have tried to complete the entire work from Mahler's sketches. I avoid this sort of thing myself. This is a bad symphony to start your Mahler studies with, but if you get to know him, you'll treasure that first movement.

DEBUSSY, ACHILLE-CLAUDE (Okay ready? uh-SHEEL klode duh-bew-SEE. Too hard even for the music geeks, so no one will bat an eye if you just call him DEB-you-see; 1862–1918)

Although he hated the term 'impressionistic' applied to his music, it is hard to think of a better term to describe it. He realized that the tonal world of Wagner was a dead-end and opened new vistas in his own direction. These fertile fields are still being plowed by many composers alive today. A master colorist (the French are like that in all the arts), he sought a radiant, subtle sound in his orchestration. Unlike many impressionists however, he was not formless. In fact, it is his mastery of form which has made his influence so long lived and pervasive.

- *La Mer*
- *Nocturnes*
- *Prelude to the Afternoon of a Faun*
- *Preludes for Piano*, Books I and II
- *String Quartet*
- *Pelleas et Melisande* (his great opera)

DELIUS, FREDERICK (1862–1934)

Delius can be described as an English impressionist. There is no one like him. When he was 22, he moved to Florida to work on an orange plantation. It was there he contracted syphilis. Moved to Germany where he met Greig. Grieg convinced ma and pa Delius to let their kid be a musician. It was a tough sell, but they said okay, and Delius moved to Paris. He became successful there and relocated to England during WWI. Nobody knew him there. After the war he returned to Paris but by then he was going blind and in the grip of paralysis. But his fame spread and, due mainly to the efforts of conductor Thomas Beecham, achieved great success before his tragic death. I am often not thrilled to be listening to Delius, but I get an afterglow from him, unique, that can last for hours.

- *On Hearing the First Cuckoo in Spring*
- *Summer Night on the River*
- *Walk to the Paradise Garden*
- *Fennimore and Gerda: Intermezzo*

STRAUSS, RICHARD (Schtrouss; 1864–1949)

German composer of magnificent tone poems for orchestra, and operas of intensity and emotional exhaustion. His handling of orchestration and use of color is directly descendent from Liszt and Wagner. Many believe that German Modern music began with his sad study for strings *Metamorphosen*. One of the great conductors of his day. Debussy, a canny observer of other musicians, said that Richard Strauss has "the frank and decisive appeal of those great explorers who walk among savage tribes with a smile on their lips."

- *Death and Transfiguration*
- *Thus Spake Zarathustra*
- *Metamorphosen*
- *Salome*
- *Four Last Songs*

NIELSEN, CARL (NEEL-sen; 1865–1931)

Danish composer, violinist and conductor. Known almost exclusively for his symphonies in our neck of the woods, but wrote a great deal more, from opera to organ music. Had the idea of 'progressive tonality.' This means that a work would begin in a certain key, symbolically transform itself through many key changes and end in a different key from the beginning. The composer Alban Berg echoed the same idea in Germany when he said to a student, "Don't automatically end in the same key you began. Think of all your theme has lived through." Remember the label name BIS. They did a remarkable job in recording his complete works.

- Symphony #4
- Quintet for Winds

SIBELIUS, JEAN (si-BAYL-yuss; 1865–1957)

Rugged, rocky and honest. Scandinavia's greatest composer to date. His music speaks of nature, the kind to be found in his Scandinavian home. The masculine frankness of his expression is very refreshing. He is not interested in effect or in prettiness. He is a rugged, austere soul who knows how to be gentle and is not afraid to be. His *Legends* and other tone poems are like sound-tracks to mind-movies. Oddly, he was very uncomfortable when out enjoying 'nature.' I have a photo of him allegedly fishing. He wore a three-piece suit and was standing bolt upright in the tiny boat looking most uneasy.

- Symphonies #2, 5
- *The Four Legends*
- other tone poems

SATIE, ERIC (sa-TEE; 1866–1925)

Economy of means, brevity, and a refusal to take himself so deadly seriously characterized this very influential French composer. He helped turned the generation after Wagner away from Serious Germanic Romanticism and all that it stood for. A bit of a clown, but like his countryman Duchamp, a serious one.

- piano works
- *Socrate* (short opera)

SCRIABIN, ALEXANDER (SKREE-ah-been; 1872–1915)

The Russian Scriabin was a theosophist. He believed in the occult power of sound and the grand synthesis of all the arts. Though primarily a piano composer, he wrote several symphonies. His last (unfinished) calls for piano, orchestra, chorus, color organ (a keyboard that controlled the color and intensity of the auditorium lights), and even an odor generator. Perhaps the strangest composer ever to have a secure place in the repertoire. A prophet and a genius.

- piano sonatas
- *Poem of Ecstasy*
- preludes and etudes for piano

VAUGHAN WILLIAMS, RALPH (Vawn Williams. If you want the music geeks to swoon and give you their magic decoder ring, pronounce his first name 'Rayf'; 1872–1958)

English composer who wrote in all major genres. Led the revival of English music in the 20th century. Influenced by Debussy and Ravel and the folk music of Great Britain. A master of melody and orchestral color.

- Symphony #5
- *The Lark Ascending*

RACHMANINOV, SERGEI (rakh-MAWN-yee-noff; 1873–1943)

Russian composer, pianist, and conductor. He is thought by many to be the foremost pianist of the 20th century. There are recordings of him playing his own works and that of the great Romantic keyboard composers before him. He was the last of a long line of major Romantics. Recalls at once Chopin and Tchaikovsky. Excelled in the melancholy temperament. Tall and taciturn with gigantic hands. His piano works have always been popular, but only recently have the two symphonies been championed so widely. Speaking of his accomplishment in piano composition, he once said, "After me—nothing."

- *The Bells*
- *Isle of the Dead*
- *Vespers*
- piano concertos (#2 and 3)
- Symphony #2
- *Rhapsody on a Theme of Paganini*
- solo piano works

SCHOENBERG, ARNOLD (SHERN-bairg; 1874–1951)

When conventional tonality reached its limits, Schoenberg formulated the '12-tone theory' in which tonality was abolished and replaced by a system of composing whereby the 12 tones of the octave were related only to one another, each as important as the rest, and not to be repeated until all 12 were used in proper order of whatever tone-row arrangement you have chosen to seed your work. (Now *there's* a quick and dirty explanation. See elsewhere in the book for better. Longer, anyway.) Though in his youth a fine composer of enormous Romantic works, he turned 180 degrees to the stark, more intellectual style of the 12-tone years. He was the most influential theorist and teacher of the first two-thirds of the last century and his ideas are still with us today in many disguises. As Einstein pointed the way past Newtonian physics, Joyce past conventional literature, Kandinsky, Klee and others past realistic and representational art, so did Schoenberg show us a way past the dilemma of tonality. Though it is only recently that we have become aware of other, more pleasing ways to accomplish the same ends, Schoenberg led the way in his theory—if not his music. Another view is that none of his shenanigans caught on, except to academics, who pretty much ruined Modern music for an entire generation with their tedious scribbles, and from which injury Contemporary music has yet to recover. He was fond of saying "I do not write *twelve-tone* music, I write twelve-tone *music*." Schoenberg actually envisioned a time when even the mailman would go his rounds whistling a tone-row. Sorry, Arnie. Not gonna happen.

- *Transfigured Night* (early gorgeous work for large orchestra)
- *Moses and Aaron* (opera)
- late orchestral and piano works

IVES, CHARLES (1874–1954)

One of the most ruggedly individualistic figures in music. His music was so advanced and unusual that he was thought, paradoxically, to be a 'primitive.' Great forerunner of John Cage. I always likened him to poet Walt Whitman in spirit.

- *The Unanswered Question*
- *Concord Sonata* for piano
- Symphony #4

HOLST, GUSTAV (1874–1934)

An Englishman who wrote much lovely music including operas and great choral works and it is a shame that his reputation rests almost solely upon *The Planets*. Mystic and austere, but not without a warm humaneness. A rare combination.

- *The Planets*

- *Three Choral Hymns from the Rig Veda*
- *St. Paul's Suite*

RAVEL, MAURICE (rah-VEL; 1875–1937)

Basque, not French, and he would thank you to remember that. Has much in affinity with Debussy but far more classical in his formal treatment. Exquisite colorist. Brilliant pianist and composer of incredible virtuoso piano solo music. Best known for *Bolero*, a slow-building, rousing sonic-spectacular that the composer described as "a 15-minute orchestration exercise with no music in it."

- *Daphnis and Chloe* (ballet)
- *Bolero*
- *L'Enfant et les sortileges* (opera)
- piano music
- *Introduction and Allegro*
- *Pavane for a Dead Princess*

FALLA, MANUEL DE (de FIE-ah; 1876–1946)

Foremost Spanish composer and pianist of the early 20th century. Combined the tunefulness and rhythmic vitality of Spanish folk music with a cosmopolitan awareness and top-notch technical foundation.

- *Nights in the Garden of Spain*
- *El Amor Brujo*
- *The Three-Cornered Hat*
- solo piano music (check out the pianist Alicia de Larrocha's recordings on Philips and Vox.)

RESPEGHI, OTTORINO (ray-SPEE-gee; hard 'g' as in great; 1879–1936)

Italian composer, conductor, pianist, string player and teacher. Studied with Rimsky-Korsakov. Brilliant and luscious scoring for his oft-played orchestral tone-poems. Somewhat of an Italian impressionist. Also, a fine arranger of old music for which he is best known in the suites from *Ancient Airs and Dances*.

- *Ancient Airs and Dances*
- tone-poems

BARTOK, BELA (BAR-tohk; 1881–1945)

Combined his great intellect for the formal side of music with a comprehensive knowledge of Hungarian folk tunes to produce some of the most imaginative music of the century. A brilliant piano virtuoso. Noted too for his vital and uninhibited approach to rhythm. Died poor and unacknowledged in New York City. His *Piano Concerto #3* was written as a love-letter to his wife, and she had exclusive performing rights to the work after he died. This helped make ends meet. It is more 'beautiful' than the first two, which are very percussive and cutting-edge.

- *Concerto for Orchestra*
- *Music for Strings, Percussion and Celeste*
- string quartets (6)
- piano concertos (3)

STRAVINSKY, IGOR (1882–1971)

After his success as a young man with his ballets (*The Rite of Spring* is often called "the birth of Modern music") he went on, in his long life, to investigate and invigorate almost every genre available to him. He is always unpredictable, but whether it is a simple Neo-Classical arrangement or a 12-tone, cerebral and austere meditation, it is unmistakably his own. Some believe him to be the leading composer of the last century. He conducted and recorded most of his orchestral music and ballets, but many are convinced he's not the man for that job. What do you think?

- The famous ballets (*The Rite of Spring, Firebird, Petroushka*)
- The austere ballets (*Apollo, Orpheus, Agon*)
- *Symphony of Psalms*

104

WEBERN, ANTON VON (VAY-bayrn; 1883–1945)

The most influential student of Schoenberg. So economical and sparse, distilled and quiet is his music that its effect is quite indescribable and unique. Though Schoenberg's theories are highly important it is the dedicated purity of Webern's music which is the more important and influential body of work. Some of his pieces are only a few minutes in length, with some movements lasting a few seconds. His music is a natural consequence of Mahler's. There exists the Complete Works conducted by Boulez, but I feel they are sometimes dry and analytical. Webern wanted these things played with passion and that's not always Boulez' strong suit.

- *String Quartet*
- *Symphony*
- *Piano Variations* (try Pollini on DG)
- cantatas
- *Six Pieces for Orchestra*

VARESE, EDGAR (vah-REZ; 1883–1965)

Only wrote about a dozen pieces but was one of the most influential of 20th century composers. Was big on percussion, electronics, and taped sounds. Way ahead of his time, which means he had to wait till the mid-1950s before he could pay his bills, but by the '60s his pieces were performed all over the Western world. *Ionisation*, a notorious piece for 13 percussionists playing about 40 different instruments, is likely his best known and a good place to start.

- *Ionisation*
- *Density 21.5*
- *Arcana*
- *Intégrales*

BERG, ALBAN (Bairg; 1885–1935)

The other well-known student of Schoenberg and the third member of that 12-tone trinity. He sought a lyrical application of the 12-tone theory and succeeded. His opera *Wozzeck* is perhaps the greatest from the last century.

- *Wozzeck*
- *Violin Concerto*

PROKOFIEV, SERGEI (pro-KO-fee-ev; 1891–1953)

Bold and colorful. Fine dramatist. Brilliant wit. Often very sarcastic. Wrote in most genres. By turns violent and gentle, he managed to express the two opposite temperaments in his personality with great success. Wrote a lot of film music, such as the great score to Eisenstein's *Alexander Nevsky*.

- *Symphony #1* (Unlike any of the others. He wanted to write a symphony that Haydn might write if he were alive in the 20th century. Incredibly charming. He also wanted to prove that he had mastered the technique of writing 'normal music' so when he got weird no one could say he just didn't know any better.)
- other symphonies (Most of these will melt your face, but some of the moments will melt your heart.)
- piano concertos (#3 is notable.)
- violin concertos (2)
- solo piano sonatas (#7, 8)
- *Romeo and Juliet* (a Romantic-style ballet)

HINDEMITH, PAUL (HIN-de-mit; 1895–1963)

Like a latter-day Telemann, he wrote not only for the professional but the amateur too. Unlike Telemann, however, he began his career as an *enfant terrible* and ended it as an ultra-conservative. He wrote in all forms. Reams of chamber music. Wrote a sonata for every instrument in the orchestra, then started over again. His work is characterized by much use of tonal/dissonant counterpoint and strong rhythmic drive.

- *Mathis der maler*
- *Symphonic Metamorphosis*

ORFF, CARL (1895–1982)

Wrote a ton of music, then wrote *Carmina Burana*, then threw all his old music away. Held conducting posts in Germany. He penned *Carmina Burana* for orchestra, chorus and soloists in 1937 when he was 42. It was, and is, a blockbuster in every sense of the word, revealing the raw, elemental power of music, an overwhelming, primitive force. *Carmina Burana* became part of a dramatic trilogy that is all of a piece and hugely entertaining. Almost all his music is dramatic in nature. Also, a world authority on musical education of children.

- *Carmina Burana*

GERSHWIN, GEORGE (1898–1937)
American composer and pianist whose mastery spanned classical and pop. Began his career in NYC as a song-plugger but moved to Paris to study with the greatest teacher of the day, Nadia Boulanger, who refused him, saying that he was fine the way he was and that she could not teach him anything. It's also possible that she realized her type of refinement would be lost on George. He wrote a great opera, and many songs that have become standards. Gershwin moved to Hollywood and composed numerous film scores until his death in 1937 from a brain tumor.

- *Porgy and Bess*
- songs

POULENC, FRANCIS (poo-LAHNK; 1899–1963)

Not really religious, not really a clown, his music was once likened to "seminarians playing baseball." Wrote lovely songs and woodwind music. His opera, *Dialogue of the Carmelites* is considered a masterpiece.

- *Dialogue of the Carmelites*
- *Gloria*
- music for winds

COPLAND, AARON (1900–1990)

Copland is probably considered to be the archetypal American composer for better or worse. Much of his music is based upon American concepts and themes with appropriate idiomatic treatment. He can be folksy, tuneful and gay, or 12-tone and severe.

- *Quiet City*
- *Fanfare for the Common Man*
- *Nonet*

- *Appalachian Spring*

PARTCH, HARRY (1901-1974)

Partch was an American composer, music theorist, and creator of musical instruments. He composed using scales of unequal intervals and was one of the first 20th century composers in the West to work with microtonal scales. He composed with scales dividing the octave into 43 unequal tones derived from the natural harmonic series; these scales allowed for more tones of smaller intervals than in standard Western tuning, which uses twelve equal intervals to the octave. (Typified by any continuous segment of the 12 white and black keys on the piano.) He built custom-made instruments in these tunings on which to play his compositions. His earliest compositions were small-scale pieces to be intoned to instrumental backing; his later works were large-scale, integrated theater productions in which he expected each of the performers to sing, dance, speak, and play instruments. Ancient Greek theatre and Japanese Noh and kabuki heavily influenced his music theatre.

- *8 Hitchhiker Inscriptions from a Highway Railing at Barstow, California*
- *The Letter (5)*

SCELSI, GIACINTO (jah-CHIN-toe SHALE-see; 1905-1988)

Italian master Scelsi is best known for writing music based around only one pitch, altered in all manners through microtonal oscillations and changes in timbre and dynamics. In middle-age he underwent a profound psychological crisis that eventually led him to the discovery of Eastern spirituality, and this radically transformed his view of music. He rejected composition and authorship in favor of sheer improvisation, an inspired 'automatic writing' of music. These were recorded on tape and transcribed by collaborators under his guidance. They were then orchestrated and Scelsi added detailed performance instructions, consulting with his performers. He wrote in most genres, heavy on the chamber music, but was almost completely unknown in his lifetime. Musicologist Harry Halbreich wrote, "A whole chapter of recent musical history must be rewritten: the second half of this century is now unthinkable without Scelsi… He has inaugurated a completely new way of making music, hitherto unknown in the West. In the early fifties, there were few alternatives to serialism's strait jacket that did not lead back to the past." Well, Scelsi achieved this and the results are fascinating. He was a genuine, and scary, musical prophet, but he still has not had his day.

- *Quattro pezzi su una nota sola ("Four Pieces on a single note", 1959).*
- *Anahit*
- String Quartets (5)

SHOSTAKOVICH, DMITRI (shos-ta-KO-vich; 1906–1975)

Russia's greatest 20th century composer. Wrote in all forms. His extroverted body of 15 symphonies is beautifully balanced by the set of 15 intimate quartets for strings. I believe these quartets to be the greatest since the 16 of Beethoven. Rarely is his work entirely free from a great sadness which sometimes barely peeks through and other times glares mercilessly. Avoided the simple sarcasms of Prokofiev but stoically bore the heavy and relentless burden of being a great artist in a repressive hell under Joseph Stalin, with whom he had several close calls.

- string quartets (15)
- symphonies (start with #5)
- *Viola Sonata*
- *Piano Trio*

MESSIAEN, OLIVIER (oh-liv-ee-ay mess-ay-AN; 1908–1992)

French composer known for his organ, piano, and intensely colorful, sparkling and exotic works for orchestra. Developed his own language based upon 12-tone and other cyclical organizational techniques applied not just to the notes but also to rhythm and dynamics. Birdsong is also a strong obsession in his music, and he uses it to great musical effect in several works. Non-Western (specifically Hindu) influence abounds. Teacher of Boulez and Stockhausen.

- *Turangalila-symphonie*
- other orchestral works
- organ works
- *Vingt Regards sur l'Enfant Jesus*
- *Catalogue of Birds*
- *Quartet for the End of Time*

BARBER, SAMUEL (1910—1981)

Samuel Barber, one of the most prominent and popular American composers of the mid-20th century, wrote effectively in virtually every genre. His music is notable for its warm Romantic lyricism, memorable melodies, and essentially conservative harmonic style, all of which put him at odds with the prevailing Modernist aesthetic of his time. Critics and academics did not like him much and this hurt his confidence and, when older, sent him into deep depression. But audiences liked him, and still do. His *Adagio for Strings* is one of the chestnuts of century.

- *Adagio for Strings*
- *Piano Concerto*

We come now to contemporary and near-contemporary composers who have enjoyed success in the concert and recital halls with many recordings to their credit. It is likely that many, but not all, of the following men and women are destined for inclusion in the pantheon of great composers. I admit that, to draw the line here is somewhat arbitrary and a judgement call.

HOVHANNESS, ALAN (hoe-VAHN-ess; 1911–2000)

American composer of Armenian ancestry, conductor and organist. Very prolific. Interested in near-eastern and eastern culture. His music is well-characterized as visionary. Mystery and a luminous spirituality pervade his entire output. Opus numbers well past 300. Suffers undue neglect because his focus is not academic-style, nor new-wave glitter, but an un-flashy calm spirituality which is certainly out of style in the West at this writing. I predict a surge in the decades ahead. Maybe America's most under-rated composer.

- *Magnificat*
- *Mysterious Mountain*
- *Fra Angelico*
- a few symphonies (67!!!)
- piano and chamber works

CAGE, JOHN (1912–1992)

Possibly the most important musical theorist of the 20th century. He made us listen to the sounds around us. He asks us—what is music? what is noise? You may think you know the answers to these questions, but will they stand up rationally? What is the nature of improvisation? What constitutes silence? Be careful if you reply 'nothing.'

- *Constructions in Metal*
- *Sonatas and Interludes for Prepared Piano*
- *Music of Changes*
- *String Quartet*
- *4'33"*
- *Etudes Australes* for piano

BRITTEN, BENJAMIN (1913–1976)

Leading British composer of the 20th century. Primarily a vocal composer (though a master in most genres), his gift for finding the memorable and essential in a situation is uncanny. A tonal composer, he is considered rather conservative, but no one would doubt his great skills of imaginative and inventive power.

- *Peter Grimes* (opera)
- *Metamorphosis after Ovid*
- *War Requiem*
- *Les Illuminations*
- *Serenade for tenor, horn & strings*

LUTOSLAWSKI, WITOLD (vee-told loo-te-SWUV-skee; the 'l' in his name isn't really an 'l'. It has a slash through it and is pronounced like a 'w'; pronounce it correctly among the nerds and they will make you their king; 1913–1994)

In Eastern Europe, the list of great composers is not the same as in the West. Composer, pianist and conductor, Lutoslawski stands like a giant in his homeland but is still barely known in the United States. Played bar-piano in Warsaw until he was 32. In 1945!!!). Early compositions were hampered severely by the 'people's music' sickness of the Soviet policy. As Poland loosened up, Lutoslawski bloomed. Employs newer developments like chance techniques within strictly defined limits and combines them with more traditional approaches.

- *Mi Parti*
- Symphonies #2, 3
- other orchestral works as they become available. (There is a beautiful boxed set of some of the great orchestral pieces on an EMI.)

XENAKIS, IANNIS (yahn-ees zen-AH-kees; 1922–2001)

In addition to being one of the most influential and intelligent composers of recent times, he is also a mathematician and architect of note. Uses stochastic theory (random processes evolving through time) and other formulas to assist him in his composition. He composes often with the aid of a computer, but unlike many lesser artists what emerges sounds like music. In fact, his compositions sound more natural and organic than those of most Modern composers who would not be caught dead at a computer terminal. One of the greatest minds of the century. Performance of his work should be widespread, but he has a terrible handicap—*his work requires rehearsals*. Not just one or two. *Lots* of rehearsals, so complex are his scores. Too expensive. Too bad. I don't see this problem going away. The Xenakis Edition on the Mode label is highly recommended.

- *Metastases*
- *ST/48*
- *Pithoprakta*
- *Polla Ta Dhina*
- *Cendrees*
- Xenakis Edition recordings on the Mode label

LIGETI, GYORGY (le-GEH-tee; 1923–2006)

One of the most renowned and at the same time most accessible of the Post-Modern composers. Works in most idioms from opera to string quartet. Seems to have fewer axes to grind than most Moderns. His *Continuum* is the greatest 20th century harpsichord work.

- *Lux aeterna*

- *Atmospheres*
- *Continuum* for harpsichord
- *Ramifications* for strings
- *Etudes* for piano

BOULEZ, PIERRE (boo-LEZ; 1925–)

Noted as a masterful conductor of lucid clarity and restraint in addition to his activities as a composer. His music, colorful and intellectual, owes much to Debussy, Schoenberg and Messiaen. Though he sometimes incorporates electronics, improvisation and chance techniques, his music is usually thorough-composed and almost always uses serial techniques in some way. A notable explorer of the interactions between orchestra, computer and synthesizer. Many find it assertively unpleasant.

- *Hammer without a Master*
- *Explosante-fixe*
- *Rituel*
- *Repons*

BERIO, LUCIANO (1925–2003)

A leader of the international avant-garde who actually managed to please audiences. Founded the first electronic music studio in Italy in 1955. He wrote a lot for voice, surely inspired by his marriage to the noted singer Cathy Berberian. In his *Sequenza III* for solo voice, he has Cathy portraying 44 emotional states in seven-and-a-half minutes, via conventional singing, coughs, sighs, sobs and odd noises. He taught in America during the '60s and then returned to Rome where he remained as a member of the Euro-royalty of Modern music till his death.

- *Sinfonia*
- *Sequenza* (14 in the series)
- *Coro*

FELDMAN, MORTON (1926–1987)

The best composer of all who collaborated with the influential John Cage. His association with the avant-garde of American painters, like Pollock, Rauschenberg and Rothko gave him the courage to discard traditional music aesthetics for a more personal approach building his works. Used a lot of graphic notation at first but drifted back to more traditional notation. His works are known for their glowing quietness and often heavenly length. His *Second String Quartet* can last about six hours.

- *The Rothko Chapel*
- *Palais de Mari*
- *Piano & Orchestra*
- *Triadic Memories*
- *For Frank O'Hara*
- *Patterns in a Chromatic Field*
- *Spring of Chosroes*

STOCKHAUSEN, KARLHEINZ (SCHTOCK-how-zen; 1928–2007)

Uses serial technique often. Webern and Messiaen are great influences upon him. Not as intellectually crystalized as Boulez. Touched and indelibly influenced every aspect of 20ᵗʰ century composition.

- *Gesang der Junglinge* (the first and perhaps only electronic music masterpiece written thus far)
- *Stimmung*
- *Mantra*
- any of the operas from the *Licht* cycle.

RAUTAVAARA, EINOJUHANI (yikes. okay, ready? AE-no-you-an-ee ROW-ta-vah-ra, with 'row' rhyming with 'now'; 1928–2016)

Best known of the recent Finnish composers. In 1955 Sibelius recommended that Rautavaara be awarded a Tanglewood scholarship to study at the Julliard School. He once quipped, "If an artist is not a Modernist when he is young, he has no heart. And if he is a Modernist when he is old, he has no brain." He did the 12-tone thing but, like most composers with a future, he ditched it about 1970. His *Symphony #7: Angel of Light* from 1994 established his international reputation. Just in time, as this is an accessible work offered at a point when the composer was starting to be considered irredeemably cerebral. He wrote in most forms, chamber, orchestra, choral and vocal

- *Symphony #7: Angel of Light*
- *Cantus Arcticus: Concerto for Birds and Orchestra*
- *Canticum Mariae Virginis*

CRUMB, GEORGE (1929–)

Intimate, exotically colorful Modern master. Exploits unorthodox methods of sound production on acoustic instruments. For example, his piano works use the inside of the piano and the wooden body of the piano itself as much or more than the keyboard. Often uses wordless vocalise. His settings of the poetry of F.G. Lorca are lovely and evocative. He was big a few decades ago and has become less visible, but I expect a resurgence.

- *Ancient Voices of Children*
- *Voice of the Whale*
- *Night of the Four Moons*
- *Black Angels*
- any of the *Macrocosmos* series
- *Apparition*
- madrigals

TAKEMITZU, TORU (ta-kay-mit-zu; 1930-1996)

Self-taught and the greatest Japanese composer of the 20th century. One of the most skilled and subtle orchestrators ever. He is famed for combining elements of eastern and western philosophy to create a sound uniquely his own, and for fusing opposites together such as sound with silence and tradition with innovation. His large output in most genres include many scores for films that are often better than the movies that used them. His colors are ravishing in their exquisiteness. Seriously under-rated.

- *Toward the Sea I*
- *A Flock Descends into the Pentagonal Garden*
- *Requiem for Strings*
- *Rain Coming*

- *All in Twilight*
- *Air for Flute solo*
- *November Steps*

PENDERECKI, KRZYSZTOF (pen-der-ET-skee; 1933–2020)

His early music put him in the forefront of the avant-garde. His use of glissandi, tone clusters and programmed improvisation were spectacular, unprecedented and viscerally exciting. In late career he turned 180 degrees to a strange neo-Romanticism (which disturbs many, as if he 'hit the wall' and then ran backwards) such as in his *Violin Concerto* and *Symphony #2*. Certainly full of surprises. Not obsessed with rigorous intellectuality, and many find this refreshing.

- *Threnody for the Victims of Hiroshima*
- *Devils of Loudon* (opera)
- *Fluorescences*
- *St. Luke Passion*
- *Utrenja*
- *Song of Songs*
- String Quartets (2)

MAXWELL-DAVIES, PETER (1934–2016)

English composer, conductor and teacher. Strikingly original, sometimes freakish sounds sprang from his pen. Close affinity to a Medieval atmosphere. Lived in near-solitude on the north-sea isle of Orkney. Wrote for his own group of great musicians called *The Fires of London*. Extremely prolific.

- The Naxos label seem to be recording his complete works

RILEY, TERRY (1935–)

Participated in the founding of Minimalism. Studied at Berkeley. Probably the most avant-garde of the minimalists. Always experimenting with electronics and music of other cultures. Early in his career, *In C* became a platform upon which the Minimalist movement was built. Since then he has never produced anything nearly as popular, though his work with the Kronos String Quartet was extraordinary.

- *In C*
- *G-Song*
- *Salome Dances for Peace*
- *Sunrise of the Planetary Dream Collector*

PÄRT ARVO (Pairt; 1935–)

In the first rank of Contemporary composers. In the '50s his work sounded like the Russians, and in the '60s he adopted serial and 12-tone techniques. By 1970 he got sick of that and by 1976 started writing actual music in his own style which he calls *tintinnabulation* (the lingering sound of a ringing bell that occurs after the bell has been struck), which in his music often involves the constant presence throughout the work of a lone unchanging three-note chord. Studied the Renaissance masters and produces music of deathly calm. Writes much religious music. Member of the Eastern Orthodox Church.

- *Spiegel im Spiegel*
- *Fratres*
- *Magnificat*
- *Symphony #3*
- *Cantus in Memory of Benjamin Britten*

REICH, STEVE (Rysh; 1936–)

Arch-minimalist. Brainiac who entered Cornell at 16. Studied at Juilliard. Met Terry Riley and performed in premier of Riley's seminal *In C*. This had a huge influence on Reich. Then met Philip Glass and for four years had a touring ensemble with him, then formed Steve Reich & Musicians which performed all over the world to great acclaim. Has immersed himself in the study of Jewish music and collaborated with his wife on works for theater.

- *Drumming*
- *Vermont Counterpoint*
- *New York Counterpoint*
- *Piano Phase*

GLASS, PHILIP (1937–)

Most minimal of the minimalists. He repeats and evolves patterns of rhythms and notes. Studied at Juilliard. Converted to Buddhism. Established the Glass Ensemble in the early '70s which became immensely popular. His opera *Einstein on the Beach* is one of the most polarizing events in music history. Many love his music; as many hate it. Few in the middle.

- *Concerto for Violin*
- *Einstein on the Beach*
- *Satyagraha*
- *Quartet for Strings #3 "Mishima"*

MONK, MEREDITH (1942–)

Singer, composer, filmmaker and choreographer. A law unto herself but I feel she has earned her place in these pages. "Bartók was someone I loved as a young woman, and also Stravinsky. And then I'm a person who loves music from the '20s and '30s, and there's a jazz singer that I love named Mildred Bailey." She also credits Janis Joplin and Joni Mitchell for inspiration. The ECM label has served her well. Her productions often feature vocalists, dancers and choruses. She stands alone and apart, and she shines.

- *Dolmen Music*
- *Atlas*
- recorded collections on ECM

TAVENER, JOHN (1944–2013)

Another convert to the Eastern Orthodox Church, Tavener is mostly regarded as a spiritual music creator. Studying at the Royal Academy in London, he became professor of composition at Trinity College. His music has an affinity with Arvo Pärt's compositions, so if you like spiritual Minimalism, dark and deep, these men might be what you're looking for. Tavener sports a slow, minimalist unfolding of his material which often employs strange vocal and instrumental combinations.

- *The Lamb*
- *Song for Athene*
- *Hymns to the Mother of God (2)*

- *Funeral Ikos*
- *The Protecting Veil*

TOWNSEND, PETER (1945-)

Frontman for The Who. He wrote the full-length stage opera *Tommy*. Wait... but isn't that rock-'n'-Roll? *Hell*, yes.

- *Tommy*

ADAMS, JOHN (1947–)

Went to Harvard but rejected the academic music scene. In 1971 he took a job as head of the composition department at the San Francisco Conservatory, a position he held until 1981. While there he came under the influence of minimalist pioneer Steve Reich and sought out the music of the previous generation of experimentalists such as John Cage and Morton Feldman. By 1980 he was popular American composer. His operas may end up his most abiding body of work and are usually based upon contemporary events. He is probably the most famous American composer at this writing.

- *China Gates*
- *Hallelujah Junction*
- *Phrygian Gates*
- *Nixon in China* (opera)
- *The Chairman Dances*
- *Harmonielehre*
- *Concerto for Violin*

ENO, BRIAN (1948–)

His name really is Brian Eno, but his *real* real name is *Brian Peter George Saint John le Baptiste de la Salle Eno*. He's an Englishman, a musician and composer, record producer, and visual artist. He is best known for essentially inventing the genre of *ambient music*. Ambient music is sonic wallpaper. It does not demand your attention and focus in the manner that most music does; rather, it eschews conventional forms in favor of using textural layers of sound to evoke an atmosphere or mood. The best of it is rewarding to both passive and active listening. It is most often instrumental or electronic, or both, and may include natural sounds. It exists on the edge of your attention. Eno is just as well-known for his contributions to rock, pop, electronic, and generative music. He describes himself as a "non-musician." No one else does. Easily one of classical and popular music's most influential and innovative figures.

- *Music for Airports*
- *Lux*

RIHM, WOLFGANG (Reem; 1952-2024)

Studied with Stockhausen, with whom he has an obvious affinity, even though he revolted against the core complexities of that generation when he became associated with the movement known as New Simplicity—a revolt against the hyper-cerebral dryness of the music scene in the '50s and '60s. Morton Feldman is also a heavy influence. He tends to follow the 12-tone system, but not religiously, and his music is unpredictable, with wide mood swings and shocking juxtapositions between harsh utter violence and gentle, lovely sounds. Extremely prolific, his deeply-felt expressionistic style, obviously Germanic, is serving him well as his reputation continues to blossom.

- *Time Chant (for violin and orchestra)*
- *String Quartets (any of 13)*
- *Oedipus (opera)*

SAARIAHO, KAIJA (KIE-yah SAH-ri-ah-ho (roll the 'r'); 1952- 2024)

Finnish composer who, at 28, moved to Germany to study at the Hochschule für Musik Freiburg under Brian Ferneyhough and Klaus Huber. She found her teachers' emphasis on strict serialism and mathematical structures stifling, saying in an interview: "You were not allowed to have pulse, or tonally oriented harmonies, or melodies. I don't want to write music through negations. Everything is permissible as long as it's done in good taste." In 1982, she began work at IRCAM researching computer analyses of the sound-spectrum of individual notes produced by different instruments. She developed techniques for computer-assisted composition, experimented with musique concrète, and wrote her first pieces combining live performance with electronics. She's done a good job making the connections between live musicians and electronic sounds as seamless as possible. So she's handy with all the techniques of the day, but it's her sensuality and passion, her color sense

120

and incredible vivacity that gives her the popularity she enjoys with her admirers.

- *Graal Théâtre (7)*
- *NoaNoa (4)*
- *A la fumée (3)*

ADES, THOMAS (1971-)

Adès might be the most accomplished overall musician alive right now. As a conductor, Thomas appears regularly with the Los Angeles, San Francisco and London Philharmonic orchestras, the Boston, London, BBC and City of Birmingham, Symphony orchestras, the Royal Concertgebouw, Leipzig Gewandhaus and the Czech Philharmonic. His concert piano engagements include solo recitals at Carnegie Hall, New York and the Wigmore Hall in London, and concerto appearances with the New York Philharmonic. And— he's widely regarded as the most important British composer of his genera- tion. His body of work spans the genres, highly emotional yet complex, and he seems un-ruled by any idea of a system, yet many find his results compelling.

- *Asyla*
- *Powder Her Face*
- *Arcadiana*

It is easy to criticize the author for omissions of favorite composers. I can think of 50 more without looking, but I must keep in mind the scope of the book. Same with composi- tions. Some of these composers are up-and-comers; some are quite fashionable now but may not last. Once you realize for yourself how small this list really is and wish you had me by the collar to set me straight on a few things—then you will be well on your way.

CR

CONTENDERS (COMPOSERS)

*H*ere follows, in alphabetical order, a list of living composers who may one day earn a place in the repertory with their compositions. The list does not represent the best living composers. It represents the most-played, for whatever reason, good or bad. Doubtless there are obscurities who will (hopefully) come to our attention in the fullness of time but, for now, labor undetected by the powers-that-be who shape the concert and recording scene. In their favor, those listed here are, at this writing, getting more performances than their peers; On the other hand, nobody is storming the doors to get a ticket to their shows. All but one of the composers listed here are still alive and kicking, one has passed but his works are still being performed. Maybe now that he's dead he'll be played more.

Péter Eötvös (1944) Hungary (PAY-ter ET-vish)
His first large-scale compositions were for film. This often reflects on his later pieces in moments of atmospheric airiness. Eötvös's works often convey a strong theatrical sense (even in the instrumental works), the movement of sound across the sonic landscape via special positioning of the players, as well as the use of electronic amplification. His music may come off as avant-garde sound to some listeners, but it is generally more accessible than that of Stockhausen (a mentor), Boulez, Ligeti, and other characters from that thorny era. As director of the Ensemble InterContemporain, he was exposed to many styles, as is evidenced in the variety of timbres and soundworlds within his music. Extended techniques such as over-pressure bowings coexist with lyrical folk songs and synthesized sounds. Eötvös provides detailed instructions on how to mix instruments for electronic manipulation or amplification.

> **Recommended:**
> *Ensemble Linea Plays* Eötvös
> Ensemble Linea; cond. Jean-Philippe Wurtz
> Budapest Music Center

Sofia Gubaidulina (1931-) Russian (so-FEE-yah goo-bye-DOOL-na)
Gubaidulina is a very religious woman, in abreaction to living in the Soviet Union. A musical child, she discovered spiritual ideas in the works of composers such as Bach, Mozart, and Beethoven. She quickly learned to keep her spiritual interests secret from her parents and other adults. These early experiences with music and spiritual ideas led her to treat the two domains of thought as one. For her, music was her escape from the Soviet system and its

consequences. Gubaidulina is a devout member of the Russian Orthodox church. In her compositions one finds the influence of electronic music and improvisational techniques, and her work is heavy with unusual combinations of contrasting elements, novel instrumentation, and the use of traditional Russian folk instruments in her solo and chamber works. Harmonically, Gubaidulina's music resists traditional tonal centers and traditional chord structures in favor of pitch clusters. She will often employ elements of the Fibonacci sequence (the next number in a series is the result of adding the preceding two numbers. Eg: 1,1,2,3,5,8,13...) or the Golden Ratio, or Phi (1.618033988749895...) (take a line segment and divide it into two smaller segments such that the ratio of the whole line segment (a+b) to segment a is the same as the ratio of segment a to segment b. The point on the line where this occurs marks the Golden Section of that line segment.) She has made these cornerstones of math theory the foundation of her personal musical style.

Recommended:
Offertorium, Hommage to T.S. Eliot
Gidon Kremer, Boston SO
Boston Symphony Orchestra; cond. Charles Dutoit
DG

Jennifer Higdon (1962-) American
She was a late bloomer and knew little of any classical music till college(!!). She liked rock and folk music. This had the interesting effect of actually making Modern and Contemporary music more compelling to her ears than old music. Incredibly persistent against people who thought her too green, she went to three top American conservatories for her education. Her composition teachers included George Crumb and Ned Rorem. She has described her own compositional process as "intuitive" and "instinctive," where she favors music that makes sense to her, rather than writing music that adheres to classical forms and structures. This seems to be where music, in general, is headed. People are sick to death (finally!) of 'systems.' Sometimes I get a Neo-Romantic vibe from her, other times Minimalism. Her most popular work is *Blue Cathedral*, a one-movement tone poem dealing with the death of her brother from cancer, which premiered in 2000. It has been performed by more than 400 orchestras since.

Recommended:
City Scape; Concerto for Orchestra
Atlanta Symphony, cond. Robert Spano

Per Nørgård (1932-) Danish (pair NAIR-gore)

Nørgård shares with the next fellow on this list, the reputation of Denmark's leading Modernist composers. He has a large catalog in all major genres. Early on, he was strongly influenced by the Nordic styles of Jean Sibelius and Carl Nielsen. In the 1960s, he began exploring the Modernist techniques of central Europe, eventually developing a serial compositional system based on the "infinity series." (Too complex to explain here.) Later he became obsessed by the Swiss artist Adolf Wölfli, who inspired many of Nørgård's works. Nørgård encountered Wölfli's work at an exhibition in 1979. After the Third Symphony (1975), Nørgård's works became more marked by conflict and polarity. Wölfli gave a kind of answer to the question that was bothering Nørgård at that period: how to establish a connection between harmony and chaos, two mutually exclusive extremes. In Wölfli's writings, harmony - in the form of the merry journey, for example - is shattered by the sudden incursion of chaos, the fall. Harmony may be quickly re-established, but one never knows when chaos will next erupt. The infinity series and the Wölfli fixation figure heavily in Nørgård's works.

Recommended:

Symphonies 1 & 8
Vienna Philharmonic, cond. Sakari Oramo
Dacapo

Poul Ruders (1941-) Danish

Born 17 years after Nørgård, Ruders has the more contemporary aura about him. Largely self-taught, he is an eclectic willing to use a variety of techniques and styles. In his works he has incorporated features of minimalism, Medieval and Renaissance-era styles, popular music sources, various tonal and atonal elements. Ruders lives a spartan life in the countryside of Denmark. The isolation has afforded him the opportunity to produce a deep and highly varied catalog which includes five operas, 45 symphonic works and concertos, and dozens of solo and chamber pieces.

Recommended:

Concertos *(for orchestra, for violin, for percussion)*
Aarhus Symphony Orchestra; cond. Thomas Sondergård

Salvatore Sciarrino (1947-) Italian (sahl-vah-TOE-ray shah-REE-no)

He is considered one of the leaders of avant-garde music in Europe. His major compositional influence was Luigi Nono, the most radical composer among well-known Italian musical figures of the post-World War II generation. Self-taught, his music uses sonorities such as harmonics, other unusual methods of tone production, and additional sounds that can be made with instruments such as tapping and key clicking. In addition, it is characterized by artful and frequent use of silence as part of the compositional structure. He has said "there [is] one thing without which no delight in sound makes sense, and that is the intensity of silence." Sciarrino's discography is extensive: there are over 70 CDs, and lots of award-winners.

Recommended:
Le Stagioni Artificiali; four other chamber pieces
various musicians
Stradivarius

Lera Auerbach (1973-) Soviet-born Jewish Austrian-American

She is a composer, conductor and concert pianist. She's written more than 100 works across every genre, including two operas, more than a dozen ballets, and many concertos. She gives concerts as a pianist and has created numerous literary works, including three Russian poetry volumes and a book of modern aphorisms in English. She has also recently appeared as a visual artist and conductor. She works with great musicians. Violinist Gidon Kremer called Auerbach "one of the most gifted artists I have ever met. Her strong talent which is evident in so many fields - performing, composing, writing - is nurtured by a deep respect towards the past, but still allows her creations to remain sincere and personal while being innovative and adventurous. Her commitment to art is always inspired by a spiritual approach." The *New York Times* wrote: "Her versatility is almost incredible. She's a passionate pianist with a lot of temperament, a natural composer and performer who can quickly grasp and transpose everything around her."

Recommended:
Preludes & Dreams *(for piano)*
Lera Auerbach, pianist
BIS

◌

THE PIANO & ITS PREDECESSORS

For the Average Classical Listener (is there such a thing? probably not, but it's a useful concept if you're writing a book), the piano and related instruments will account for much of your listening. Their historical importance, vastness of repertoire, and sheer number of recordings in which these instruments appear call for a brief overview of their development.

Clavichord

The *clavichord* is the earliest keyboard instrument, invented in the early 15th century. Starting with a compass of only 3 1/2 octaves with a single string to each note, by the time the clavichord flowered and finally entered obscurity around 1800 it spanned more than five octaves, each note double-strung.

A small brass blade, the *tangent*, stands on each key just below its string. When the key is depressed, the tangent strikes the string. The dynamic range of the clavichord is very quiet, from *ppp* to *p*, or in other words triple-pianissimo to piano, or—almost inaudible to very quiet.

Clavichords come in two flavors, fretted and unfretted. Fretted clavichords were the earliest type. Like a guitar or violin these would sound several notes from the same set of strings by striking the string in different places along its length. This approach means an instrument with fewer strings to tune, a narrower and lighter case, keys more equal in length bass to treble, less tension on the soundboard so often a louder sound. Which was good.

The disadvantage of unfretted clavichords comes if the music wants a note that isn't available in the key you chose to tune the instrument in. The early types of Renaissance and early Baroque clavichords were fretted but this did not pose a problem with music of that period because the music was simpler and rarely ventured outside of its home key. If you are playing a piece in C, you're probably not going to have to use a C#, so it just is not available. But, more chromatic music written later does present the problem of non-existing notes. These types are suitable if only the early repertoire is going to be played.

For the later Baroque and early Classical literature an unfretted clavichord is the ticket. Here each note has its own pair of strings so is completely independent of whatever else is being played. The disadvantages of the unfretted design are that there will be more strings to tune, the case will be broader because of more strings, and it will be much heavier in order to have the strength to withstand the additional tension of those added strings.

The most wonderful thing about the clavichord is its expressiveness. Unlike the harpsichord, the clavichord can vary its loudness—from barely audible to merely quiet, but vary nonetheless, depending upon the force with which the key is struck. On a harpsichord, your cat's paw pressing down on a key will produce the same volume from the string as a sturdy wallop from an angry pro arm-wrestler.

The expressiveness of the clavichord is enhanced by the unique effect known as *bebung*. This is a vibrato obtained on the clavichord by alternately increasing and decreasing the pressure of the finger on the key after the string has been sounded. Press harder, the pitch goes up; relax pressure and the pitch goes down to normal. You cannot use a bebung to lower the tuned pitch of the string, just raise it or bring it back to normal. Still, in the right hands it's a hypnotically beautiful effect.

From 1800 to about 1950 the clavichord all but disappeared from musical consciousness. Now there are makers all over the world, probably more than during its heyday. It's safe to say there is really nothing new written for the clavichord these days, but Renaissance, Baroque and early Classical keyboard music (like early Haydn) sounds great on it.

The clavichord is a deeply personal instrument. It is never used in ensemble with other instruments. It's just too quiet. Recitals featuring the instrument are also very rare for the same reason, though it's a great treat to sit near a good player while they play for you. It's sublime in the sitting room on a quiet night, maybe with the fireplace aglow, or by the bedside to end the day.

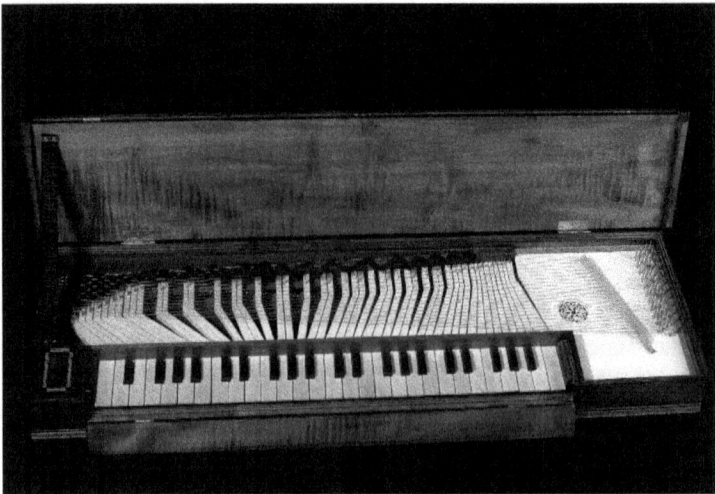

An early fretted clavichord

A late, large, unfretted double-strung clavichord

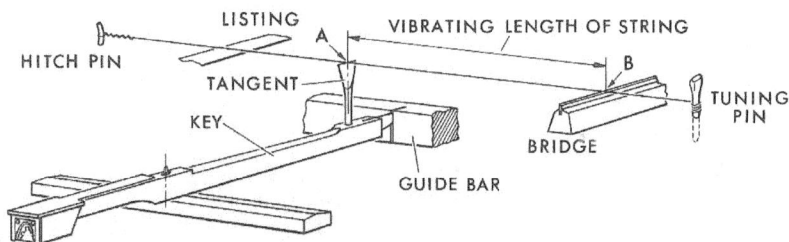

The action of a clavichord. Very simple. Press key, brass tangent hits string.

A note about listening to a clavichord recording. If it is recorded at a realistic level, your impulse will be to crank the volume. Resist this. Keep it quieter than you're used to. Reach out to it with your soul; don't force it to come to you.

If you have read all this, you simply must see this short video. It will explain everything much more clearly than all the ink I have just spilled:
https://www.youtube.com/watch?v=9WuVVE2t-Vk

Harpsichord

The virginal and spinet are essentially economy, space-saving home amateur versions of the harpsichord and are rarely featured in recordings. We will not discuss them.

The harpsichord had its day as the main keyboard for performances of Renaissance and Baroque music. During the late 18th century, with the rise of the piano, it gradually disappeared from the musical scene. Bach himself tried out a few pianos, but there is no record of his being very impressed at the early efforts. In the 20th century, the harpsichord made a resurgence, being used in historically informed performances of older music, and even in new compositions

When a key is pressed on a harpsichord, a string is plucked by a crow-quill (or nowadays a trimmed piece of Delrin plastic). Hit the key hard or press it soft, the volume level stays the same. Volume could be increased by having more than one string sound with a single key press, but there was no way to graduate the volume level smoothly. This was one reason why the piano eventually replaced the harpsichord. The piano is simply more expressive in its possibilities.

The largest harpsichords have a range of just over five octaves, and the smallest have under four.

An early single keyboard Italian harpsichord

While many harpsichords have one string that sounds when a key is pressed, more elaborate harpsichords can have two or more strings sounding on a key press. These additional strings are called *choirs* of strings. This provides two advantages: the ability to achieve another level of volume and to vary tonal quality.

Different *choirs* of strings can be designed to have distinct tonal qualities, usually by having one set of strings plucked closer to the place where the string is anchored, called the *nut* (the other end of the string is wrapped about the *tuning pin*), this emphasizes the higher harmonics, and produces a thinner, nasal sound quality. The mechanism of the instrument, called *stops* permits the player to select one choir or the other. So having one key pluck two strings at once changes not just volume but also tonal quality; for instance, when two strings tuned to the same pitch are plucked simultaneously, the note is not just louder but also richer and more complex.

A particularly vivid effect is obtained when the strings plucked simultaneously are an octave apart. This is normally heard by the ear not as two pitches but as one: the sound of the higher string is blended with that of the lower one. When describing a harpsichord it is customary to specify its choirs of strings, often called its *disposition*. Strings at *eight foot pitch* sound at the normal expected pitch, strings at *four foot pitch* sound an octave higher. Harpsichords occasionally include a *sixteen-foot pitch* choir (one octave lower than eight-foot) or, rarely, a *two-foot pitch* choir (two octaves higher).

When there are multiple choirs of strings, the player can control which choirs sound. This is usually done by having a set of jacks for each choir, and a mechanism for turning off each set, so that their plectra miss the strings.

Harpsichords with two keyboards provide flexibility in selecting which strings play, since each manual can be set to control the plucking of a different set of strings. In addition, such harpsichords often have a mechanism called the *coupler* that couples manuals together, so that a single keyboard plays both sets of strings. The most flexible system is the French *shove coupler*, in which the lower manual slides forward and backward.

Harpsichords may be equipped with a *stop* that, when engaged, places a strip of leather against the strings. The muted sound resembles a lute or nylon strung guitar and is called a *lute stop*. There may also be a *peau de bouffle* stop, which when engaged plucks the strings with leather quills instead of the plastic plectra.

Example of harpsichord stops controller (Christopher Hogwood Instruments)

Like birds, harpsichords are usually much lighter than you would guess by looking at them. They are made of wood (not birds, harpsichords), sturdily but cunningly braced, with metal fittings.

A large harpsichord stands alone on legs and may be styled in the manner of other furniture of its place and period, Contemporary included. Early Italian harpsichords were so light in construction that they were treated more like a guitar, easily carried about, and simply placed on a tabletop ready to play. (Until the late 18th century people usually played standing up.)

Harpsichords have been decorated in a great many ways, with paint, paper printed with patterns, with leather or fabric coverings, or sometimes with highly elaborate artwork.

The Flemish instruments served as the model for 18th century harpsichord construction in other nations. The Ruckers family and the Dulcken are well regarded. Instruments from the peak of the French tradition, by makers such as the Blanchet family and Pascal Taskin, are among the most widely admired of all harpsichords, and are frequently used as models for the construction of modern instruments. In England, the Kirkman and Shudi firms produced sophisticated harpsichords of great power and sonority. German builders, being Germans, extended the sound range of the instrument by adding the sixteen foot and two foot choirs, sounding respectively an octave below and two octaves above the standard (eight-foot) pitch of the key when pressed.

Among the most famous composers who wrote for the harpsichord were the members of English virginal school of the late Renaissance, notably William Byrd. In France, look to Baroque masters Jean-Phillipe Rameau and four books of *ordres* by François Couperin. Domenico Scarlatti penned 555 harpsichord sonatas, all of them worthy of a listen. Georg Friedrich Handel composed numerous suites for harpsichord, and of course the towering genius J. S. Bach, whose solo works (for instance, the *Well-Tempered Clavier* and the *Goldberg Variations*), continue to be performed very widely, often on the piano. Bach was also a pioneer of the harpsichord concerto, both in works designated as such, and with his *Fifth Brandenburg Concerto*.

Single manual by Tom Pixton of Boston, made in 1980

A late Flemish double manual harpsichord

Simplified view of harpsichord action

Fortepiano

The fortepiano is an early incarnation of our modern grand piano. It was invented by Bartolomeo Cristofori around 1700 and flourished up to the early 19th century. Usually it refers to the late-18th to early-19th century instruments for which Haydn, Mozart, and the younger Beethoven wrote their piano music. Starting in Beethoven's time, the fortepiano began a period of steady evolution culminating in the late-19th century with the basic structure of the modern grand piano. The fortepiano became obsolete and was absent from the musical scene till the 20th century. It has been revived due to interest in historically informed performance and made again in studios all over the Western world, though there is scarce music being written nowadays for the fortepiano.

Like the modern piano, and unlike the harpsichord, the fortepiano can vary the sound volume of each note, depending on the player's touch. The tone of the fortepiano is quite different from that of the modern piano, however, being softer with less sustain.

The fortepiano has leather-covered hammers and thin, harpsichord-like strings made of brass and iron. (Modern pianos have steel strings, the lower strings of which are wound with copper winding.) The fortepiano uses *straight stringing*, with all strings parallel to each other and perpendicular to the keyboard; the modern piano is *cross-strung*, with strings crossing in an 'X' shape. Cross-stringing helps to focus sound on the center of the soundboard to create large masses of sound, which is very appealing for music of the late 19th century, aiding the long unfolding melodies of Romantic music. However, the short phrases of 18th century music demand subtle and frequent finger articulations. Playing Mozart or Haydn melodies with all the required nuances is easier on a fortepiano than on a modern grand.

The fortepiano has a much lighter case construction than the modern piano and, except for later examples of the early 19th century (already evolving towards the modern piano), it has no metal frame or bracing.

The range of the fortepiano was about four octaves at the time of its invention and gradually increased. Mozart wrote for instruments of about five octaves. Beethoven gradually expanding his range to about six and a half octaves. (The range of most modern pianos, attained in the 19th century, is 7⅓ octaves, or 88 keys.)

The action and hammers are significantly lighter that our modern piano, giving rise to a much lighter touch, which in well-constructed fortepianos is also very responsive. Smaller, lighter hammers required less distance to travel to hit a string, making keys more responsive.

The key dip on a fortepiano is much shallower than on a modern grand. A modern piano's keys depress approximately 9mm; a Viennese fortepiano of the late 18th century dipped around 2.5mm. A well-regulated fortepiano excelled at brisk passagework. Also the keys of the fortepiano are narrower than modern piano keys by approximately 1mm.

Pedals, of which modern pianos have two or three, gradually came into use only during the second half of the 18th century and were not the rule until the beginning of the 19th. More common early on were hand stops or knee levers to do the damping and sustaining.

Some fortepianos of Beethoven's time had as many as seven pedals, to quiet the piano to different degrees, sustain various registers while damping others, buff stops, and novelty effects. The number of pedals gradually decreased over the course of the 19th century to include a *una corda* pedal, *sostenuto* pedal, and sustain. More about those later.

Cristofori fortepiano replica in the workshop of maker
David Sutherland of Ann Arbor, Michigan

Cristofori, the inventor of the fortepiano, is remembered today for his ingenious piano action, which in some ways was more subtle and effective than that of many later instruments, including the current. Cristofori also used thicker, tenser strings, mounted on a frame considerably more robust than that of contemporary harpsichords. As with virtually all later pianos of the era, Cristofori used pairs of strings throughout the range, that is, two string per note.

Cristofori was also the first to incorporate a form of soft pedal into a piano, the mechanism by which the hammer shifts a bit to strike only one of each pair of strings. Cristofori uses a hand stop here, not a pedal.

It was Gottfried Silbermann who brought the construction of fortepianos to the German-speaking nations. Silbermann, who worked in Freiberg, made pianos based on Cristofori's design around 1730. (His previous experience had been in building Bach's favorite organs, as well as harpsichords and clavichords.)

Silbermann is credited with the invention of the forerunner of the sustain pedal, which removes the dampers from all the strings at once, permitting them to vibrate freely. Again, the Silbermann device was a hand stop, and thus could be changed only at a pause in the music. These hand stops eventually evolved into the more convenient knee levers, then finally to the pedals of today.

Replica of Gottfried Silbermann fortepiano by Paul McNulty

Johann Andreas Stein, who worked in Augsburg, Germany, was a pupil of Silbermann. Stein's fortepianos used a Viennese action, with the striking end closer to the player than the hinged end. This Viennese action was simpler than the Cristofori action, and very sensitive.

A fortepiano by Johann Andreas Stein (1775)

Another important Viennese builder was Anton Walter, a friend of Mozart's who built instruments with a somewhat more powerful sound than Stein's. The fortepianos of Stein and Walter are widely used today as models for the construction of new fortepianos.

A replica of Mozart's Anton Walter fortepiano by Urbano Petroselli of Perugia, Italy

By the late 18th century there were two very prominent schools of fortepiano building—the Viennese school and the English school.

Viennese instruments had a much more focused and clear tone, and clearer distinction of voices. English instruments preferred thicker and grander textures. Viennese instruments had extremely efficient dampers which discontinued the sound the instant the key was released. English instruments had purposely inefficient dampers which resulted in an afterglow sound after the release of a note. A remnant of this effect can still be heard at the very top register of modern pianos, where there are no dampers. Thus while Viennese instruments had a more 'speaking' quality appropriate for Mozart and Haydn, the English instruments a more 'singing' quality (foreshadowing of Romantic long-lined phrases), which Haydn makes use of in his last sonatas. English instruments were bigger in almost every respect–they were louder, heavier, and had a longer decay of sound.

In Germany, another important builder from this era was Conrad Graf, who made Beethoven's last piano. Beethoven couldn't hear it. Graf's pianos are a better fit for Brahms and Schubert than Beethoven and Mozart—heavy-sounding at the expense of clarity and transparency.

John Broadwood's piano that he gave to Beethoven (1817)

In England, John Broadwood and a few other fellows produced an English grand action with an escapement and check which enabled a louder, more robust sound than the Viennese one, though it required deeper touch and was less sensitive. The early English grand pianos by these builders were very imposing with elegant, restrained veneer work on the exterior. Unlike contemporary Viennese instruments, English grand fortepianos had three strings rather than two per note.

The Broadwood company survives to this day and was an important innovator in the evolution of the fortepiano into the piano. Broadwood, in collaboration with Jan Dussek, a piano virtuoso active in London in the 1790s, developed pianos that gradually increased the range to six octaves. The firm shipped a piano to Beethoven in Vienna, which the composer evidently treasured. He wrote the *Hammerklavier Sonata* on it. He also wrecked it with his increasing number of violent fits as he became more and more deaf. It has since been lovingly restored.

Action of a Stein fortepiano

Modern Piano

We will not discuss vertical pianos (spinet pianos, 'studio' pianos, huge old uprights like the one in your grandparents basement, consoles) or square pianos because they are always a compromise to the glories of a large modern grand—the piano exclusively used in modern classical recordings.

Pianist and composer Franz Liszt enjoyed smashing pianos. You know how Pete Townsend used to smash his guitar on stage? Well, Liszt did that sort of thing a long time before. Mainly, he did it to teach makers a lesson: *start making pianos that I can play in large halls and through which I can express all my emotions.* Other virtuosi aped Liszt's destructive behavior. The makers had no choice here. They complied.

In the period from about 1790 to 1860, the Mozart-era piano underwent tremendous changes that led to the modern form of the instrument. This revolution was in response to a preference by composers and pianists such as Liszt and other virtuosi for a more powerful, sustained piano sound. This was the time of the Industrial Revolution which gave us better piano wire for strings (strings breaking in this era was more the rule than the exception), and most importantly, massive iron frames that could withstand the tremendous tension of the strings were being produced. This played havoc with the delicacy of the light, wooden-framed Viennese sensibility, but it made the piano a mighty presence in a large hall, capable of intense expression.

Early technological progress in the late 1700s owed much to the above-mentioned firm of Broadwood. They quickly gained a reputation for the splendor and powerful tone of their instruments, with Broadwood constructing pianos that were progressively larger, louder, and more robustly constructed than anything the Viennese had devised, but as mentioned, at the expense of delicacy of expression. They sent pianos to both Haydn and Beethoven and were the first firm to build pianos with a range of more than five octaves: five octaves and a fifth during the 1790s, six octaves by 1810 (Beethoven used the extra notes in his later works), and seven octaves by 1820. The Viennese makers tried to follow these trends, but they could never muster the power and presence of the new line. Sensibilities had shifted.

By the 1820s, the center of piano innovation had shifted to Paris, where the Pleyel firm manufactured pianos used by Chopin and the Érard firm manufactured those used by Liszt. In 1821, Sébastien Érard invented the double escapement action, which incorporated a repetition lever that permitted repeating a note even if the key had not yet risen to its maximum vertical position. This facilitated rapid playing of repeated notes, a musical device exploited by Liszt.

Chopin's Pleyel piano, a delicate beauty

Other improvements of the mechanism included the use of firm felt hammer coverings instead of layered leather or cotton. Felt is a more consistent material, permitting wider dynamic ranges as hammer weights and string tension increased. The sostenuto pedal (see below), allowed a wider range of effects.

But the one innovation that helped create the powerful sound of the modern piano was the use of a massive, strong, cast iron frame. Also called the *plate*, the iron frame sits atop the soundboard, and serves as the primary bulwark against the force of string tension that can exceed 20-tons in a modern grand. The increased structural integrity of the iron frame allowed the use of thicker, tenser, and more numerous strings. In 1834, piano wire made from cast steel was introduced, refined over the decades leading ultimately to our sophisticated modern form of steel alloy piano wire.

Several important advances included changes to the way the piano was strung. The use of a choir of three strings, rather than two for all but the lowest notes, enhanced the richness and complexity of the higher octaves. Research into where exactly the string should be hit by the hammer greatly increased the power and character of the sound. Cross-stringing allowed greater length to the bass strings. Cross-stringing came into its own about 1860 with Steinway's patent.

There are many sizes of contemporary grand pianos used in recordings. Probably the smallest acceptable size in the world of professional classical recordings would be a seven-footer. This is known as a B size, represented most commonly by the Steinway Model B. But the mainstay is the D size, represented most commonly by the Steinway Model D, which comes in at nine feet. This is the piano that is most often used in recordings and concerts.

The Steinway Model D. Nine glorious feet of pianotastic awesomeness

Steinway is probably the industry standard, due to sheer numbers as well as high-quality, and an artist support network that spans the globe. To be a Steinway Artist is quite the thing. Some of these Steinway Artists actually prefer other pianos, but Steinway takes care of their own very well, and a successful concert artist can usually count on a decent piano being provided when they need one.

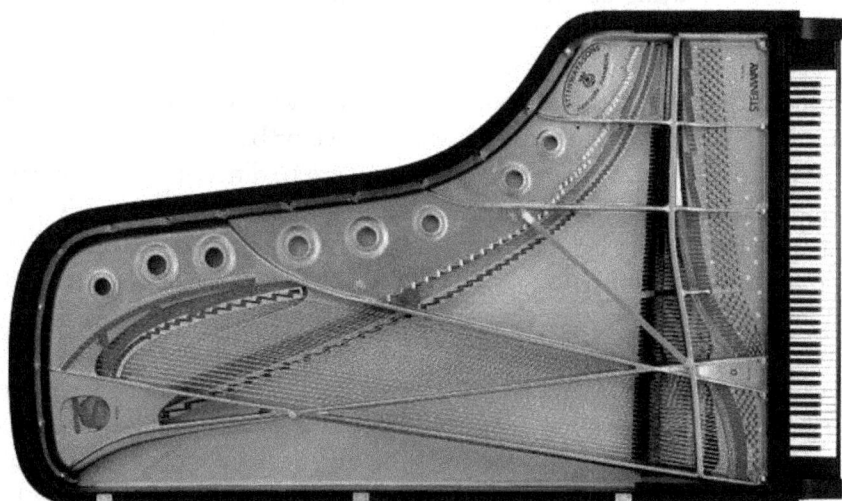

Cast metal frame (on this Steinway D) is the key to modern piano sound and stability

Other great pianos being made today include Mason & Hamlin, Bluethner, Shiguru Kawai, and Fazioli. That's my list from personal experience. Others will have their own favs.

Pianos have had pedals, or some related mechanism since the earliest days. (In the 18th century, pianos often used levers pressed upward by the player's knee instead of pedals.) Most grand pianos in the US have three pedals: the soft pedal (*una corda*), *sostenuto*, and sustain pedal (from left to right, respectively), while in Europe, the standard is two pedals: the soft pedal and the sustain pedal.

The sustain pedal (or, damper pedal) is often simply called *the pedal*, since it is the most frequently used. It's placed as the rightmost pedal in the group. It lifts the dampers from all the keys, sustaining all played notes. In addition, it alters the overall tone by allowing all strings, including those not directly played, to reverberate freely.

The soft pedal or *una corda* pedal is placed leftmost in the row of pedals. In grand pianos it shifts the entire action/keyboard assembly to the right so that

145

the hammers hit two of the three strings for each note. (In the earliest pianos the action shifted so that hammers hit a single string, hence the name *una corda*, or 'one string.') The effect is to soften the note as well as change the tone.

On grand pianos, the middle pedal is a *sostenuto* pedal. This pedal raises the dampers only on notes that are already being held down on the keyboard at the moment the pedal is pressed. This allows pianists to let chords ring in the left hand while playing detached, unsustained notes with the right hand. There is not a whole lot of call for this pedal in the literature, but when you need it, you need it.

In the early years of piano construction, keys were commonly made from sugar pine. Now they are usually made of spruce or basswood. Spruce is typically used in high-quality pianos. Black keys were traditionally made of ebony, and the white keys were covered with strips of ivory. Ivory is beautiful. Also it is non-glairy in bright light, perfectly micro-textured and absorptive of sweat so that it's not slippery. However, since ivory-yielding species are now endangered and protected by treaty, or are illegal in some countries, makers use plastics almost exclusively.

Early attempts at ivory replacement were terrible. Pianos from great makers in the mid-20th century had ugly glaring white plastic keyboards that were slippery! (I'm looking at *you*, Steinway). Yamaha invented a plastic called Ivorite that they claim mimics the look and feel of ivory. It has since been imitated by other makers and the issue is pretty much resolved. Keyboards are very nice and playable now, with no elephant assassinations required.

Almost every modern piano has 52 white keys and 36 black keys for a total of 88 keys. Some piano manufacturers have extended the range further in one or both directions. For example, the Imperial Bösendorfer has nine extra keys at the bass end, giving a total of 97 keys and an eight octave range. These extra keys are sometimes hidden under a small, hinged lid that can cover the keys to prevent peripheral visual disorientation for pianists unfamiliar with the extra keys, or the colors of the extra white keys are reversed (black instead of white).

The extra keys are added primarily so the commonly-used bass strings nearer the edge of the soundboard are moved closer to the center, increasing resonance and tone quality. The extra strings (for which almost no music has been written) resonate sympathetically with other strings whenever the damper pedal is depressed and thus give a fuller tone.

Eight extra keys on Bösendorfer Imperial Concert Grand

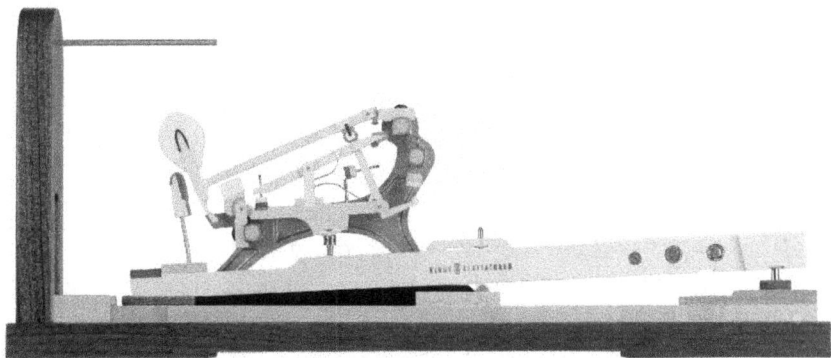

Steinway grand action (There are over 12000 parts in a typical concert grand piano.)

CR

THE ORGAN

*A*n organ is a keyboard instrument in which sound is produced by pipes or reeds to which wind is supplied through a mechanism under the control of the organist. They are the largest, most complicated, most grandiose, most versatile, and most expensive of musical instruments. Conventional pipe organs consist of five main parts: (1) the keyboard or keyboards and other controls that collectively are called the console, (2) the pipes that produce the tone, (3) the mechanism, or action, and (4) the wind generator. (5) the stops which allow the organist to control which ranks of pipes sound at a given time.

The first pipe organs weren't conceived as musical instruments. They were more like a science experiment demonstrating the principles of hydraulics. This took place about 200 BC in Greece through the efforts of a Greek engineer named Ctesibius of Alexandria. In Europe, it took another thousand years for the principle to be applied to what we have come to know as the Pipe Organ.

Around 900 AD the first pipe organs appeared in Europe, but they would have been hard to recognize as such. These new music machines were operated using sliders instead of keys. The Benedictine order of the Catholic church is likely responsible for this development. New churches were springing up and the new organs were part of the growing music scene.

The wind chest was made of wood and molded metal, and the entire organ could be placed within a wall, showing only the pipes. Wind was made using one, two or three bellows.

It was in the Medieval era that sliders were replaced with a keyboard, sometimes two or more. The number of pipes used was greatly expanded, increasing the total available notes to around 40 in this era.

Since the 14th century, the organist's feet received a keyboard of their own. The pedal board is basically like the keyboard but controls the longer, deeper bass pipes. Only a few pedals at first, but organs today normally have pedal keyboards of up to 32 notes.

The development of the chromatic keyboard (all 12 keys per octave, laid out much as the piano keyboard is today) was a game-changer for the nascent organ, enhancing playability and clarifying construction goals. By 1361 the cathedral organ at Halberstadt, Ger., a unique oddity at the time, had three chromatic keyboards and pedals; the keys, however, were quite huge and hard to press. It took another century for the keyboard to achieve the size and shape about as we enjoy today. It took even longer for keyboards to achieve the balance and feel to allow for any real artistic expression.

During the Middle Ages and the Renaissance, three small, portable forms of the organ were popular.

Positive Organ

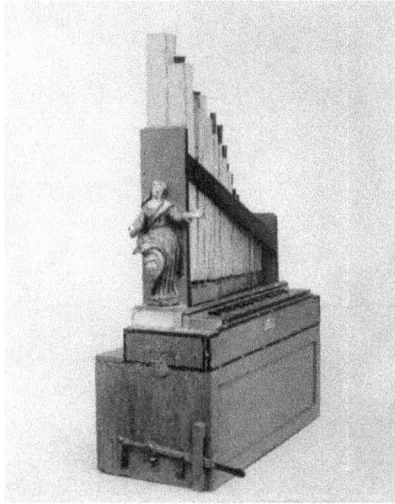

The Positive Organ was used in chamber music and it was capable of being moved, usually by two men, either on carrying poles or on a cart.

Portative Organ

The Portative Organ could be toted about by the player and sported but a single set of pipes and a keyboard of very short range. The player worked the bellows with one hand and played the keys with the other. These were used in processions and in instrumental ensembles.

Regal

The Regal had one or more metal reed stops which were of the clarinet type. In the first part of the Renaissance period the name Regal was applied to any small organ which served a similar purpose, even though it did not wholly consist of reed pipes. It was larger than the Portative Organ and had more keys.

It was during the late 1400s that the *Blockwerk* (the main chest of pipes on a Medieval organ which operated together rather than with individual stops for each rank) was divided into different sounds.

The pressing of any one key opened wind to a specific row of pipes that were designed to produce a certain type of sound. Organ builders fashioned stops that imitated various instruments, such as the krummhorn and the viola da gamba. Stops kept wind from operating all of the other pipes in the same row. By 1500, the average organ in western Europe probably consisted of 10 separate stops.

Renaissance Organ

Eventually organs became ever more elaborate and capable of producing more colors than ever before. At this time there was a great splitting off of national styles of organ building and playing. Differences arose for about every aspect of the organ imaginable, from the operation of keys and the number of keyboards, to the types of stops and how they were operated. Northern European organs were louder than Italian organs. Different types of wood locally available influenced the design (and resonance) of wind boxes.

The Baroque period was organ building's "golden age," as virtually every important refinement was brought to a culminating art. Builders such as Arp

Schnitger and Gottfried Silbermann constructed instruments that were in themselves artistic masterpieces, displaying both exquisite craftsmanship and beautiful sound. These organs featured well-balanced mechanical key actions, finally giving the organist precise control over the pipe speech.

Silbermann Organ

Bach's favorite dashboard: the Silbermann Organ Console

Because of the increasing interest in orchestral and operatic music, the organ fell out of favor during the 18th century, and by 1800 it survived only in the church setting.

During the Romantic period, the organ became more symphonic, capable of creating a gradual crescendo (increase in volume). New technologies and the work of organ builders such as Eberhard Friedrich Walcker, Aristide Cavaille-Coll, and Henry Willis made it possible to build larger organs with more stops, more variation in sound and timbre, and more divisions. Enclosed divisions became common, and registration aids were developed to make it easier for the organist to manage the great number of stops. The desire for louder, grander organs required that the stops be voiced on a higher wind pressure than before. More, bigger, louder, with massively increased complications was the new philosophy.

Cavaille-Coll Organ

Cavaille-Coll Console

Organists found that they could play effective arrangements of orchestral music on the new Romantic-style organ. Since orchestral music was popular and good orchestras were rare, the organ suddenly regained an immense popularity hardly rivaled by that of the 17th and 18th centuries, when it was the acknowledged "king of instruments." Organ builders naturally responded by making their instruments increasingly orchestral in character.

Organ builders began to lean towards specifications with fewer mixtures and high-pitched stops. They preferred to use more 8' and 16' stops in their specifications and wider pipe scales. These practices created a warmer, richer sound than was common in the 18th century. Organs began to be built in concert halls and composers such as Camille Saint-Saens and Gustav Mahler used the organ in their orchestral works.

Albert Schweitzer, organist, philosopher, and later medical missionary was a fanatical disciple of the organ music of J.S. Bach and was a pioneer in recordings of his organ music. (He even had a pipe organ in his African missionary living quarters.). In 1906 he wrote a scholarly and passionate plea for the reformation of organ-building that would address the inadequacies of the bloated 19th century organ for the performance of the music of Bach and his contemporaries. It took 20 years for the revival of earlier styles of organ building to begin in earnest. Historically-minded organ builders began designing and building organs based tonally and structurally upon Baroque models. They returned to building mechanical key actions, voicing with lower wind pressures and thinner pipe scales, and designing specifications with more mixture stops. They also restored old organs that had been 'improved,' back to their original specifications.

These Baroque-style organs could not serve large-scale works by Romantic and later composers, but their musical qualities and sensitivity to the player's touch make them artistically superior to the overstuffed and unwieldy all-purpose organs, some of which have more than 150 ranks.

The late 20th century has seen a decline in production of pipe organs, with several large manufacturers going out of business in the United States. Many new organs, even in churches, are digital. They play, through loudspeakers instead of pipes, digital samples taken from pipe organs. The best of these sound impressive to the uninitiated, cashing in on the dumbing-down of current society. But they are fakes and must be tolerated as an economic expedient.

Organ Anatomy & Physiology

On pipes, action, wind systems, stops, consoles, keyboards, couplers, enclosures, expression pedals, combination action & casing.

Pipes

The pitch of each note is determined by the length of its pipe; the longest pipe emits the deepest note, the shortest pipe the highest note. If two comparable pipes sound an octave apart, the effective length of the higher-pitched pipe is exactly half that of the lower-pitched. The timbre and volume of the sound produced by a pipe depends on the volume of air delivered to the pipe and the manner in which it is constructed and voiced, the latter adjusted by the builder to produce the desired tone and volume which cannot be readily changed while playing.

Organ pipes are made from either wood, metal, or more rarely glass and produce sound ("speak") when air under pressure ("wind") is directed through them. As one pipe produces a single pitch, multiple pipes are necessary to accommodate the musical scale.

155

Organ pipes are divided into flue pipes and reed pipes. Flue pipes produce sound by forcing air through a fipple, like that of a recorder, whereas reed pipes produce sound via a vibrating reed, like that of a clarinet or saxophone.

Pipes are arranged by timbre and pitch into *ranks*. A rank is a row of pipes mounted vertically onto a windchest. The stop mechanism admits air to each rank. For a given pipe to sound, the stop governing the pipe's rank must be selected and engaged, and the key corresponding to its pitch must be depressed. Ranks of pipes are organized into groups called *divisions*. Each division generally is played from its own keyboard and conceptually comprises an individual instrument within the organ.

Since there is just one pipe for each note, a keyboard with 61 notes (5 octaves) would have 61 pipes, one for each note of that rank. If a keyboard of 61 notes controls a group of 10 ranks of pipes, there will be 610 pipes playable from that keyboard. There are many more pipes in an organ than the ones you typically see.

Action

An organ contains two *actions*, or systems of moving parts.

- The stop action allows the organist to control which ranks are engaged.
- The key action admits wind into a pipe when a key is depressed.

In a mechanical stop action, each stop control is physically connected to a rank of pipes. When the organist activates the stop control, the action allows wind to flow into the selected rank. This control is usually a *stop knob*, which the organist activates by drawing it towards himself. This is the origin of the idiom "to pull out all the stops." Tracker action has been used from antiquity to modern times. Despite the extra effort needed in playing (the slight delay from keypress to sound produced takes some getting used to), many organists prefer tracker action because of a more intimate feel and control of the pipe valve operation.

A key action which physically connects the keys and the windchests is a mechanical or tracker action. Connection is achieved through a series of rods called trackers. When the organist depresses a key, the corresponding tracker moves, allowing wind to enter the pipe.

The most recent development is the electric action which uses electrical current to control the key and/or stop mechanisms. Electricity may control the action indirectly through air pressure valves (pneumatics), in which case the action is electro-pneumatic. When electricity operates the action directly without the assistance of pneumatics, it is commonly referred to as direct electric action.

Wind system

The wind system consists of the parts that produce, store, and deliver wind to the pipes.

Playing the organ before electricity required at least one person to operate the bellows. When signaled by the organist, a *calcant* would operate a set of bellows, supplying the organ with air. Because you had to pay calcants who could be pricey, annoying and/or unreliable, organists would usually practice on other instruments such as the clavichord or harpsichord. By the mid-19th century bellows were also being operated by water engines, steam engines or gasoline engines, and yes, noise could be a big problem. Starting in the 1860s bellows were gradually replaced by wind turbines which were later directly connected to electrical motors. This made it possible for organists to practice regularly on the organ, with only the electric bill to consider. Most organs, both new and historic, have original electric blowers or have been converted to their use, although some can still be operated manually. The wind supplied is stored in one or more regulators to maintain a constant pressure in the windchests until the action allows it to flow into the pipes.

Stops

Each *stop* usually controls one rank of pipes. The name of the stop reflects the stop's timbre and construction

To facilitate a large range of timbres, organ stops exist at different pitch levels. A stop that sounds at unison pitch when a key is depressed is referred to as being at 8' (pronounced "eight-foot") pitch. This refers to the length of the lowest-sounding pipe in that rank, which is approximately eight feet. For the same reason, a stop that sounds an octave higher is at 4' pitch, and one that sounds two octaves higher is at 2' pitch. Likewise, a stop that sounds an octave lower than unison pitch is at 16' pitch, and one that sounds two octaves lower is at 32' pitch.

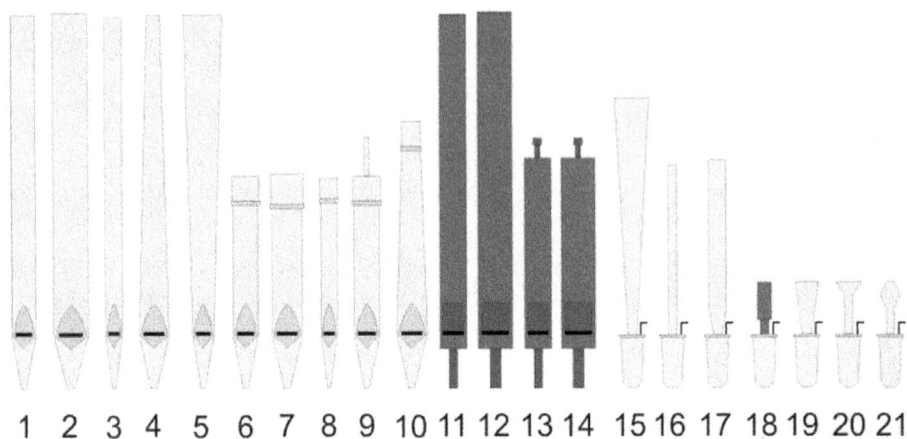

Common types of organ stops

1-10: metal flue pipes
1: open diapason
2: open flute
3: gamba
4: spire flute
5: cone flute
6: stopped diapason
7: stopped flute
8: quintaton
9: chimney flute
10: stopped spire diapason

11-14: wooden flue pipes
11: open diapason
12: open flute
13: stopped diapason
14. stopped flute

15-21: reed pipes
15: trumpet
16: cromorne
17: dulcian
18: wooden regal
19: trumpet regal

20: bell regal
21: double bell regal

All pipes shown produces a tone of the same pitch.

Console

The controls available to the organist, including the keyboards, couplers, expression pedals, stops, and registration aids are accessed from the *console*. The console is either built into the organ case or detached from it.

A very large and complex 20th century organ console

Keyboards

Keyboards for the hands are known as manuals, the keyboard played by the feet is a pedalboard. Every organ has at least one manual (most have two or more), and most have a pedalboard. Each keyboard is named for a particular division of the organ (a group of ranks) and generally controls only the stops from that division. The range of the keyboards has varied widely across time and between countries. Most current specifications call for two or more manuals with sixty-one keys and a pedalboard with thirty or thirty-two pedals.

Often the organist needs to play two or more simultaneous parts to give prominence to a melody against a quieter accompaniment, use two contrasting colors (stops), or to play loud and soft passages in rapid succession. None of these effects can be achieved on an organ with one manual. For this reason, organs of more than about seven or eight stops usually have two manuals, each controlling its separate wind-chest and stops. Some later organs sport as many as seven or eight manuals.

Pedalboard

Couplers

A *coupler* allows the stops of one division to be played from the keyboard of another division. For example, a coupler labelled 'Swell to Great' allows the stops drawn in the Swell division to be played on the Great manual. Coupling allows stops from different divisions to be combined to create various tonal effects. It also allows every stop of the organ to be played simultaneously from one manual.

Octave couplers, which add the pipes an octave above or below each note that is played, may operate on one division only (for example, the Swell super octave, which adds the octave above what is being played on the Swell to itself), or act as a coupler to another keyboard (for example, the Swell super-octave to Great, which adds to the Great manual the ranks of the Swell division an octave above what is being played).

Enclosure and expression pedals

Enclosure refers to a system that allows for a structural solution to regulate the volume. In a two-manual organ with Great and Swell divisions, the Swell will be enclosed. In larger organs, parts or all of the Choir and Solo divisions may also be enclosed. The pipes of an enclosed division are placed in a chamber called the *swell box*. At least one side of the box is constructed from horizontal or vertical palettes known as swell shades, which operate like Venetian blinds; their position can be adjusted from the console. When the swell shades are open, more sound is heard than when they are closed. The swell also mutes the timbre of a stop, which is not always desirable. Sometimes the shades are exposed, but they are often concealed behind a row of facade-pipes or a grill.

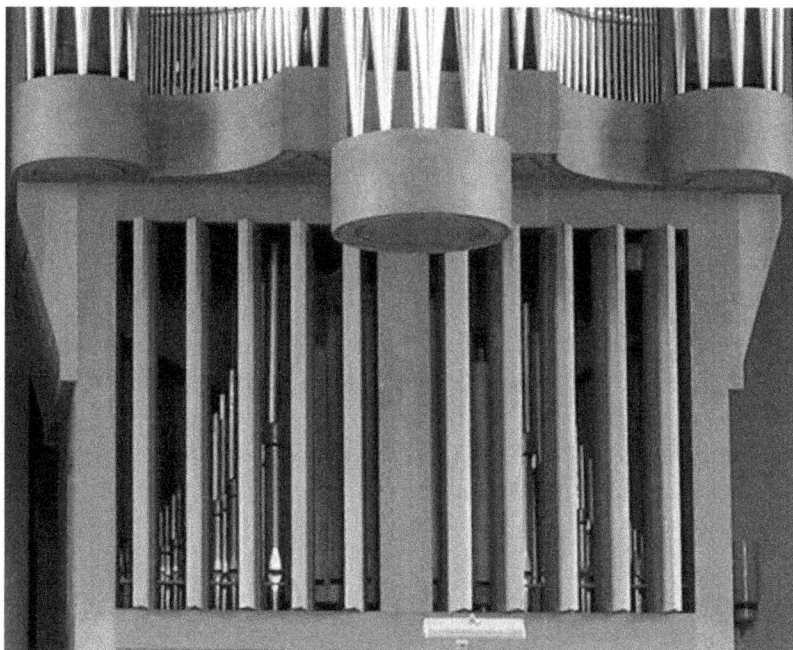

Swell shades open

The most common method of controlling the louvers is the balanced swell pedal. This device is usually placed above the center of the pedalboard. An

161

organ may also have a similar-looking crescendo pedal, found alongside any expression pedals. Pressing the crescendo pedal forward cumulatively activates the stops of the organ, starting with the softest and ending with the loudest; pressing it backwards reverses this process. It is used to death by lazy or unimaginative organists.

Combination action

Organ stops can be combined in countless permutations, resulting in a great variety of sounds. A combination action can be used to switch instantly from one combination of stops (called a registration) to another. Combination actions feature small buttons called pistons that can be pressed by the organist, generally located beneath the keys of each manual (thumb pistons) or above the pedalboard (toe pistons). The pistons may be divisional (affecting only a single division) or general (affecting all the divisions) and are either preset by the organ builder or can be altered by the organist. Modern combination actions operate via computer memory and can store several channels of registrations.

Casing

The *case* houses the pipes, action, and wind. The console may also be incorporated in the case in organs both great and modest. The case acts acoustically to blend the organ's sounds and a good design will help in projecting the sound into the room. The placement of the organ in the space is of highest importance and can make the difference between a successful installation and a failure. The case often is designed to complement the building's architectural style and it may contain ornamental carvings and other decorations, but one often finds a hypermodern organ design in an old church. The visible portion of the case is called the *facade*, containing pipes which may be either sounding pipes or dummy pipes solely for decoration—a philosophical horror to purists. The facade pipes may be plain, burnished, gilded, or painted.

CR

EVOLUTION OF THE ORCHESTRA

People have been putting instruments together in various combinations for thousands of years. But it wasn't until about the last 400 years that musicians started forming into combinations that turned into the Modern Symphony Orchestra, surely the greatest musical instrument on the planet.

In the Medieval and Renaissance eras, when musicians got together, they used whatever instruments were around. If there were a couple lute players, a harp, and a flute or two, then that's what they used. By the 1500s the word 'consort' was used to mean a group of instrumentalists, and sometimes singers too, making music together or 'in concert.'

Early Renaissance composers usually didn't say what instrument they were writing a part for. They meant for the parts to be played by whatever was around. But around 1600 in Italy, the composer **Claudio Monteverdi** wanted what he wanted. He knew just what instruments he required to accompany his opera *Orfeo* (1607), and he specified exactly which instruments should be included: fifteen viols (of different sizes), two violins, four flutes (two large and two medium), two oboes, two cornetts (small wooden trumpets), four brass trumpets, five trombones, a harp, two harpsichords, and three small organs.

Piffaro, Michigan-based Renaissance band

Baroque

Music of the Baroque period was decorative and filled with embellishments (much like the paintings of that time). The music contained very few directions in the score such as dynamic markings (how loud or soft) and tempos remained the same within each movement of a piece, rarely changing. Sometimes, even tempo was not specified.

So **Monteverdi's** orchestra was already starting to look like what we think of as an orchestra: instruments organized into sections; lots of bowed strings; lots of variety. This was the beginning of the Baroque. From this time on the orchestra developed still further. The violin family—violin, viola, cello, and double bass—replaced the viols. Musical leadership in the Baroque orchestra came from the keyboard instruments, with the harpsichordist, or sometimes the organist, acting as leader.

Orchestras during this time were unstandardized, usually small and consisted of perhaps:
4 first violins
4 second violins
2 violas
2 cellos
1 double bass
Other string instruments were also occasionally used, which are no longer used today. These include the viola da gamba, viola d'amore, violoncello piccolo, violetta, and violone.

When called for, a small wind section (one player per part) was used, which may include:
flute
recorder
bassoon
Other wind instruments were also occasionally used, which are no longer used today. These include the oboe d'amore and the oboe da caccia.

Brass sometimes included:
trumpet
trombone
horn
Other brass instruments were also occasionally used, which are no longer used today. These include the cornette, various sizes of trumpets, corno da caccia and corno da tirarsi.

Timpani was used sparingly in the percussion section.

Basso Continuo parts (or simply 'continuo') were almost universal in the Baroque era, provided the harmonic structure of the music, it's underpinnings and scaffolding.

The makeup of the continuo group is often left to the discretion of the performers, or simply what is available for the task. The combinations varied enormously in the Baroque period.

At least one instrument capable of playing chords must be included, such as a harpsichord, organ, lute, theorbo, guitar, or harp. In addition, any number of instruments that play in the bass register may be included, such as cello, double bass, bass viol, or bassoon. The most common combination, at least in modern performances, is harpsichord and cello for instrumental works and secular vocal works such as operas, and organ for sacred music

Conductors: Because orchestras were small and works contained little change in tempo or dynamic, no conductors were needed. In most cases, the leader or harpsichordist used his head or free hand to begin the piece and give the final cutoff.

Typical 'orchestra' such as Bach may have used (Victoria Baroque Players)

Classical

Music of the Classical period was much more reserved, less concerned with busy counterpoint, with balance being a main focus. The ornamentations and complexities of the Baroque period had fallen out of style.

In the early Classical period, the string sections of orchestras began to grow in number. In the late Classical period, around **Beethoven's** time, orchestras were substantially larger in all sections of the orchestra. The total number of musicians ranged from 30-50 and in some cases even higher. The great variety of instruments that could be found in the Baroque orchestra had sifted down to essentially the same instruments we use today. (Note, however, that the only instrument from this era that has come down to us completely unchanged is the trombone.)

A typical Classical orchestra may be constituted thus:
8 first violins
8 second violins
4 violas
4 cellos (eventually with their own part, not just doubling the double basses)
2 double basses
2 flutes
2 oboes
2 clarinets (from late Haydn on)
2 bassoons
2 or 4 horns
2 trumpets (eventually used independently instead of always doubling the horns)
2 timpani

Conductors: Musicians were still experimenting with ways to keep large numbers of players in time. Batons were uncommon, and conductors often used rolled up pieces of music into a scroll and waved them in the air.

Typical Classical Era-size orchestra (Australian Brandenburg Orchestra)

Romantic

Music of the Romantic period conveyed feelings, and all the baggage and complexity that feelings entail. It had many more expression markings and tempo changes written in. Composers used nature as an inspiration for their works. Many tone poems were written, taking music out of the abstract world and into a realm of sound painting. In the Late Romantic period, composers from many nations used folktunes from their native countries as inspiration for their compositions, a movement known as Nationalism.

Orchestras exploded in size during the Romantic Period. Large concert halls were built which could accommodate these huge new orchestras. String sections alone as large as 60+ players were combined with a large compliment of woodwinds, brass, and percussion. Orchestras also began to use a standard of seating that is still used today. New instruments were introduced, many simply to increase the range of existing instruments. They include harp, modern tuba, English horn, bass clarinet, Eb clarinet, modern double bassoon, bass trombone, xylophones, drums, celestes, harps, bells, and triangles.

A typical Romantic-era orchestra is hard to pin down. The sky was the limit. Here is what **Mahler** required for his Symphony No. 8, entirely untypical but an example of how gargantuan the possibilities were. Its premiere performance featured 1,028 performers.

Woodwinds
2 piccolos (1st doubling 5th flute)
4 flutes
4 oboes

english horn
3 B♭ clarinets
E♭ clarinet
bass clarinet
4 bassoons
contrabassoon

Brass
8 horns
8 trumpets (four offstage)
7 trombones (three offstage)
tuba

Percussion
4 timpani
bass drum
cymbals
triangle
tam-tam
2 tuned bells in A and A♭
glockenspiel

Keyboards
organ
celesta
piano
harmonium

Strings
2 mandolins
2 harps (preferably doubled)
1st violins
2nd violins
violas
cellos
double basses

Choral and Vocal Forces
3 soprano solos
2 alto solos

tenor solo
baritone solo
bass solo
2 full choirs
children's chorus

Conductors: In the Romantic era conductors were a standard part of the orchestra, if for no other reason just to keep everything from falling apart. They would stand on a podium and use a baton to lead, as they do today. Their function became more than just a timekeeper and cue giver. It was now the conductor's job to interpret the compositions and convey musical gestures to the musicians (and audience) that would produce the desired musical effect.

The New York Philharmonic Orchestra

Modern

Early in the last century, composers tried to convey impressions created by sights, sounds, fragrances, even tastes. Other composers smashed the molds of traditional harmonies to bits and replaced the old ways with personalized, synthetic systems of composing. Eventually, all the rules were tossed aside and by this writing there is nothing from the past that is still standing as an iron-clad rule or requirement to be deemed 'classical music.' It's a judgement call. History, of course, is the best judgement call, but that hasn't yet been made of the current scene.

Today, the size of an orchestra will vary according to the requirements of the piece it is performing. they can be as large as 100+ or as small as 24. Compositions today may require an instrument not usually found in an orchestra.

The 'standard' orchestra still exists, though numbers are declining. They are generally smaller than orchestras of the Romantic heyday, usually contracting with 100 or so players. They have mostly become museums of music. In order to stay relevant, modern orchestras are experimenting with expanding repertory to include pop music, film and television music, as well as concert music, so their repertoire now encompasses a great range of styles. The big orchestras stick to the later Classical, Romantic and Modern repertory because specialized orchestras that feature original instruments and performing practices have claimed the Baroque and early Classical era as their own. Few people these days care to hear a light, fleet-footed **Vivaldi** concerto played by such as the massive Berlin Philharmonic. It's like watching an elephant dance.

Various electronic instruments (e.g. ondes martenot, synthesizers) have been added to the orchestral landscape, as well as digital computer accompaniments. There has been much development in the percussion section. It is not uncommon to see vast amounts of percussion used in modern orchestras, including a range of tuned instruments, unusual or exotic untuned instruments, and many effects. As early as 1913, **Igor Stravinsky's** *Rite of Spring* included triangle, tambourine, guiro, 2 antique cymbals, and tam-tam, and by 1926, **Edgard Varèse** included 39 tuned and untuned percussion instruments in his massive orchestra for his *Arcana*. Pretty much any instrument from any part of the world is now acceptable for use in a symphony orchestra.

Conductors: All symphony orchestras use them. Usually they have a music director who does most of the concerts, along with various jet-setter guest conductors who fly in to share the schedule, giving the music director some free time and allowing him or her to guest conduct for *other* orchestras. One way the role has changed is that modern music directors need to help get asses in the seats, not just conduct. They need to *fundraise*, because just being an excellent conductor won't get you the job anymore. Charisma, baby.

Also, the age of the conductor-as-ruthless-tyrant is past. Early in the last century, one of these authoritarian beasts could call a musician out, embarrass him or her in front of colleagues and then fire them on the spot. Maybe throw your viola on the floor for good measure. Now there are unions, and violence and vulgarity are out. So is sexual abuse, which was rampant.

CR

20 GREAT CONDUCTORS

Those who want to investigate history's great conductors will require more than what I provide here. Your best bet is a single-volume study by Norman Lebrecht. The book is The Maestro Myth: Great Conductors in Pursuit of Power. *A masterful overview that is light on hero-worship and doesn't avoid the dirt and scandal, of which much. It's a couple decades old but that doesn't matter much. It's available in all the usual places.*

Most of the conductors featured here are dead or old. They are from the Golden Age of classical music performance and the age we are in now is not it. The new breed of baton-wavers are pretty much interchangeable. They are mostly all satisfactory. Lots of them are women because equity or something, which has become more important than talent. It is likewise with soloists, who are all technically perfect and all essentially interchangeable. I don't see any hope in the near term. I hope I am wrong. I often am.

Most conductors are like most people in any profession—unremarkable. A few are worse than no conductor at all, and some are amazing geniuses who have transformed the art.

Even before Bach's day, there was usually a 'leader of the band.' The person most respected, or simply willing to take charge was often the *de facto* leader. He or she set the tempo and acted as a sparkplug to the event.

'Do orchestras even need conductors?' is a question asked perennially by culture wags trying to stir the pot. Yes. They do. There are exceptions, natch—the Orpheus chamber orchestra comes to mind—but they sound like a chamber orchestra without a conductor, and they won't be playing any large orchestral works.

On the other hand, conductors need to know when they ought to pull back. Lennox Mackenzie, chairman and sub-leader of the London Symphony has a cogent tale to tell:

"I remember a conducting masterclass when [Colin Davis] berated one of the young conductors for working too hard—moving his arms around too much. He took over, briefly, on the podium and set the orchestra off in a movement of Beethoven. Then he stopped conducting completely, the orchestra carried on, and he explained to the young man, 'The orchestra is on a roll. It's not going to stop. You don't have to do anything.' But of course every now and again, Sir Colin would give a small gesture which would indicate a dynamic or a piece of expression that made the orchestra sound totally differ-ent. I realized at that point I was in the presence of greatness."

If you get yourself to YouTube you can watch some rehearsals recordings. They are most instructive. Beating time and looking handsome is what we see on stage, but the details, in number and type, are astonishing. This is where they earn their money, in *rehearsal*, making what they do on stage look effort-less takes an enormous amount of effort.

No conductor does everything well. You don't want Herbert von Karajan conducting Bach with his elephantine band. If you want him at all, you want him doing Romantic-era repertory. Likewise, Christopher Hogwood conduct-ing late-Beethoven would be a wayward choice; it's simply not the sort of thing he did very well.

Here follows a list, not of 'The 20 Greatest Conductors in History,' but of 20 great conductors *from the golden age of classical music from whom we have a sub-stantial body of recordings*. So Arthur Nikisch isn't here because he's a bit early, and the great Carlos Kleiber isn't listed because he made so few recordings.

The influence upon classical music and its interpretation that these men have is unassailable. Note that many of the best of these have a strong flavor about their work and lots of listeners are passionately against their interpreta-tions and avoid them.

It's a small list, but within their degree of specialization, these fellas will very rarely steer you astray. (Every aficionado alive will take issue with this tiny list. I am comforted by the fact that no one would agree with *their* list, either.)

• ARTURO TOSCANINI (ITALY, 1867-1957)

SUPERPOWER: *The marriage of Passion and Clarity*

Toscanini grew up in Parma, Italy. After graduating from the conservatory in 1885, Toscanini immediately found work with travelling orchestras in Italy. In 1886 he joined a company that journeyed to Rio de Janeiro, Brazil, to stage some operas. On that particular trip the company conductor one day refused to lead, so with no prior preparation Toscanini made his conducting debut on June 25, 1886 with Verdi's *Aida*. He was 19 at the time.

He conducted various orchestras in Italy, 1887-1908; by 1898 Toscanini was named chief conductor and artistic director at La Scala, and he became well known there for introducing new operas and symphonic works. He also gained a reputation for his unorthodox attitudes; he was dismissed in 1903 for refusing to permit encores. There was absolutely nothing frivolous about Toscanini.

He led the Metropolitan Opera orchestra, New York City, 1908-15; back to Italy at the outbreak of World War I to conduct benefit performances for the country's soldiers, 1915-26; conductor of New York Philharmonic-Symphony Orchestra, 1926-36; conductor of Palestine Symphony Orchestra, 1936; He hated the Fascisti and moved to New York where NBC created an orchestra just for him 1937-54; guest conductor of numerous symphony orchestras in U.S. and Europe. Made numerous recordings on RCA Victor label.

For more than half a century, Arturo Toscanini was one of the world's most respected conductors, a musical powerhouse whose performances packed orchestra halls—and filled the radio waves—in every major city in the United States. Toscanini dominated the classical music world, leading the debut performances of numerous important operas and symphonies.

Toscanini conducted entirely from memory. Nearsighted from childhood, he memorized hundreds of intricate operas, symphonies, and concertos. He was very lively, often brisk in his interpretations. He was passionate but precise in his music, and obsessive about sticking to the composer's intentions.

But he was often brutal to his musicians, shrieking out chestnuts such as:

I hate you all because you destroy my dreams!

After I die, I shall return to earth as a gatekeeper of a bordello and I won't let any of you enter!

Can't you read? The score demands 'con amore,' and what are you doing? You are playing it like married men!

God tells me how the music should sound, but you stand in the way!

- # BRUNO WALTER (GERMANY, 1876-1962)

SUPERPOWER: *He married Profundity to Grace.*

Walter, like so many, started as a pianist and made his debut as a conductor in 1894 at the Cologne Opera. By 1900 he was at the State Opera in Berlin, and in the following year he became Gustav Mahler's associate in Vienna— the beginning of what was to be a lifetime spent in promotion of Mahler's music.

As a young man he suffered from a paralyzing neuralgia and, after consulting a number of specialists, he decided to seek help from Sigmund Freud. While the young Walter expected months of psychological investigation, Freud, after a physical exam and a single visit, prescribed sojourns in Italy and Sicily. Walter obeyed immediately. His subsequent treatment with Freud resembled therapy by suggestion such as was common in the 19th century. When Walter asked Freud if he would be able to play in front of an audience because he feared a relapse, Freud took upon himself the responsibility, assuming the role of a protective paternal figure and inducing an almost hypnotic effect upon Walter, traces of which were still discernable 40 years later.

Walter conducted the premieres of Mahler's *Das Lied von der Erde* (1911) and the *Ninth Symphony* (1912). After Mahler passed, Walter moved to the

177

Munich Opera (1914–22) and from 1922 conducted at Salzburg. Here he developed a passion for Mozart. Walter was a great Mozartean.

He was at the Berlin Municipal Opera (1925–29) and Furtwängler's successor in Leipzig with the Gewandhaus Orchestra (1929–33). He fled the Nazis, leaving his work in Germany behind, moving first to Vienna (1936–38), briefly to Paris, and finally to the United States (1939). He conducted frequently at the Metropolitan Opera and the New York Philharmonic.

His style is gracious. He was rarely argumentative. Mozart suits him. And his Mahler is not only great, it is authoritative.

By concentrating on precision, one arrives at technique, but by concentrating on technique one does not arrive at precision.

- ## OTTO KLEMPERER (GERMANY, 1885-1973)

SUPERPOWER: *Crushing afflictions and liabilities overcome by indomitable spirit that is audible in his work.*

When he was old he looked a lot like Frankenstein's monster, towering and intimidating. A bad fall in 1951 forced him to conduct seated in a chair. A severe burning accident disfigured and further paralyzed him, which resulted from his smoking in bed and trying to douse the flames with the contents of a bottle of spirits of camphor nearby. (This serious, formidable man lent karmic balance to the universe through his son Werner, who played Colonel Klink on the old *Hogan's Heroes* TV series.)

Klemperer studied in Frankfurt and Berlin and on the recommendation of Mahler was made conductor of the German National Theatre at Prague in 1907. From 1910 he conducted opera at Hamburg, Barmen, Strassburg, Cologne, Wiesbaden and Berlin. Mahler inculcated the young man with the *avant-garde*. When refracted through the prism of Klemperer's romantic character, this contributed to his unique style.

Klemperer's early reputation was made conducting opera. He moved to Strasbourg in 1914 where he was appointed first conductor and musical director of the opera house and a professor and the director of the conservatory there. In 1916, Klemperer became Strasbourg's general music director. The next year he moved to Cologne, whose *avant-garde* tastes suited his own and where, as first conductor, he expanded his reputation. Klemperer remained in Cologne for seven years, leaving to accept an appointment as general musical director in Wiesbaden.

Three years later, in 1927, Klemperer was appointed general musical director of the Kroll Opera in Berlin. He served in that capacity until 1931, the year the company went out of existence. This was the heyday of the Weimar Republic. Culturally, Berlin was at its notorious between-the-wars zenith. Under Klemperer, the Kroll became one of the most renowned experimental companies in the world. The list of composers whose works were performed reads like a who's who of European Modernism: Schoenberg, Stravinsky, Hindemith, and Kurt Weill among others. Klemperer also gave all-Bach concerts and sometimes mixed Bach with contemporaries such as Hindemith and Weill.

After leaving the Kroll, he took the position of second conductor at the Staatsoper (State Opera). Being a Jewish musician (albeit one who had converted to Christianity), and a controversial one at that, Klemperer foresaw difficulties with the Nazi regime. He fled to America.

In many respects, Klemperer's sojourn in America was the nadir of his life and career. Lifelong severe depression (made worse by unfamiliar surroundings and culture) continued to plague him, and he found the respect that he had garnered in Europe had all but vanished in the New World. He settled almost immediately in Los Angeles, where a thriving community of intellectual refugees had made their homes, But L.A. was a city where serious music was nothing more than a backdrop to cinema. Klemperer was fortunate enough to be given the opportunity to conduct the Los Angeles Philharmonic after the departure of Artur Rodzinski for Cleveland.

In addition to his duties at the L.A. Philharmonic, Klemperer was a guest conductor for the New York Philharmonic during the 1934-35 and 1935-36 seasons. In 1937, he spent six weeks reorganizing the Pittsburgh Symphony. However, his behavior outside the concert hall became more erratic and the ensuing publicity he received damaged his reputation in the United States. His tenure at the L.A. Philharmonic lasted until 1939. Just before the start of the 1939-40 season, Klemperer was diagnosed with a brain tumor. The surgery and the stroke he suffered afterward ended his career in Los Angeles.

The stroke left Klemperer partially paralyzed. Conducting was out of the question. It could only have deepened the torment he experienced during bouts of depression. The remainder of his stay in America was a long slide into obscurity. Ironically, as he went about the task of rehabilitating his body (Klemperer, at six feet four inches had the physical strength to match his will), rumors of insanity persistently followed him. By the time he was able to again take up conducting, he was left to promote his own concerts, including one at Carnegie Hall. During the war years he received little work.

In 1947, Klemperer returned to Europe, first to Prague, the location of his first conducting post, then on to Budapest for the 1948-49 and 1949-50 seasons. He began making recordings during these years. After leaving Budapest, Klemperer moved on to East Berlin, where he conducted opera until government interference became too great. Klemperer thereupon returned to the United States, but his woes returned. This was the beginning of the Cold War and Klemperer had spent most of the post-war period in the Eastern Bloc. His passport was confiscated, and he found himself under scrutiny by the FBI. He was rescued from this latest debacle by British record producer, Walter Legge. It proved to be the Renaissance of his career.

At that time, London was filled with refugees eager to hear the classic German repertoire, which Klemperer brought to the Philharmonia. The recordings he made with the Philharmonia received international praise. Beginning as a guest conductor, Klemperer was appointed musical director by 1955. In 1959 he was named the Philharmonia's principal conductor for life. It was during this final stage of his career (which lasted until 1972) that the recognizable figure of Klemperer as an indomitable, deliberate, acid-tongued personality gained acceptance among the general public.

In these final years, Klemperer made the recordings upon which his reputation rests. The pace of many of these recordings is slow, critics have conceded, yet they confirm him as a master of the core German repertoire of Mozart, Beethoven, and Bach.

Those musicians who performed under his baton recall his sternness and indomitable spirit, which enabled him to overcome physical and psychological challenges.(He also suffered from bipolar disorder, which grew worse over time.)

He was never very tactful, reserving some of his sharpest barbs for colleagues such as Wilhelm Furtwangler, whose work he admired but whose collaboration with the Nazi government he could not abide. The antagonism that Klemperer felt toward Furtwangler, however, was nothing compared to that which he felt toward Herbert von Karajan, who had actually joined the Nazi party. By the time the war had ended, Klemperer had re-embraced Judaism and someone like Karajan was not merely a rival, but anathema to him.

His work is solid as a rock and full of intensity and attention to detail. His tempos were faster when he was young, although this is surprisingly common among conductors (and organists). His Mozart, Mahler, Bruckner and Beethoven require your attention.

A musicologist is someone who knows everything about ology,
but nothing about music.

• WILHELM FURTWÄNGLER (GERMANY, 1886-1954)

SUPERPOWER: *He improvised the written score as in a dream yet compelled a great orchestra to somehow follow his lead.*

Furtwängler studied in Munich and got his break as an assistant to conductor Felix Mottl (1907–09). He became director of the Mannheim Opera in 1915 and in 1920 succeeded Richard Strauss as conductor of the Berlin Opera concerts. In 1922 he followed Arthur Nikisch (who would figure prominently on this list if we had recordings by him) as conductor of the Gewandhaus concerts in Leipzig. He also led the Berlin Philharmonic Orchestra (1922), the Vienna Philharmonic Orchestra (1930), the Bayreuth Festivals (1931–32), and the Berlin State Opera (1933). What a list!

He conducted in Germany during most of the Nazi regime. So he was a Nazi? No, no, and no. Controversy arose when he led an orchestral version of Paul Hindemith's opera *Mathis der Maler* with the Berlin Philharmonic in

1934—Hindemith had been denounced by the Nazi propaganda chief Joseph Goebbels and the work banned. Furtwängler resigned his position, but he returned to the orchestra in 1935. Although he was offered and accepted the post as conductor of the New York Philharmonic in 1936, but that did not work out well. The hostility of American musicians to his alleged Nazi associations caused him to resign. The Chicago Symphony Orchestra offered him the baton in 1949, but he got the same treatment there, even though by then he had been formally exonerated of accusations of Nazi complicity.

He's known for his passionate, romantic style, and excelled as a conductor of Beethoven and Richard Wagner. He wasn't much for details. He was into the spirit of a work so much that he was often accused of sloppiness. He had no definable beat at the podium and players would often have to guess when a piece would begin, so imprecise were his beats and cues. That said (and it had to be said), he was one of the greatest musicians that has ever lived. Here are his words:

> *"I am told that the more you rehearse, the better you play. This is wrong. We often try to reduce the unforeseen to a controllable level, to prevent a sudden impulse that escapes our ability to control, yet also responds to an obscure desire. Let's allow improvisation to have its place and play its role. I think that the true interpreter is the one who improvises. We have mechanized the art of conducting to an awful degree, in the quest of perfection rather than of dream…*
>
> *Music making is something else than searching to achieve an accomplishment. But striving to attain it is beautiful. Some of Michelangelo's sculptures are perfect, others are just outlined, and the latter ones move me more than the first perfect ones because here I find the essence of desire, of the wakening dream. That's what really moves me: fixing without freezing in cement, allowing chance its opportunity.*

• YEVGENY MRAVINSKY (RUSSIAN, 1903-1988)

SUPERPOWER: *Old school, hard-boiled perfection; sober, autocratic... yet exciting*

You like Russian music? You need to know this guy.

His professional life started with the Imperial Ballet as a rehearsal pianist. In 1923, he enrolled in the Leningrad Conservatory, where he studied composition. He graduated in 1931 joined the Bolshoi Opera from 1931 to 1937 as rehearsal conductor, with a stint at the Kirov from 1934. In 1938 he gave all that up after winning first prize in the All-Union Conductors' Competition in Moscow, to become principal conductor of the Leningrad Philharmonic. Huge job. He remained there until his death, ignoring many guest-conducting offers from abroad.

Under Mravinsky's direction the Leningrad Philharmonic came to be regarded as one of the finest orchestras in the world, although the world had comparatively few opportunities to hear it aside from the rare tour (about 30 performances in 25 years, starting in 1956), some dim Soviet recordings, and a very few highly acclaimed records for Deutsche Grammophon and Erato.

His rep rests on his fine performances of Mozart, Beethoven, Bruckner, Wagner, Sibelius, Bartók, Stravinsky, and anything Russian or Soviet. His reputation only rose upon his retirement from the Leningrad Philharmonic, particularly with the posthumous release in 1995 by Melodiya and BMG Classics of 20 CDs surveying Mravinsky's work from the 1940s into the 1980s.

Mravinsky gave world premieres of six symphonies by Shostakovich: *Nos. 5, 6, 8* (which Shostakovich's dedicated to Mravinsky), *9, 10* and finally *12* in 1961. His refusal to conduct the premiere of Shostakovich's *Symphony No. 13* in 1962 caused a permanent rupture in their friendship.

He premiered Prokofiev's *Symphony No. 6* in Leningrad the year of its composition (1947). He also conducted works by Bartók and Stravinsky. Mravinsky made commercial studio recordings from 1938 to 1961. His issued recordings from after 1961 were taken from live concerts. His final recording was from an April 1984 live performance of Shostakovich's *Symphony No. 12.*

Recordings reveal Mravinsky to have an extraordinary technical control over the orchestra, especially over dynamics. He was also a very exciting conductor, frequently changing tempo in order to heighten the musical effect for which he was striving, often emphasizing the brass instrumentation.

Surviving videos show that Mravinsky had a sober appearance at the podium, making simple but very clear gestures, often without a baton. Mravinsky's rehearsal manner was said to be autocratic and brutal, and the resulting performances were tightly clenched. Yet they were also technically precise, finely detailed, subtly colored, and highly dramatic. Despite all this, his readings had a spontaneity that has been compared to those of Wilhelm Furtwängler.

To sear art and music into the minds of the people - audiences and performers - that is my principal concern, my ultimate aim.

• HERBERT VON KARAJAN (AUSTRIA, 1908-1989)

SUPERPOWER: *Established 'the standard performance' against which others were judged for a huge portion of the repertory.*

Karajan was a child prodigy at the piano and studied at the Mozarteum in Salzburg from age eight (!). He made his conducting debut in 1929 at Salzburg, and landed a conducting position in Ulm, Germany, later that year. In 1934 he was appointed Kapellmeister at Aachen and stayed till 1941. During that period he also occasionally conducted the Berlin State Opera. He left Germany for Italy in 1944 (or 1945). He helped found the London Philharmonia in 1948, and in 1955 he became music director of the Berlin Philharmonic. And there he made his great career.

Was he a Nazi? Some say he was a Nazi Party member from 1933 to 1942, though the records are fuzzy. He wasn't so much a true believer, he was just the sort of guy who would sell his grandmother's eye teeth for a leg up on a great career. Anyway, he was exonerated by an Allied tribunal after World War II, but his American debut in 1955 was hotly protested. Lots of high-level Jewish musicians in New York City.

He became principal conductor for the Vienna State Opera from 1956 to 1964, and the Salzburg Festival, an annual music festival with which he was associated throughout his later career with great pride. He was also a chief conductor at La Scala, Milan, and a guest conductor at the New York Philharmonic. But for all that and more, his center was the Berlin Phil. He resigned in April 1989, a few months before his death.

Karajan's musical interpretations were noted for their precision and objectivity (though sometimes his 'perfection' can be a little characterless), though he seemed to relax into a more personal style in his later years. Many musicians complained that he shut himself off from them during a performance, closing his eyes most of the time as if he were conjuring the whole show from inside himself. He's known for setting the bar for recordings of music from Beethoven (he did four complete symphony cycles) through the composers of the first half of the 20th century. He did Bach, Haydn, Mozart, too—but one is advised to look elsewhere.

The art of conducting consists in knowing when to stop conducting to let the orchestra play.

• GEORG SOLTI (HUNGARY, 1912-1997)

SUPERPOWER: *Energy and drama, vitality and never-ending curiosity.*

Solti studied at the Liszt Academy of Music in Budapest with Béla Bartók and Zoltán Kodály. At 18 he joined the coaching staff of the Budapest Opera and made his conducting debut there in 1938. A Jew, he fled to Zürich at the outbreak of the war, but in Switzerland, it seems, only a citizen of the nation could conduct professionally. An awesome pianist, he won the Geneva International Piano Competition in 1942. After the war he became music director of the Bavarian State Opera in Munich (1946–52), the Frankfurt Opera (1952–60), and the Royal Opera at Covent Garden (1961–71). He became a British citizen in 1972 and was knighted that same year.

From 1969 to 1991 he was music director of the Chicago Symphony Orchestra and is credited with reestablishing that orchestra's international reputation. He was chief conductor of the Orchestra of Paris (1972–75) and acted as musical adviser to the Paris Opéra from 1971 to 1973. He served as the principal conductor and artistic director of the London Philharmonic Orchestra from 1979 to 1983.

As a conductor Solti was best known for his dynamic and deeply felt interpretations of operas, symphonies, and other large-scale German works from Mozart through Mahler. He was big on attention to detail and his ability to evoke a wide range of tonal colors from an orchestra. He made many highly praised recordings from the late 1940s as both conductor and as pianist.

In 1958–65 Solti made the highly acclaimed first complete set of recordings of Richard Wagner's opera cycle, *The Ring of the Nibelung,* which was released in 1966. This is his greatest hit among acres of great hits. He won 32 Grammy Awards, more than anyone in recording history.

His early style was very intense, but he mellowed out as he aged. His conducting style was always clear and direct with no nonsense. Although he was one of the more acrobatic conductors, his movements were never superfluous. He was obsessed with making the form of the music clear. Solti had a commanding presence both on and off the podium, but no one ever called him tyrannical, and musicians respect his businesslike attitude on the podium.

He never listed to his own recordings, of which almost 300 in his career. He said:

> *My entire learning process is slow,*
> *because I have no visual memory.*

> *Although both sides of my family were religious, I was never forced*
> *to practice the Jewish faith. I did not really rebel against it, but then,*
> *as today, I disliked organized religion.*
> *I have a strange inhibition about praying with others.*

> *I have a theory that there is something abnormal about children who*
> *like to practice instruments They are either geniuses or, more often,*
> *completely untalented. I certainly did not like to practice, and the*
> *teacher who hit me, and the view of the park,*
> *did not help to improve my attitude.*

• CARLO MARIA GIULINI (ITALY, 1914-2005)

SUPERPOWER: *Magisterial and urgent, yet utterly natural.*

Giulini studied at the Academy of Saint Cecilia. He played the viola in the resident orchestra there and got to observe the work of such greats as Wilhelm Furtwängler, Otto Klemperer, and Bruno Walter. He was forced to join the army in 1942 but went into hiding because he refused to fight alongside Germans.

His own conducting debut took place at the Academy in 1944 when he was also appointed musical director for Italian Radio. In 1950 he organized the Milan Radio Orchestra, and those broadcasts brought him to the attention of Toscanini and Victor de Sabata. Three years later he succeeded Sabata as principal conductor of La Scala. From there his reputation soared and he conducted festivals all over Europe.

In 1967 Giulini backed off the opera career and turned his attention to conducting symphony orchestras. He had grown disheartened with working in opera houses, where he said he had to contend with insufficient rehearsal time, musically obtuse directors and too many singers interested more in jet-setting international careers than in substantive work. He restricted his appearances, and even the Metropolitan Opera was never able to engage him.

In his new career, Giulini did lots of work with the London Philharmonia and the Chicago Symphony. From 1973 to 1976 he conducted the Vienna Symphony Orchestra and in 1978 succeeded Zubin Mehta as chief conductor of the Los Angeles Philharmonic, a post he held until 1984.

Giulini's conducting style was often compared to that of Toscanini. A Romantic conductor, he performed few Modern works and was best known for his interpretations of the music of Giuseppe Verdi, Wolfgang Amadeus Mozart, Gustav Mahler, and Anton Bruckner. He enjoyed recording and did so extensively.

Here's how the New York Times described Giulini in his obituary: "Far from being an autocratic conductor or a kinetic dynamo of the podium, Mr. Giulini was a probing musician who achieved results by projecting serene authority and providing a model of selfless devotion to the score. His symphonic performances were at once magisterial and urgent, full of surprise yet utterly natural."

My intention always has been to arrive at human contact without enforcing authority. A musician, after all, is not a military officer. What matters most is human contact. The great mystery of music making requires real friendship among those who work together. Every member of the orchestra knows I am with him and her in my heart.

• LEONARD BERNSTEIN (USA, 1918-1990)

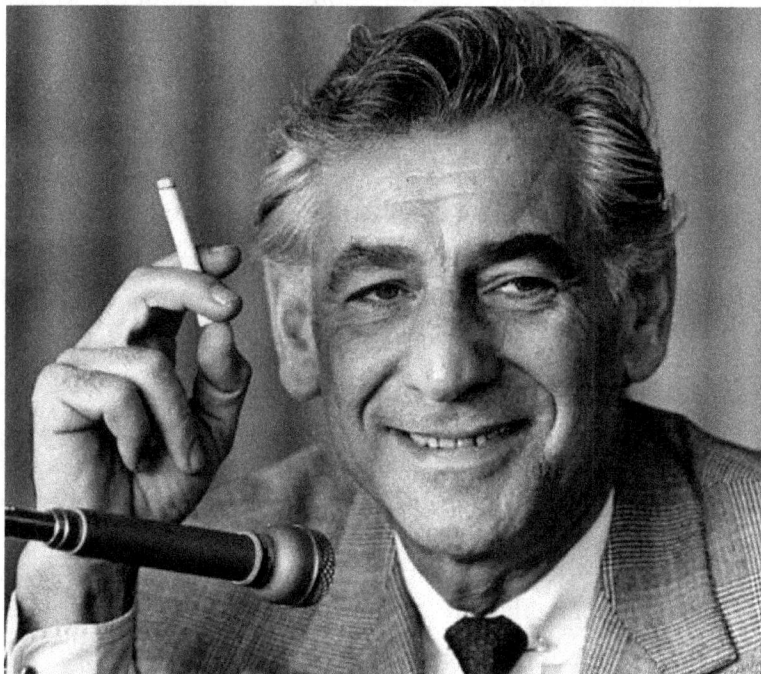

SUPERPOWER: *Mesmerizing charisma and worldwide respect*

Bernstein attended Harvard University where he took courses in music theory, then the Curtis Institute of Music, Philadelphia (1939–41), where he studied conducting with Fritz Reiner and orchestration with Randall Thompson, then the Berkshire Music Center at Tanglewood, Massachusetts, where he studied conducting with Serge Koussevitzky. In 1943, age 25, Bernstein was appointed assistant conductor of the New York Philharmonic. That year, a fairy tale came true and Bruno Walter called in sick for a concert. Lenny stepped in and the rest is history.

He subsequently conducted the New York City Center orchestra (1945–47) and appeared as guest conductor in the United States, Europe, and Israel. In 1953 he became the first American to conduct at La Scala in Milan. From 1958 to 1969 Bernstein was conductor and musical director of the New York Philharmonic, becoming the first American-born holder of those posts.

Lenny's popularity increased through his appearances not only as conductor and pianist but also as a commentator and entertainer. Bernstein explained classical music to young listeners on such television shows as Omnibus and

Young People's Concerts. After 1969 he continued to write music and to perform as a guest conductor with several symphonies throughout the world.

As a composer Bernstein wrote the music for the great American musical *West Side Story*. He wrote reams more music, but they sink under the radar as the years pass.

Bernstein was held in high regard amongst many musicians, including the members of the Vienna Philharmonic, the London Symphony Orchestra, of which he was president; and the Israel Philharmonic Orchestra, with which he appeared regularly as guest conductor. He was probably the main conductor from the 1960s onwards who acquired a superstar status like Herbert von Karajan, another controversial figure.

Bernstein's conducting was characterized by extremes of emotion as he nimbly danced and twerked along with the beat. His manner in rehearsal was the same as in concert. As he got older his performances tended to be even more extreme which often divided critical opinion. There is no conductor who is so equally loved and reviled as Bernstein. He was a pop star, and his pop star sensibilities he wore on his sleeve. Many find him vulgar.

In addition to being an active conductor, Bernstein was an influential and selfless teacher of conducting. He directly taught or mentored many conductors who are performing now, including John Mauceri, Herbert Blomstedt, Edo de Waart, Paavo Järvi, Seiji Ozawa, Helmuth Rilling, Michael Tilson Thomas, and Jaap van Zweden. These are big names.

*Conducting is like making love
to a hundred people at the same time.*

*To be a success as a Broadway composer,
you must be Jewish or gay. I'm both.*

*To achieve great things, two things are needed: a plan,
and not quite enough time.*

- ## NEVILLE MARRINER (BRITAIN, 1924-2016)

SUPERPOWER: *Everything he touched he made agreeable and appealing.*

Marriner was a violinist and teacher, and eventually conductor who had one of the most prolific recording relationships in classical music history with the Academy of St. Martin in the Fields, a London chamber ensemble that he founded in 1958 and for which he served as the music director till 2011 and then president of the ASMF until his death.

During his early career as a violinist, he played with a number of small ensembles, including the Jacobean Ensemble, where he performed with the early-music specialist Thurston Dart. Marriner also played in the London Philharmonia (1952–56) and the London Symphony Orchestra (1956–68).

Encouraged by conductor Pierre Monteux, Marriner began to conduct, specializing in Baroque music. Now this was well before the 'original instrument/authentic performance movement' was underway. But even today, some 60 years since he started the group, the ASMF still sounds good in the Baroque and Classical repertory, never bloaty or ponderous. Even so, when the authenticity movement hit stride, the new gang bludgeoned Marriner pretty hard about his sticking to modern instruments and techniques. Especially Christopher Hogwood, who should have been more gracious about it.

Marriner also directed and conducted the Los Angeles Chamber Orchestra (1969–78), the Minnesota Symphony (1979–86), and the Stuttgart Radio Symphony Orchestra in Germany (1986–89). He did lots of guest conducting worldwide. In the late 1970s Marriner gave opera a try, had good success with Mozart and Rossini, which surprised many.

He was the second-most recorded conductor of all time, only Herbie von K edging him out. No one would accuse Marriner of having been a profound conductor, but he shines in other ways. In fact, 'shine' is a good word for what he did to his music. His Baroque and Classical works were buoyant and graceful. He was also a champion of 20th century British string music.

> *I just wish, maybe, that I'd started conducting earlier. I was about*
> *40 when I started. Apart from that I don't really have any regrets.*
> *Is that bad?*

• COLIN DAVIS (BRITAIN, 1927-2013)

SUPERPOWER: *A generous collaborator who made everyone the best they could possibly be.*

Davis was a clarinetist, a very odd instrument for a conductor. He was in fact barred from early conductor classes because he had no aptitude for the piano. He was never serious about the clarinet, for that matter, it was just something to play till he got his hands on a baton, which he finally learned how to do at the Royal College of Music in London. He was appointed assistant conductor of the BBC Scottish Symphony Orchestra in 1957. Two years later the fairy tale happened when he was asked to substitute for an ill Otto Klemperer in a performance of Mozart's *Don Giovanni*. That was the launch pad of a great career.

From 1961 to 1965 Davis was musical director of Sadler's Wells Opera, and from 1967 to 1971 he served as principal conductor of the BBC Symphony Orchestra. In 1971 he succeeded Georg Solti as musical director of the Royal Opera House, Covent Garden. Davis was music director and principal conductor of the Bavarian Radio Symphony Orchestra from 1983 to 1992. He was named principal conductor of the London Symphony Orchestra in 1995, having first conducted the orchestra in 1959 and been principal guest conductor since 1975. He was also principal guest conductor of the New York

Philharmonic from 1998 to 2003. Many other major orchestras engaged him as guest conductor.

Davis was the foremost modern interpreter of the composer Hector Berlioz, whose complete orchestral and operatic works Davis recorded. His Sibelius recordings are universally praised, and he did almost everything that interested him very well.

Davis was a hothead in his younger years, and his relationships with musicians and musical organizations were often rocky. After succeeding Georg Solti in 1971 at Covent Garden, he was booed by the audience and reacted by booing back and sticking out his tongue. In later year he was nothing like that. He was gracious and thoughtful. Davis was an energetic figure on the podium, his upper body tense and his arm gestures large and decisive. But he also exuded an air of security and generosity that gave his performances dignity and balance.

Opera director David McVicar noted, "His approach was predicated purely on an innate and instinctive understanding of the music, and the depth of both his knowledge and empathy was extraordinary. He didn't tend to say much in rehearsals. He'd smile benignly, mostly, and just watch intently. But he certainly knew what he wanted, and if he didn't like something he'd pipe up, expressing himself in terms that you simply couldn't argue with – they made so much sense. Instead of micromanaging the singers, he collaborated with them, letting them sing, while with his orchestra he was a fantastic technician. He had that wonderful talent of knowing how to watch and accompany. Few conductors have that ability."

He approached both the musicians and the music with respect, remarking in an interview:

> The less ego you have, the more influence you have as a conductor. And the result is that you can concentrate on the only things that really matter: the music and the people who are playing it. You are of no account whatever. But if you can help people to feel free to play as well as they can, that's as good as it gets.

> Conducting is like holding the bird of life in your hand: hold it too tight and it dies, hold it too lightly and it flies away.

> The road to success and the road to failure are almost exactly the same.

> To lose your temper is only useful once a year.

• BERNARD HAITINK (HOLLAND, 1929-2021)

SUPERPOWER: *Married Meticulous and Exciting*

Haitink studied at the Amsterdam Conservatory, then joined the Netherlands Radio Philharmonic as a violinist. At the age of 25, Haitink won a place in a conductors' course sponsored by Netherlands Radio, and at the end he won a contract to conduct four radio concerts. The prize was a post at the Hilversum Radio Philharmonic.

He studied conducting with Ferdinand Leitner at the Netherlands Radio Union's annual conductor's courses, 1954–55, and became their second conductor in 1955. His association with the Concertgebouw Orchestra of Amsterdam began in 1956, but one day that year a guest conductor cancelled an appearance with the Royal Concertgebouw Orchestra, and Haitink was asked to step in. The old fairytale strikes again.

He was appointed the RCO co-conductor in 1961 and permanent conductor in 1964. He also served as artistic adviser (from 1967) and artistic director

(1970–79) of the London Philharmonic Orchestra. In 1972 Haitink turned his attention to opera, which led to his appointment in 1978 as music director of the Glyndebourne Festival in East Sussex, England. He became music director of the Royal Opera House, Covent Garden, in London in 1986, and he held that post until 2002. In 2002–04 he was principal guest conductor of the Staatskapelle Dresden, and in 2006–10 he led the Chicago Symphony Orchestra as principal conductor. Maestro Haitink retired in 2019.

Haitink was not an adventurous conductor, best known for his recordings of Mahler, Bruckner, Beethoven, and Liszt. His conducting was noted for its careful attention to detail combined with an uncommon strength of character and conviction. You can be meticulous, or you can be exciting. Pick one. Haitink picked *both*, and that was his superpower.

Max Raimi, who played viola under Haitink in Chicago, observed: "Because his technique was so unfussy and drew so little attention to itself, it was almost universally underestimated. With a minimum of motion, he could give you every single particle of information you needed. I always could play with confidence and freedom under his baton. I read once that he admonished student conductors, saying "Don't distract the musicians—they are very busy playing the music!"

I don't think an opera house is ever a place
that can make you entirely happy.

• NIKOLAUS HARNONCOURT (AUSTRIA, 1929-2016)

SUPERPOWER: *Transformed classical music; put his personal stamp on all he did by annihilating the accumulated grime of centuries of baseless 'traditions.'*

Harnoncourt was born into a distinguished aristocratic family descended from royalty and Holy Roman emperors, and he spent much of his childhood in Meran Palace, his mother's ancestral estate in Graz, Austria. Following the war he studied cello and viola da gamba at the Vienna Music Academy and then cofounded (1949) the early-music Vienna Viola da Gamba Quartet with fellow musician Alice Hoffelner, whom he married in 1953, the same year he founded Concentus Musicus Wien.

Harnoncourt was a suburb cellist and played with the Vienna Symphony Orchestra under Herbert von Karajan from 1952 to 1969. When Harnoncourt applied for the position its principal conductor Herbert von Karajan engaged him *without an audition*, finding sufficient reason "just in the way he sits." But for the young artist, Karajan stood for everything Harnoncourt opposed in music making. The two parted ways over Harnoncourt's remark that Karajan was "a good Porsche driver." The older musician never forgot it.

Thereafter, he divided his time between directing the Concentus Musicus and serving as a guest conductor, leading and recording with various orchestras. Harnoncourt's most ambitious undertaking was a joint project (1971–89) with Dutch harpsichordist Gustav Leonhardt in which the Concentus Musicus and the Leonhardt Consort recorded all 193 (there are 100 more— lost!!) of Bach's sacred cantatas.

He was a monumental champion of early music, but nobody was safe from his baton, and many of his recordings outside of the Baroque were considered outside his bailiwick by many. He recorded Schumann, Brahms, Dvořák, Alban Berg, even Gershwin's *Porgy & Bess.* among other decidedly non-Baroque composers. He recorded Verdi's *Aida,* which was almost universally panned. These performances were distinguished by their bracingly astringent qualities. While some found such readings mannered and idiosyncratic, others relished their freshness and vigor. He made more than 500 recordings.

He had little regard for 'tradition' and how you were 'supposed to do things.' Many of his recordings upset people. He went to the source and made his own case for everything he did, re-thinking everything with his giant brain and huge energy.

During his reign as conductor royalty, early music became more established and the distinction between historical and mainstream gradually faded. Harnoncourt was at the center of this transformation. His career also coincided with the demise of the conductor as feared tyrant. To the end of his life he remained fundamentally opposed to the cult of the autocratic conductor— the only man he acknowledged as 'maestro' was his hairdresser, he joked. His rehearsal process was collegiate, with musicians as partners.

Conducting without a baton, Harnoncourt used his hands, eyes, and his emotional and intellectual presence. (He had a face that he could make horror-movie scary, with chilling and terrifying bugged-out eyeballs that he used to great effect.) Lacking in his gestures, however, was a clear indication of the beat. "We don't even look at him," one orchestra member revealed. Added a colleague, "We only play to see him look happy."

Even when I was small, I always took the opposite point of view. I'm not someone who agrees. At age 10, I told my father out of the blue, 'Politeness is a lie.'

I have always encouraged musicians to tell me immediately if something in my explanations sounds suspicious. And if, in return, they can convince me of something - and that has happened - then that's what we'll do.

Art isn't a pretty accessory - it's the umbilical cord that connects us with the divine. It ensures our humanity. To be beautiful, music must operate on the outer fringes of catastrophe.

- CLAUDIO ABBADO (ITALY, 1933-2014)

SUPERPOWER: *Soft-spoken perfection. Effortless leadership.*

Born in Milan, Abbado began training under his father before entering Milan's Giuseppe Verdi Conservatory to study piano. After graduation in 1955, he continued piano classes with Friedrich Gulda and began learning conducting from Antonio Votto. Over the next three years, Abbado pursued conducting with Hans Swarowsky, conductor of the Vienna State Opera Orchestra. In class at the Vienna Academy of Music, Abbado sometimes sang in the Singverein choir under Herbert von Karajan, his mentor and role model. Abbado further refined his orchestral skills at the Accademia Chigiana in Siena under Alceo Galliera, conductor of the Philharmonia Orchestra, and Carlo Zecchi, leader of the Czech Philharmonic. He led the Teatro Communale in Trieste, conducting Sergei Prokofiev's *Love for Three Oranges* at the age of 25.

In 1965, Karajan signaled formal acceptance among the music community by introducing Abbado at the Salzburg Easter Festival conducting Mahler's

Second Symphony. Abbado valued the older musician's guidance and compared him to a sage, compassionate father. After his stint at the Teatro alla Scala, Abbado left Italy in 1965 to lead the Vienna Philharmonic. He returned in triumph in 1968 to become opera conductor of Milan's La Scala, the mecca of Italian opera.

Energetic and visionary, Abbado began leaving his mark on the musical scene by establishing the European Community Youth Orchestra in 1978 and by conducting the Chamber Orchestra of Europe three years later. After serving as principal conductor of the London Symphony Orchestra in 1979, he established Milan's La Filarmonica della Scala in 1982. Returning to the United States, he was principal guest conductor of the Chicago Symphony from 1982 to 1986.

Late in the 1980s, Abbado kept up the pace of fine music by serving from 1983 to 1988 as the London Symphony Orchestra music director. Concurrently with his other projects, he assumed the baton of the Vienna State Opera in 1986, the year that he founded Vienna's Gustav Mahler Youth Orchestra.

In 1989, Abbado succeeded his friend and mentor Herbert von Karajan as the first Italian-born artistic director of the Berlin Philharmonic and inaugurated a 12-year career marked by variety and flexibility unknown under past masters.. Instrumentalists under his direction discovered a taskmaster devoted to removing even a hint of imperfection or uncertainty with long hours of rehearsal and refinement. As conductor of the Berlin Philharmonic, which most Europeans consider the height of orchestral attainment, he chose not to renew his contract. His resignation, effective in 2002, dismayed the German musical elite, who expected their maestros to die in office.

His command of the repertory extends from the Classical masters to the latest representatives of the avant-garde. His concert programs are as likely to include works of more difficult, unpopular Modern composers as they are the classics. Abbado established a reputation for musical excellence on the fine edge between scholar and performing genius. A meticulous reader of scores, he mastered symphonic detail to such a degree that his conducting has often overshadowed the lead singers in his operatic efforts.

The main attraction at an Abbado concert is leadership, a character trait he claims to have derived from Wilhelm Furtwangler, one of Germany's most beloved maestros. Unlike the prima donnas of an earlier generation, Abbado throws no tantrums, yet manages to elicit from orchestra, choir, and soloists a high quality of sound and execution.

Abbado tended to speak very little in rehearsal, sometimes using the simple request to orchestras to "Listen." This reflected his own preference for communication as a conductor via physical gesture and the eyes, and his perception that orchestras did not like conductors who spoke a great deal in rehearsal. In performance, Abbado often conducted from memory, noting that he felt more secure without a score, and that communication with the orchestra was easier.

Clive Gillinson characterised Abbado's thus: "…he basically doesn't say anything in rehearsals, and speaks so quietly, because he's so shy, so people can get bored. But it works because everyone knows the performances are so great. I've never known anybody more compelling. He's the most natural conductor in the world. Some conductors need to verbally articulate what they want through words, but Claudio just shows it, just does it."

Many people learn how to talk, but they don't learn how to listen.
Listening to one another is an important thing in life.
And music tells us how to do that.

I love the sound of snow… You can hear it even if you are only
standing on a balcony. [The sound] is only minimal, not even a real
noise: a breath, a trifle of a sound. You have the same thing in
music: if in the score there is a pianissimo marked that ends in
nothing. Up there you can feel this 'nothing.'
With an orchestra it is very difficult to achieve it.
The Berlin Philharmonic manage it sometimes.

- NEEME JÄRVI (ESTONIA, 1937)

SUPERPOWER: *Facility, flexibility and adaptability. Resurrected much fine music from nations and traditions formerly marginalized.*

Järvi graduated with degrees in percussion and choral conducting from the Tallinn Music School, then studied conducting with Mravinsky and Rabinovich at the Leningrad Conservatory till 1960. In 1971 he won first prize in the Accademia di Santa Cecilia conducting competition in Rome. He was active in Tallinn as music director of the Estonian State Symphony from 1960 to 1980, and of the Estonian Opera Theater from 1964 to 1977.

He subsequently served as principal guest conductor of the City of Birmingham Symphony in England and in 1982 he became music director of the Göteborg Symphony in Sweden; also was principal conductor of the Scottish National Orchestra in Glasgow from 1984 to 1988. In 1990 he became music director of the Detroit Symphony. His guest conducting engagements have taken him to most of the principal music centers of the world.

Järvi became Music Director of the New Jersey Symphony Orchestra in 2005 until 2009. In September 2005, Järvi became Chief Conductor of the Residentie Orchestra of The Hague, as Chief Conductor through 2013. In August 2009, the Estonian National Symphony Orchestra announced the appointment of Järvi as its next music director, for an initial contract of three years. In November 2010, Järvi resigned over the dismissal of the orchestra's director. In September 2010, the Orchestre de la Suisse Romande named Järvi as its ninth artistic and musical director, as of 2012, with an initial contract of three years.

Järvi's discography includes almost 500 recordings for labels such as BIS, Chandos, Orfeo and Deutsche Grammophon. He is best known for his interpretations of Romantic and 20th century classical music, and he has championed the work of his fellow Estonian Arvo Pärt. His interpretations of Jean Sibelius with the Gothenburg Symphony are also well regarded.

Järvi has carved a reputation for the spontaneity of his performances, often changing his interpretation from one concert to the next and frequently "going with the moment." Some orchestras hate it. They want more precise directions in rehearsal, fewer surprises in concert. Others love the creativity and freedom of expression implied in Järvi's intuitive style

Recording had always been his first love. Day-to-day administration, of the sort required of a modern music director, is not his thing. He works best as a conductor who breezes in, excites an orchestra, gets quick results and moves on.

In America, the [musicians'] connection with the conductor is as with management - it becomes political. You cannot conduct properly in this environment. I hate this enemy situation between management and orchestra members.

What is a career, actually? Nobody can destroy my career. Only I can destroy my career if I am a bad conductor. I've gone to lesser known orchestras in Scotland and Sweden, Detroit, but I have enjoyed the places I've been, and had success. I like the close community relations, and to solve problems.

- ## RICCARDO MUTI (ITALY, 1941)

SUPERPOWER: *Forceful, uncompromising, full of integrity yet brings such intimacy to his performances; Hard to work with but too great not to.*

Born in Naples, Muti took violin and piano lessons at home, then studied composition and piano at the San Pietro a Majella Conservatory in Naples. One of his teachers there was future *Godfather* soundtrack composer Nino Rota. Switching to conducting, Muti attended the Verdi Conservatory in Milan. His breakthrough was a win in Italy's Guido Cantelli Competition in 1967. That led to a conducting appearance with the orchestra of the Italian national RAI radio network the following year. In 1969 he became principal conductor of the Maggio Musicale (May Music Festival) in Florence, one of Europe's most prominent annual classical music events. He remained in that post until 1981.

The early 1970s saw Muti filling a sequence of guest conducting slots, each more prestigious than the last. Holding a conducting job with the Civic Theatre in Florence, he appeared at the Salzburg Festival in Austria in 1971 and with the Berlin Philharmonic and the Philadelphia Orchestra in 1972. The

Philadelphia Orchestra appearance proved to be the beginning of a long love affair with Muti for concertgoers in that heavily Italian-American city; Muti became principal guest conductor of the Philadelphia Orchestra in 1977, and in 1980 he took over the music directorship of the orchestra from its legendary conductor Eugene Ormandy.

From 1974 to 1982 Muti also served as conductor of London's Philharmonia Orchestra, adding the post of music director in 1979. He continued to conduct opera performances in Europe's top theaters in the late 1970s and early 1980s.

In 1986 Muti became music director of the La Scala opera house in Milan, Italy. He is current music director of the Orchestra Giovanile Luigi Cherubini. Muti has also held posts at the Maggio Musicale in Florence, the Teatro alla Scala in Milan, the Salzburg Whitsun Festival, and the Chicago Symphony Orchestra.

He also never quite succeeded in coming to terms with the American cultural scene:

> *I always felt the accent was more on entertainment than the cultural experience. When I made tours around the U.S., I was shocked to find reviews written on a page called 'entertainment': topless show next to Bruckner [Symphony No.] 7. That says it all. It says culture is something to consume, not to engage with. When I go to a concert or opera, my attitude is to go to a place where I make my mind work.*

Muti gave up his music directorship in Philadelphia in 1992 but stayed on as conductor laureate and continued to appear with the orchestra. By that time, Muti was one of the best-known conductors in the world. He was also unafraid to exert his power and influence. Even early in his career he had walked away from productions in Florence, Milan, and Paris, rather than compromise over artistic questions. In 1992 he pulled out of an appearance at Austria's prestigious Salzburg Festival because he disliked the ultramodern interpretation of Mozart's *La clemenza di Tito* being mounted by the director. Seemingly safely ensconced at La Scala, he turned down the top post in American classical music, the conductorship of the New York Philharmonic Orchestra, in 2000.

Controversy began to engulf Muti at La Scala itself, however, as the opera house closed down for a massive renovation in 2003. Muti objected to what he saw as the dumbing-down of La Scala's programming in its temporary home, and he attempted to convince the La Scala orchestra to cast a no-confidence vote against the general manager. The move backfired; the orchestra musicians refused to go along and lodged a complaint against Muti, alleging that he had refused to hire prominent guest conductors who might detract from his own power.

Among Muti's detractors was film director Franco Zeffirelli, who was quoted as saying that Muti was "drunk with himself, drugged by his own art and his own personal vanity; he can only talk about himself; he's become a caricature of a conductor."

Riccardo Muti is, as you might guess, a conductor in the old style—fiery, demanding, and charismatic. He idolized another Italian autocrat of the podium, Arturo Toscanini. Famous off the podium for wrangling with administrators and presenters, he sometimes ended up in the headlines. Yet there have been few other figures in the world of classical music who could command similar attention, and though Muti has had detractors as well as admirers, no one has doubted his energy and sheer force of personality. Muti is considered by many to be the world's greatest conductors of the operas of Verdi.

Controversy flared once again in 2004, when he backed out of a La Scala-designed production of Verdi's *La forza del destino* at England's Royal Opera House, after British administrators demanded a small change in the stage sets—the replacement of a solid brick wall with a curtain—that they said was necessary for safety reasons. Muti was then lambasted as a prima donna in Britain's famously merciless newspapers.

After La Scala reopened in late 2004, things deteriorated for Muti in Milan once again. He persuaded the opera company's board to force the general manager out, but the orchestra players refused to accept the decision and organized several wildcat strikes. On March 16, 2005, they convened a meeting of all of the theater's 700 or 800 employees, who voted overwhelmingly to ask for Muti's resignation. Muti resigned his post on April 2. No one thought that this marked the end of Muti's career.

The most remarkable quality of his performance is in the intimacy of a passionate lover that he brings to his music.

The conductor's stand is not a continent of power,
but rather an island of solitude.

A conductor should guide rather than command.

• CHRISTOPHER HOGWOOD (BRITAIN, 1941-2014)

SUPERPOWER: *Transformed our concepts of Baroque and Classical music.*

He was born in Nottingham. Christopher was a great organizer of family events, and at the age of 10 persuaded the rest of the family to sing the Hallelujah Chorus from a score of *Messiah* that he had managed to get hold of. He read classics and music at Pembroke College, Cambridge, then went on to study performance and conducting under Raymond Leppard, Mary Potts and Thurston Dart, and later with Rafael Puyana and Gustav Leonhardt. During his college years, Hogwood toured England in a repurposed laundry van and demonstrated Medieval instruments.

After graduating in 1964, he won a British Council scholarship to study harpsichord in Prague with Zuzana Ruzickova, then as a harpsichordist, he joined the Academy of St. Martin in the Fields, a pacesetter for Baroque and Classical performance led by the eminent conductor Neville Marriner.

In 1967, he co-founded the Early Music Consort with a like-minded Cambridge chum, David Munrow. The group achieved a degree of prominence after recording the themes to BBC series such as *The Six Wives of Henry VIII* but went fallow after Munrow's suicide in 1976.

Meanwhile, Hogwood formed the Academy of Ancient Music (AAM). They used gut strings, shorter bows and lower tuning, causing the music to sound in a different key that modern tunings present. But they had "a certain clarity and speed" that Hogwood felt was lacking in their modern descendants.

Hogwood's philosophy with the orchestra, and in all his projects, was to attempt to understand and recreate the composer's intentions, in terms of both notation and performance. To this end he would return to the original sources, correct publishing errors, and evaluate textual alterations in subsequent editions. Much of the repertoire the orchestra performed was given in editions prepared by Hogwood himself.

In 1986 Hogwood was appointed artistic director of the Handel and Haydn Society in Boston, Massachusetts. Other significant appointments included music director of the Saint Paul Chamber Orchestra of Minnesota (1987-92; principal guest conductor 1992-98) and artistic adviser to the Australian Chamber Orchestra (1989-93). In 2006 he took the title of emeritus director of the AAM.

Hogwood appeared in many of the world's leading opera houses, including Covent Garden, the Paris Opéra, the Deutsche Oper and the Sydney Opera House. His performance of Purcell's *Dido and Aeneas* at La Scala, Milan, in 2006 was well received. He also recorded many operas to high acclaim, including those by Purcell, Handel, Haydn and Mozart.

Hogwood's accomplishments as a keyboard player were demonstrated in recordings of works by many of the great masters from the Renaissance to early Classical. His discography also includes a wide range of chamber and vocal repertoire of the early periods, as well as Neo-Classical music by such composers as Martinů, Stravinsky, Britten, Copland, Tippett and Honegger. His love of the clavichord was evident in his 'Secret' series: *Secret Mozart, Secret Bach* and *Secret Handel.*

Industrious, too, as an editor, Hogwood prepared countless volumes of pieces by Renaissance and Baroque composers. Of his numerous books, the most substantial were an authoritative biography of Handel (1984, revised 2007). In the later decades of his career, he worked increasingly in repertoire of the 19th and 20th centuries, preparing editions of, among others, Mendelssohn, Martinů, Elgar, Brahms and Stravinsky.

Though the complete Mozart symphonies and piano concertos (with Robert Levin), along with Handel's *Messiah* were perhaps the best-known of

Hogwood's many successes, his performance of Beethoven's *Ninth Symphony* is a good candidate for the worst recording of the work in the history of recorded music, probably in the entire galaxy. It lacks a speck of grandeur, passion, or indeed anything remotely Beethovian. It's wimpy and sterile, bloodless. It is a travesty of the highest order. Avoid it.

The 1840s Cambridge house in which he lived was filled with books, watercolors and an impressive collection of musical instruments, predominantly clavichords, both original and period reproductions. He rarely watched television or films, he once said, preferring to immerse himself in the culture of previous eras.

His technique on the podium was clean and stylish, if not especially precise. Hogwood had a charisma that was irresistible to ticket buyers used to formal and formidable conductors in white-tie-and-tails. He long sought to abolish artificial barriers between the conductor and the patrons. During one outdoor NSO concert, a rain cloud burst while the orchestra played Handel's *Water Music*. Hogwood, soaked through, turned to the audience after concluding the piece. "See?" he said, "It works."

The AAM was pioneering in the element of democracy in its music-making. Recognizing that his players brought often deep levels of understanding and experience to the ensemble, Hogwood happily accepted the role of umpire. "I'm for democracy to the point of anarchy," he once declared. The notion of an autocratic maestro dictating performance practice to such professionals was a nonsense to him, and other ensembles (including many not specializing in early repertoire) began to adopt a similar policy.

According to Ernest Fleischmann, who invited Hogwood to conduct the Los Angeles Philharmonic in 1981, "initially the musicians found him a little strange. He didn't have the greatest conducting technique, but he's the most stimulating force in years." His habit of talking about the music during concerts took many by surprise, annoyed many, but audiences were largely won over.

There's nothing wrong with playing things historically completely incorrectly. Music is not a moral business, so you can play absolutely in a style that suits you and pleases your public. It may be completely unrecognizable to the composer, but so what, he's dead.

Every piece of music should be looked at as a painting that dissolved off the wall when you closed the gallery door. If all the colors dripped down into a huge pot and you took this pot, along with a recipe of how to reassemble the colors back into Van Gogh's 'Sunflowers,' you would be very careful to get all the reds and the yellows in the right places, and not to paint it bigger or smaller than it was. I think music carries with it this responsibility.

• JOHN ELIOT GARDINER (BRITAIN, 1943)

SUPERPOWER: *He brings intense scholarship alive without a hint of pedantry.*

Gardiner was born in Fontmeli Magna, in southwestern England. He was raised on a farm and his parents enlisted him in the local church choir as a child. When he was six his parents took him to hear a lecture given by Nadia Boulanger on Monteverdi and to hear the composer's *Vespro della beata vergine*. Gardiner listened to a taped radio broadcast of that work time and time again.

Gardiner had learned some of the early-music repertoire by the time he was 13. His family members enjoyed singing at home, and that's where Gardiner developed a rudimentary knowledge of Renaissance and early Baroque-period choral music.

He became a self-taught musician, and by the time he reached his teenage years he demonstrated an aptitude for conducting music. He attended King's College, Cambridge. As an undergraduate, he served as secretary of the King's College Music Society and sang and played the violin in Berlioz-revival performances led by Colin Davis.

After obtaining his master's degree in history, Gardiner decided he needed formal music training. He started by studying with harpsichordist with musicologist Thurston Dart. He earned a certificate of advanced studies in music from King's College in 1966 and moved to Paris where he studied with Nadia Boulanger for two years. He also studied with Antal Dorati and apprenticed himself to the BBC Northern Orchestra in Manchester for two years.

He founded the Monteverdi Choir in 1964 and its complement Monteverdi Orchestra in 1968. Although he conducted all types of music, he is a renowned authority in a variety of 17th and 18th century styles and conducted Gluck's *Alceste* for the British Broadcasting Corporation (BBC) and *Iphigenie en Tauride* at Covent Garden in 1973. The Monteverdi Orchestra was renamed the English Baroque Soloists in 1978 after switching to original-period instruments.

He became principal conductor and music director of the Canadian Broadcasting Corporation's Vancouver Orchestra, 1980-83; artistic director of the Gottingen Handel Festival in Germany from 1981-89; music director of the Opera de Lyon, founded Orchestre de l'Opera de Lyon, 1983; led symphony orchestras all over the USA and Britain as a guest conductor, also the Oslo Philharmonic. In 1990 he created a new period-instrument orchestra called the Orchestre Revolutionnaire et Romantique that was identical in personnel to the English Baroque Soloists.

He is too much in demand for any record company to hold him and thus has made hundreds of recordings with Erato, Philips, ARC, Argo, and London labels included annual releases of Bach's major choral works, the complete Mozart piano concertos, and a complete cycle of Beethoven concertos. He has his limits, like anyone, and has overshot the mark with his attempts at Italian Romantic operas, which were universally reviled.

He doesn't like to use a score when he conducts. He has a phenomenal memory. His style is joyous and affable. His temper may be his undoing. He recently punched a performer for disobeying. Maybe it's his age, but if he doesn't get his act together he may find himself dis-engaged from the scene.

[on choosing to adopt the use of period instruments] *I'd come up against a brick wall. I was doing concert performances of Rameau's operas, and we tried as hard as we could putting gut strings on modern instruments and getting the wind players to listen to period instruments, and it was just the wrong tools. It was like painting a landscape using thick bristle brushes.*
You needed something more subtle.

If you think about it, the written page of music is so limiting. It's one stage: the moment when the butterfly is being pinned to the board and chloroformed. What you are trying to do as a conductor is to get to the previous stage, where it is still fluid in the imagination of a composer.

- ## SIMON RATTLE (BRITAIN, 1955)

SUPERPOWER: *Stylistic mastery from Baroque to Contemporary.*

As a boy, Rattle learned to play piano, violin, and percussion. At age 10 he performed as a percussionist with the Liverpool Philharmonic Youth Orchestra (known then as Merseyside Youth Orchestra). He also began conducting at a young age. In 1974, not yet 20 years old, he graduated from the Royal Academy of Music, University of London, having won first prize in the John Player International Conductors' Competition. That paved the way to an assistant conductor position with the Bournemouth Symphony Orchestra (1974–77). From 1977 to 1980 he was the assistant conductor of the Royal Liverpool Philharmonic Orchestra. During that period, Rattle conducted his first opera, Leoš Janáček's *The Cunning Little Vixen*, at the 1977 Glyndebourne Festival in Sussex, England.

In 1980 he began an 18-year tenure as principal of the City of Birmingham Symphony Orchestra. While still with the CBSO in 1992, Rattle also became the principal guest conductor of the British period-instrument ensemble called the Orchestra of the Age of Enlightenment

In 2002 Rattle became the principal conductor and artistic director of the Berlin Philharmonic Orchestra. Rattle stretched the repertoire of the Berlin

219

Philharmonic to include many 20th century and Contemporary composers as well as more British and American composers in their regular roster of performances. Rattle's commitment to Contemporary music led to unique collaborations with composers, such as Sofia Gubaidulina, and to crossover performances, as with the jazz musician Wynton Marsalis.

Rattle has made more than 200 recordings and is well known for his performances of works by Mahler as well as by Schoenberg and other composers of the Second Viennese School.

His range is spectacular. As a musician Rattle has an insatiable curiosity that spans the earliest music (he is an expert conductor of music performed on period instruments) to the thorniest Modern compositions. He holds Modern masters such as Boulez and Messaien in the kind of high regard usually reserved by others for Beethoven and Brahms and Mozart.

His style is energetic on the podium. He will even mime ridiculously if that's what it takes to do the job. New Statesman's Dermot Clinch described one of Rattle's displays at the podium. "Sometimes he bent his knees, puffed his cheeks and mimed a straw-chewing yokel, to encourage a proportionate rustic attitude in his players during Beethoven's *Pastoral Symphony,"* wrote Clinch. "During the pizzicato interlude in *Mahler's Second Symphony*, he dropped his hands to his sides and encouraged his band just to pluck 'n' swing."

Conductors start getting good when everybody else retires.

My worst and best qualities are rashness: the good part of it is due to youth, which is, of course, why I'm not a great conductor.

The better the orchestra, often the harder it is to conduct, not the other way around.

If you think the music business is the be-all and end-all of life, you're in big trouble.

• ESA-PEKKA SALONEN (FINLAND, 1958)

SUPERPOWER: *Perfect contemporary conductor; sees the past, groks the present, and is anticipating and participating in the future.*

Salonen was the music director of the Los Angeles Philharmonic (1992–2009). In 2008 he was appointed principal conductor and artistic advisor of the Philharmonia Orchestra in London.

Salonen studied French horn (unique among star conductors), conducting, and composition at the Sibelius Academy in Helsinki (1973–77) and composition with private teachers in Italy (1979–81). In 1979 he made his conducting debut with the Finnish Radio Symphony Orchestra. He burst onto the international scene in 1983 with his performance of Gustav Mahler's *Third Symphony* with the Philharmonia in London.

Like other international star conductors, Salonen works with many of the world's most highly regarded orchestras. He is also active in the international music festival circuit and made numerous recordings for the German label Deutsche Grammophon. Salonen's programming emphasized Contemporary music, though he did not ignore the Classical repertoire; in 2006 he completed a cycle of Beethoven symphonies. Among the composers he featured were the best known from the Baltic region, including Estonian Arvo Pärt and Finns Jean Sibelius, Kaija Saariaho, and Magnus Lindberg. Salonen recorded much of Austrian composer György Ligeti's work, collaborating with the composer until Ligeti's death in 2006. Of particular interest were Salonen's collaborations with American stage director Peter Sellars on such productions as *The Tristan Project* (2004), a multimedia concert presentation of Richard Wagner's opera *Tristan und Isolde*; one act was played on each of three successive evenings, and all were accompanied by a video by Bill Viola.

A composer for much of his life, he rather lamely followed the usual path of the brainiac melody-hating style that everybody despises except academics, until he woke from that nightmare in the mid-'90s. He now understands the role of organic melody in his writing.

His style on the podium is clean, lively and virtuosic, and he can be brutal if it's called for. His players love him.

Anyone who composes and conducts at the same time is immediately suspect, because he must be faking one or the other.

Conducting is intensely social. You work with a hundred people every day. You collaborate, you try to focus their thoughts, you try to give them a concept, you try to inspire them, and it's actually exhausting.

You know, in some ways conducting is counter-intuitive. It's like winter driving in Finland - if you skid, the natural reaction is to fight with the wheel and jam on the brakes, which is the quickest way to get killed. What you have to do is let go, and the car will right itself. It's the same when an orchestra loses its ensemble. You have to resist the temptation to semaphore and let the orchestra find its own way back to the pulse.

CR

Wow… that is one tiny list. One thing about it, though, the entire standard orchestra repertoire is covered by these guys so well that you wouldn't need anybody else. You might want a bunch of others, but you wouldn't need them. I'm pretty sure I could get a consensus on that even though every aficionado would be annoyed to admit it.

Okay, the more progressive among you are furious! Where are the women?! I think that the truth of the situation is by turns thought-provoking, shameful and hard to bear.

From the earliest days of the modern orchestra to a few short years ago, no one would seriously dispute that any woman truly capable of leading a huge (mostly male) band of self-important virtuoso musicians, would have less than a snowball's chance in hell of ever getting near the podium of a major orchestra.

But were there any masterful and brilliant women truly up for the task? Nobody knows. They weren't allowed to play, *but it does not logically follow from this that they existed.* This is not a popular point to make, but it is, as I said—logical.

A musician friend of mind takes a strong anti-PC stand. "A female conductor," he says, "is analogous to a male belly-dancer." He elaborated. "Or consider this: you're about to engage in a huge and bloody battle with the enemy. Your commander, the one who will lead the charge up the hill, comes into view and it's… a woman? If people were honest, which they aren't anymore, most would admit that this vision would be uncomfortable and uninspiring."

I responded, "What about Joan of Arc?"

He laughed and admitted that I got him on that point. "It's true that the anointed ones have to be acknowledged, but how many Joans are there?"

Conductors are not like painters or writers. Conductors have traditionally been a combination of kindly father and all-powerful Jehovah-God. Alpha-male chiefs. There is nothing *remotely* feminine in this traditional concept of the orchestra conductor. All that is changing since the turn of the 21st century. Has the change been for the better?

Decidedly not. (Stay with me here.)

Women are being appointed to high and mid-level orchestras all over the world at an astounding rate. Is this because, now that all prejudice has been thrown aside, these women are finally being acknowledged as a shining new army of geniuses?

No.

I would not be surprised if, in 20 years, *most* high and mid-level posts were held by women, but it will have little to do with their genius at the podium.

It's the fashion. It's 'social justice' at work and the crusade isn't over. Expect quotas soon in the makeup of orchestras. The second violins need a lesbian Latina, and we require a transexual in the brass section. Sound crazy? Stay tuned.

Don't misunderstand—it's way past time that the real prejudices were cast away! But it's the fashion. Orchestras, most of which are in poor health, need stay 'relevant.' They need to be *cool*. And they'll need to abide by guidelines and regulations.

So this means some better men are currently being passed over for jobs because they have penises; and some jobs are going to women who are less worthy simply because, well… you know.

The consequence is that musicianship will suffer because other concerns are displacing musical concerns. This is not to say that 'great' women conductors cannot emerge, it's just that it isn't being done in a way that won't cast doubt and suspicion among those paying attention.

A great leveling-out is occurring; one conductor (and instrumental soloist) is becoming pretty much like another as the schools churn them out by the hundreds—generals without armies. Their authority has diminished much further from the conductors of the past, most of whom were *not* tyrants, and there may be few if any new 'legendary' conductors that will rise up to the demi-god status of the old days.

This all bodes poorly for the future of the orchestra, and for recordings, and for classical music in general. Conductors of status 'get asses in the seats,' as the bean-counters like to say. The Bad Old Days were bad in many ways, but there were heroes minted back then, living legends ramrodding orchestras into performances of mythical status. These days? Not so much…

I hope I'm wrong about a lot of this, but the writing is certainly on the wall.

CR

CONTENDERS (CONDUCTORS)

*B*elow find my top contenders, in alphabetical order, for the pantheon of greatness. Most are young, but a few seasoned souls made the list who are teetering on the edge of lasting eminence. I don't kid myself that there is even a single connoisseur that views these lines who would agree with my list. But this list isn't for them. They have their own list.

Gustavo Dudamel (1981)

Dudamel was born in Barquisimeto, Venezuela. Studied violin from age 10.

His first orchestra was the Simón Bolívar National Youth Orchestra, which he still directs. He made his US conducting debut with the Los Angeles Philharmonic in 2005. In 2007 he was named the LAP's music director as of the 2009-2022.

Also: Gothenburg Symphony for season 2007/2008. 2014 Honorary Conductor. He does mucho guest conducting. He is scheduled to become the Music and Artistic Director of the New York Philharmonic in 2026.

Dudamel is a charisma machine. Audiences and the press love him. His style is his own and his enthusiasm is genuine and infectious. If he has another few years at near his current pace and influence, he may to be recognized as one of the greats.

His Mahler and Beethoven recordings are highly praised.

Go here for a good, long (if a little outdated) piece about him:

https://www.nytimes.com/2018/11/01/magazine/gustavo-dudamel-los-angeles-philharmonic.html

Valery Gergiev (1953) (GER-jiff)

Gergiev was born in Moscow, Russia. Studied piano as a boy and in conservatory.

He became artistic and general director of the Mariinsky Theatre (previously called Kirov Theatre) in St. Petersburg in 1996. In 2015 he became conductor of the Munich Philharmonic Orchestra also the Bolshoi Theatre. Gergiev was dismissed from Munich Philharmonic after he refused to condemn the 2022 Russian invasion of Ukraine. He is a Putin supporter and this has caused incredible tumult in his career outside of Russia. He is roundly despised by much of the classical orchestra industry for his views.

Also: Gergiev conducted the Kirov Theatre in Leningrad (now St. Petersburg) in 1978. From 1981 to 1985 he was the principal conductor of the Armenian State Orchestra. He was principal conductor of the Rotterdam Philharmonic Orchestra (1995–2008) and the London Symphony Orchestra (2007–15) and of the Munich Philharmonic. He has founded several music festivals worldwide.

Gergiev is arguably the 21st century's foremost interpreter of Russian operatic repertory. He is known for his charismatic stage presence and passionate performances heavy on dark sonorities in the lower strings, precisely calibrated explosions of percussion, and a tendency to choose what Alex Ross has called "lugubrious tempos."

He stands out in the Classical Russian opera repertoire; symphonic works by Rachmaninov, Shostakovich, and Borodin; as well as a fine partner in the complete Prokofiev piano concertos

Mirga Gražinytė-Tyla (1986) (MEER-gah grah-zhee-NEE-teh tee-LA)

Gražinytė-Tyla was born in Vilnius, Lithuania. Does not play an instrument (!).

She was named Music Director of the City of Birmingham Symphony Orchestra in 2016 to 2022.

In February 2019, Gražinytė-Tyla signed an exclusive long-term recording contract with Deutsche Grammophon. She is the first female conductor ever to sign an exclusive recording contract with DG.

Also: She is, on and off, one of the world's busiest guest conductors, in demand seemingly everywhere.

She is married and she likes to have babies, which has put a dent in her career path. Many are waiting to see how her career will play out.

She may become the 'Joan of Arc' I mentioned in the last chapter. Everyone who has seen or heard her has gushed over her, but without particulars—just the usual silly clichés one uses to describe conductors they like. Interesting thing about her: she is small, totally feminine, even girly. She dances on the podium. Her body sings. I can imagine her hypnotizing the crusty old guard musicians against their will like Ann mesmerized King Kong. Check her out on YouTube or buy a few discs. She has that certain indefinable something extra.

She is a champion of composer Mieczyslaw Weinberg, and her discs on DG are highly praised.

Jakub Hrůša (1981) (YA-kub ha-ROOSH-ah. Roll that 'r'.)
Hrůša was born in Brno, Czechoslovakia. Studied piano and trombone as a youth.

He is Chief Conductor of the Bamberg Symphony, Principal Guest Conductor of the Philharmonia Orchestra, and Principal Guest Conductor of the Czech Philharmonic.

Also: He is a frequent guest with many of the world's greatest orchestras.

A specialist in the music of Eastern Europe, also praised for his Mahler interpretations. He has all the proper virtues in abundance.

The Dvorak recordings are very nice, also his *Vanessa*, complete opera by Samuel Barber, is highly regarded.

Paavo Järvi (1962) (PAH-vo YARE-vee)
Järvi was born in Tallinn, Estonia. Son of Neemi. Studied percussion when young.

He is Chief Conductor of the Tonhalle Orchester-Zürich, also the NHK Symphony Orchestra until 2022, and Artistic Director of Die Deutsche Kammerphilharmonie Bremen and the Estonian Festival Orchestra.

Also: He is Conductor Laureate of the Frankfurt Radio Symphony, Music Director Laureate of Cincinnati Symphony Orchestra and Artistic Advisor of the Estonian National Symphony Orchestra. He is a frequent guest conductor for many of the world's great orchestras.

Järvi has recorded for such labels as RCA, Deutsche Grammophon, PENTATONE, Telarc, ECM, BIS and Virgin Records. The Sibelius orchestral recordings are very fine, also his 2-disc set of music by Arvo Part.

Susanna Mälkki (1969) (SOO-sah-na MAL-kee)
Mälkki was born in Helsinki, Finland. She was a world-class cellist.

She is Chief Conductor of the Helsinki Philharmonic Orchestra, and Principal Guest Conductor of the Los Angeles Philharmonic. In September 2014, she was named the next chief conductor of the Helsinki Philharmonic Orchestra, from 2016 – 2023.

Also: Mälkki was Principal Guest Conductor of the Gulbenkian Orchestra (2013-17) and Music Director of the Ensemble Intercontemporain (2006-13). She is a guest conductor in high demand wordwide.

Mälkki is likely the conductor best versed and most familiar with Contemporary music than any of her peers here. This one reason that she's on this list. She is on top of things. Formidable. Almost all of her recordings are of music written recently.

Andris Nelsons (1978)

Nelsons was born in Riga, Latvia. Studied piano, but mainly trumpet when young.

He is currently music director of the Boston Symphony Orchestra and the Leipzig Gewandhaus Orchestra. He was previously music director of the Latvian National Opera, chief conductor of the Nordwestdeutsche Philharmonie, and music director of the City of Birmingham Symphony Orchestra. He is heavy demand as guest conductor everywhere.

Nelsons focusses on the heavy Romantic repertory, operas very much included, in the German and Slavonic traditions.

His recordings, which are many, are at the heart of the repertory, starting with Beethoven.

Yannick Nézet-Séguin (1975) (yah-NEEK nay-ZAY say-GHEN)

Nézet-Séguin was born in Montreal, Canada. Was a virtuoso-level pianist.

In 1979, at age 18, van Zweden became one of the two first chairs of the Concertgebouw Orchestra. He was the youngest violinist ever to assume that position, which he held until 1995. He performed as a soloist with many other orchestras.

He is currently music director of the Orchestre Métropolitain (Montréal) since 2000, the Metropolitan Opera since 2017, and the Philadelphia Orchestra since 2012.

Also: He was also principal conductor of the Rotterdam Philharmonic Orchestra from 2008 to 2018. He does many guest spots, many in Great Britain.

His specialty is the standard repertory, with a flair for the dramatic.

His recordings show a passion for Bruckner. Try his *Seventh Symphony.*

Jaap van Zweden (1960) (Yahp van ZVAY-den)

Van Zweden was born in Amsterdam, Netherlands. Was a virtoso violinist when younger, and the youngest concertmaster ever of the Concertgebouw Orchestra.

He is currently music director of the Hong Kong Philharmonic Orchestra (since 2012) the New York Philharmonic (since 2018), and the Seoul Philharmonic.

Also: Van Zweden was chief conductor with the Orkest van het Oosten (Orchestra of the East, or the Netherlands Symphony Orchestra) (1996-2000). He was chief conductor of the Residentie Orchestra in The Hague (2000-2005), and chief conductor and artistic leader of the Radio Filharmonisch Orkest (RFO; Netherlands Radio Philharmonic) (2005-2012). He was chief conductor of the Antwerp Symphony Orchestra (2008-2011). Van Zweden led the Dallas Symphony from 2009 to 2019.

I think it's safe to say that no conductor of his stature today has split critics and listeners so far apart with his conducting.

Wagner, Brahms and Beethoven figure heavily in his recorded catalog.

CR

INSTRUMENTAL SOLOISTS

The situation with instrumental soloists at this writing echoes that of the conductors: *absolute technical perfection and little to distinguish one from the other.* Often, too often, these folks distinguish themselves by one gimmick or another that makes record companies think they might capitalize on the up-and-comer as they struggle to find something, anything, to set them apart from their peers. For women soloists, appearing on stage and photo shoots as close to naked as they can get away with is working out brilliantly for some. For a few of the males, especially pianists, beating the hell out of their instrument, playing too fast, and peppering a piece with ten climaxes instead of the one written into the score seems like a savvy strategy.

There *are great soloists alive today and more upcoming,* but so far precious few have distinguished themselves by the glories of their *character.*

So I have again reverted to the best of the Golden Age of classical recordings, from about 1930 to the start of the new century. The soloists listed below are men and women you will surely encounter if you decide to explore art music seriously. They are inevitable. These people had a personality that is outstanding enough that one can identify them in a previously unheard piece just by listening. That is very difficult to do with most of the new breed of instrumentalists unless they are cultivating one or another kind of vulgarity that makes them easy to identify.

I have chosen to highlight the three most popular categories of concerto artists: *pianists, violinists, and cellists.* Surely every instrument in the orchestra can claim dozens of masterful solo players throughout the ages, and there are concertos written for every instrument of the band. The Baroque period features hundreds of concertos for violin, cello, flute, oboe, or bassoon with small orchestra. But as the form evolved the concerto became longer, more complex, and emotionally variable. Therefore, the violin, cello, and piano rose to the top as the most expressive, and these three categories are by far the most popular in concert and in recordings from the Classical era to the present.

Making this list was very painful. Picking only 10 (12 pianists) is a setup for failure—every aficionado in the world will hate me for what I have done here, on account of those masters whom I have omitted for the sake of brevity. But hey... I gave it a shot.

They are listed in order of birthdate.

10 Great Cellists
from the Golden Age of Classical Recordings

Pablo Casals (1876-1973)

PC was a Spanish and Puerto Rican cellist, composer, and conductor. He made many recordings of solo, chamber, and orchestral music, including some as a conductor, but he is best remembered for the pioneering recordings he made of the *Cello Suites* by **Bach**.

Gregor Piatigorsky (1903-1976)

Born in Russia, **Piatigorsky** trained at the Moscow Conservatory and was principal cellist of the Berlin Philharmonic under **Wilhelm Furtwängler**. When **Richard Strauss** heard him perform, he said, 'I have finally heard my *Don Quixote* as I thought him to be.' He made several recordings for RCA with **Arthur Rubinstein** and **Jascha Heifetz**, earning them the nickname of *The Million-Dollar Trio*.

Pierre Fournier (1906–1986)

Fournier overcame childhood polio to enjoy a glittering career for over half a century. His tone is refined and elegant. **Martinů** and **Poulenc** dedicated sonatas to him, and he gave the premieres of concertos by **Martinů, Roussel**, and **Martin**. His recordings of the *Beethoven Cello Sonatas* with **Artur Schnabel**, his solo **Bach**, the **Brahms** *Double Concerto* (with **David Oistrakh**), and the **Dvořák** *Cello Concerto* with Szell are highly-prized by aficionados.

János Starker (1924-2013)

The Hungarian-American cellist was a child prodigy who made his first public appearances at age six. He was principal cellist of the Budapest Philharmonic Orchestra, Dallas Symphony Orchestra, Metropolitan Opera Orchestra and Chicago Symphony Orchestra, and as a soloist made more than 150 recordings, including five recordings of the **Bach** *Cello Suites.*

Mstislav Rostropovich (1927-2007)

Regarded by many as the greatest cellist of the second half of the 20th century, he was a passionate campaigner for human rights who used his fame to further his beliefs and political opinions. His musicianship has been characterized as "emotional largesse and deep sincerity." He played premieres and/or commissioned 117 works by the likes of **Prokofiev, Shostakovich, Britten, Messiaen, Lutosławski, Khachaturian, Piazzolla, Schnittke,** and **Penderecki.**

Anner Bylsma (1934–2019)

AB was a Dutch cellist who played on both modern and period instruments in a historically informed style. For six years, from 1962 to 1968, he was the principal cellist of the Royal Concertgebouw Orchestra. He recorded the six suites for unaccompanied cello by **Bach**, the first of its kind on a period instrument.

Lynn Harrell (1944-2020)

As a player he was known for his beautiful, penetrating tone and for the richness of his sound. He was principal cellist of the Cleveland Orchestra from 1964 until 1971 before beginning his acclaimed career as a soloist. He was a frequent partner with violinist Itzhak Perlman and pianist Vladimir Ashkenazy. He was also a revered teacher at several schools including the Royal Academy of Music in London (including three years as Principal), the Julliard in New York, the Cleveland Institute of Music, the Aspen Music Festival, and the Los Angeles Philharmonic Institute.

Jacqueline du Pré (1945-1987)

JdP was an English cellist whose extraordinary talent and emotive performances earned her a place among the greatest musicians of her time. At the age of four she is said to have heard the sound of the cello on the radio and asked her mother for "one of those." Du Pré gained early recognition, winning Britain's most prestigious cello award at age 11 and making her official debut at Wigmore Hall at 16. Her heart-on-sleeve recording of the **Elgar** *Cello Concerto* achieved legendary status and epitomized the rapturous nature of her playing style. Tragically, du Pré's career was cut short due to multiple sclerosis.

Yo-Yo Ma (1955-)

Born in France to Chinese parents and raised in the USA. He has an incredibly diverse repertoire, from classical to contemporary. A child prodigy, Ma began giving public concerts at the age of five. By seven, he was performing for presidents Eisenhower and Kennedy. Ma is known for his smooth, lyrical tone, and technical facility. He has so far recorded more than 90 albums

Steven Isserlis (1958-)

SI is an acclaimed soloist, chamber musician, educator, broadcaster and author.
Committed to authentic performance, Isserlis is also a keen exponent of contemporary music. He has received universal acclaim for his scholarly musicianship, technical mastery, command of phrasing and use of distinctive gut strings.

10 GREAT VIOLINISTS
FROM THE GOLDEN AGE OF CLASSICAL RECORDINGS

Jascha Heifetz (1901 – 1987)

For many people, Heifetz is the greatest violinist of all time. By age two, he had a violin in his hand. He focused on absolute clarity. He bowed with swift economical strokes, a precision left hand free of extraneous movement. His facial impassivity and high-velocity execution created the impression of someone in a trance. His playing sustained a remarkable level of intensity. Though an outstanding exponent of **Bach** and **Beethoven**, his repertoire was centered on the Romantic period.

Nathan Milstein (1903-92)

Almost painfully self-effacing and indifferent to fame and fortune, Milstein approached things more by stealth, gently seducing his listeners into a world of extraordinary refinement. He was above all celebrated for his unique tonal luster. He coaxed the sound out of his violin by taking unusually long bow-strokes at a low pressure and was no less gentle with the fingers of his left hand which were more about precision than strength, resulting in intonation of ringing purity.

235

David Oistrakh (1908 – 1974)

DO was the preeminent violinist in Soviet Russia. His was crowned by a seamless, singing legato, apparently unbroken by any change in bow direction. **Prokofiev, Shostakovich** and **Khachaturian** all wrote major works for him. An eloquent, lyrical player who emphasized the similarities between breathing and bowing. Memorable interpretations of concertos by **Brahms, Beethoven**, and **Tchaikovsky**

Yehudi Menuhin (1916-1999)

A prodigy who created a sensation playing the **Mendelssohn** *Violin Concerto* at age seven. Many feel that his finest recordings were those of his youth, since they seem less studied and more spontaneous. His playing in general was characterized by sweetness of tone and an unusual spirituality of atmosphere. His most famous recording was made in 1931 at the age of 15 of **Elgar's** *Violin Concerto* conducted by the composer.

Arthur Grumiaux (1921-1986)

Arthur Grumiaux was one of the great aristocrats of the violin but was also a remarkable pianist, as witness a unique 1957 recording he made of **Brahms** and **Mozart** sonatas *playing both parts!* The complete opposite of a temperamental maestro. Grumiaux's recordings of **Bach** and **Mozart** are highly prized among aficionadi.

Sigiswald Kuijken (1944-)

SK is a Belgian violinist, violist, and conductor known for playing on period and original instruments. At the encouragement of the Deutsche Harmonia Mundi label and **Gustav Leonhardt**, founded his own orchestra, La Petite Bande, to perform Baroque and Classical works. He is noted for using the older technique of resting the violin on the shoulder without a shoulder rest, rather than held under the chin. He has also performed as conductor of symphonies of the Romantic era.

Gidon Kremer (1947 –)

GK became a sensation in the West when conductor **Herbert von Karajan** in 1976 proclaimed Kremer "the greatest violinist in the world" after recording the **Brahms** concerto with him. His playing tends toward a thoughtful austerity rather than extraversion. His catalog contains nearly 200 recordings.

Reinhard Goebel (1952-)

RG established himself as a Baroque violin soloist and inspirational director of the period-instrument Musica Antiqua Köln. Its focus was on historical performance of late 17th - and early 18th century German music. Composers such as **Heinichen, Schmelzer, Biber, Telemann** and members of the **Bach** family featured prominently. Severe right-arm tendonitis restricted his solo playing from 1990.

Anne-Sophie Mutter (1963 –)

A-SM combines technical virtuosity, beauty of tone, and exceptional charisma. At age 13, She was invited by **Herbert von Karajan** to perform with the Berlin Philharmonic Orchestra. After this collaboration she became one of the best-known instrumentalists on the planet. Her repertoire includes traditional classical violin works from the Baroque period to the 20th century, but she also is known for performing, recording, and commissioning new works by present-day composers. She often studies the letters, original scores, and other historical documents by the composer to guide her interpretation.

Joshua Bell (1967 –)

JB is known for his unique performance style of 'dancing' with the flow of the music. This is particularly apparent when he is playing and conducting simultaneously, which he does often. Bell also was involved in a psychology experiment for the Washington Post where he performed **Bach** at a subway station for 45 minutes. Whilst a thousand people passed him, only seven people stopped to listen.

12 Great Pianists
from the Golden Age of Classical Recordings

Sergey Rachmaninov (1873-1943)

Considered by many the greatest pianist of them all, SR was first and foremost a composer, hailed in Russia as the natural successor to **Tchaikovsky**, who championed him. He could comfortably stretch a 13th on the piano (five more notes than an octave).He had a direct, earnest quality, shorn of humor, deeply serious, with each gesture committed toward conveying the overall meaning.

Artur Schnabel (1882-1951)

AS was revered as the leading exponent of the **Beethoven** *piano sonatas*; he was the first to record them all and his interpretations set the benchmark. They are amazing – he sounds like he's improvising them into existence. He was not a virtuoso. Mistakes abound, but they don't seem to matter, such is the overwhelming musicianship. His repertoire was limited to those composers with whom he felt most empathy, namely **Bach, Mozart, Beethoven, Schubert** and **Brahms**. Here you'll find granite strength and a disarming simplicity.

Artur Rubinstein (1887-1982)

AR was perhaps the best **Chopin** performer of all time. He had a photographic memory. When he came to give his first performance of **Franck's** *Symphonic Variations*, he learned it on the train journey to the venue, working out the fingerings on his knee-caps! He loved wine, women, cigars, and art. He played in public for eight decades.

239

Claudio Arrau (1903-1991)

The great Chilean pianist could read music before words. He's perhaps best-known for his interpretations of the music of **Beethoven**, but his devotion to **Liszt** was extraordinary. Arrau ennobled **Liszt**, which can be a challenge. He regarded the late **Schubert** masterpieces for piano as "the supreme challenge." His musical style has been described as "aristocratic," but you wouldn't hear him describe himself this way. "I try to play the way a cat jumps." Also seek him out for, **Chopin, Schumann**, and **Brahms**.

Sviatoslav Richter (1915-97)

SR was mostly self-taught. He wasn't a big fan of making recordings, so his best albums are of live performances. A highly sensitive artist, he loathed the limelight (literally – in his later years he performed on a darkened stage). His repertoire was the most enormous of any pianist. Perversely, he never performed **Beethoven's** *Second, Fourth or Fifth Piano Concertos.* He couldn't love them.,

Arturo Benedetti Michelangeli (1920-95)

He was perhaps the most reclusive, enigmatic and obsessive among the handful of the world's legendary pianists. ABM's repertory was small, honed carefully over many years – certain **Mozart** concertos and **Beethoven** sonatas, and a few works by **Schumann, Brahms**, **Ravel**, **Debussy, Grieg** and **Chopin**. Incredibly fastidious, it was said that no one ever heard him make a mistake in performance or rehearsal. ABM was a connoisseur of the piano mechanics and insisted his concert instruments be in perfect condition.

240

Alfred Brendel (1931-)

"I did not come from a musical or intellectual family... I have not been a child prodigy. I do not have a photographic memory; neither do I play faster than other people. I am not a good sight-reader." None of that matters. He performed all **Beethoven** *sonatas* in London in 1962, and recorded them for Vox (adventurous, chancy). In the 1970s he became an exclusive Philips artist and recorded them again (mature, cerebral). He is celebrated for his interpretations of all the important classical and Romantic masters.

Glenn Gould (1932-82)

GG is best known for performances of **Bach**. Also for audibly humming along while he played, on a tiny chair with sawn-off legs, and his exacting demands for recording and performing conditions. He could play most of the repertory from memory. He eschewed live performance and preferred studio recordings, No **Chopin, Liszt** or **Schumann**; He butchered **Mozart**. He revered **Schoenberg, Beethoven, Brahms** and **Gibbons**.

Vladimir Ashkenazy (1937-)

VA's piano playing is bright and incisive, with clear articulation and an intellectual depth that does not interfere with warmth. He has exceptional control over tone color. Recordings include the complete piano works of **Rachmaninov** and **Chopin**, the complete sonatas of **Beethoven**, **Mozart's** piano concertos as well as works by **Scriabin, Prokofiev** and **Brahms.** He has also recorded **Bach's** *Well Tempered Clavier.*

241

Martha Argerich (1941-)

MA is arguably the greatest living pianist. Volatile, explosive, quixotic, astounding and mesmerizing are common critical terms used in her reviews. She is notoriously reclusive and reluctant to pander to the conventional publicity hype. Her repertory is astonishingly versatile, extending from **Bach** to **Shostakovich** and demonstrating a particular commitment to **Schumann**. She loves **Beethoven** "more than anything" and considers **Prokofiev** and **Ravel** her "best friends."

Maurizio Pollini (1942-2024)

MP was noted for performances of some of the most monumental works of contemporary music and for pairing such works with standard repertory of the 19th century. His repertory extended from **Bach** to **Stockhausen**. Later in his career, Pollini conducted piano concertos from the keyboard and sometimes led performances of opera. Pollini's recording catalog comprised some 150 CDs and many LPs.

Mitsuko Uchida (1948-)

The child prodigy daughter of a Japanese diplomat, Uchida grew up largely in Vienna, where she gave her first recital aged 14. She's a highly expressive yet finely controlled performer, with a vibrant immediacy of touch and the capacity to create enveloping atmospheres in just a few notes. Best known for her performances of **Mozart**, **Beethoven** and **Chopin** she's also made world-class recordings of works by **Schubert** and **Schumann** as well as the works of the Second Viennese School's **Schoenberg, Berg,** and **Webern.**

ON AUTHENTICITY

*I*s it not reasonable, if one really wishes to hear how a composer conceived his music, that it should be performed in a manner as close to his or her wishes as possible? This seems to go without saying. Why then is there such controversy surrounding this issue? There are many sides to this question, some more valid than others to the rational person. Let's examine some.

(+) is a composer and hard-boiled musicologist

(-) is a dedicated music lover and collector of recordings

This is my recollection of an actual conversation I had with a guy who isn't as smart as me. Okay—some have taken issue with that assessment. And no, I am not going to tell you which of these two guys is me.

಄

(+) Let me start by stating the obvious: We should hear a piece of music performed the way it was conceived by the composer. There. What could be more obvious than that? I win. Let's go home.

(-) Stay put. You say that because you're a composer.

(+) Do not.

(-) Do so. A lot has changed since the time of the Renaissance. For instance, I have this great recording of Monteverdi's *Magnificat* recorded in 1940 in terrible sound ...

(+) Sound quality is a boring issue. Not essential. Talk performance.

(-) We agree on that. Now, should I dump this beautiful record? It's as non-authentic as it gets. A mass of Verdi-loving Italians Caruso-ing their hearts out. Yet never have I heard such devotion, such a single-minded, fervent sound from the heart. This performance lives. I suppose this is not essential also?

(+) Of course, it is. It is most essential that it lives, as you say. But here's the thing: that work, and that composer are so great that any fine group from any century or country can make that work glow with the spirit the composer imbued it with, even if he completely disregards the letter. But think of the ideal! How much superior would a performance be that glowed with the spirit you described, performed in the style and tradition of Monteverdi himself!

(-) I don't know. How much?

(+) Plenty. Listen you, I know the recording you're talking about. You played it for me once. It was beautiful.

(-) Right. See?

(+) But it wasn't Monteverdi.

(-) Sure, it was. I'll get the record.

(+) No, I mean - they were his notes. But if he walked into the room he might not recognize his music. See, he only knew the tradition before him. These singers are steeped in the tradition of Arch-Romantic Italian Opera. If Monte did recognize the music as his own, he would think that there was something very wrong with the performance. He would be put off.

(-) But this music has a life of its own now. It's great enough not to have been left behind in the evolution of mankind. It's kept pace. This is what makes great music great!

(+) You have a point, but you see, I know the tradition Monte comes from. I have a sympathy for that era. Besides, I'm younger than you and never cared much for Romantic Opera anyway. I'm contemporary with the authentic school. I got in on the bottom floor. The first early music I heard at least made some attempt to capture the reality of the style in which it was written.

(-) I'll lay down and die.

(+) Just submit. Let's talk instrumentation. The only instrument in the orchestra which has not changed since the time of one so late as Beethoven, is the trombone. Baroque composers didn't just use oboes. They used a whole *palette* of different oboes—none of which sounds like the oboe of today! The brass has changed very drastically. Ever hear a natural horn or trumpet? Different instrument, my man. No valves. Every tone and nuance had to be produced by the mouth and hand of the player. Some of the instruments that Monteverdi used aren't even approximated by *any* modern orchestral instruments. As a composer, this is the easiest reason for me to relate to. If I write a small chamber piece using recorders, I don't want to hear it done by the Berlin Philharmonic using a battery of modern metallic and shrill-sounding flutes. Yet this represents the violence that was done routinely to works like Bach's *Brandenburg Concertos*, which are scored for small chamber ensemble, containing instruments the timbre of every one of which is different from that of its modern counterpart. Think of the tremulous vibrato that our modern string players dish out to all music regardless of its appropriateness. Vibrato was an ornament. Even Schubert wouldn't like it. Had enough?

(-) Yes, but not for the reason you think. Should our greatest contemporary musical creation, the Orchestra, be forever denied the privilege to play these beautiful works? You mentioned the Bach *Brandenburgs*... ever see many Ingmar Bergman movies?

(+) Sure. Why? Now what does that ...

(-) Be patient. Would those movies, say, *The Seventh Seal*, would that be a better movie if were in color?

(+) No.

(-) The greatness, the essence of that film, perhaps because it is so great, doesn't require color to do its magic. And, I submit to you, either does Bach.

(+) Hmmm ... I only agree that there are differences in the degree of need for proper colors. Do you deny the greatness of the French Baroque masters? Rameau, Couperin, Charpentier ...

(-) Of course not.

(+) Do you know why their works have been buried for years in obscurity, and are only now seeing the light of day?

(-) Oh oh.

(+) Right. Ha! Imagine the French without their color! You can no more deprive Rameau of color than you could deprive Monet. Think of a black-and-white *Water Lilies*. Or even one with the colors all screwed up, if you get my analogy.

(-) An extreme case. Valid perhaps, though I've enjoyed modern orchestral performances of the French Baroque, rare as they are.

(+) Hmph.

(-) Let's move to another point.

(+) You'd better.

(-) What about Beethoven. How can you insist that a work as powerful and gigantic as...

(+) The *Hammerklavier Sonata*

(-) ...yes. For an extreme, but valid example. How can you insist upon hearing that only on a tinkle-y fortepiano!

(+) I don't.

(-) Wait. What?

(+) Only a mindless pedant would expect to hear the colossal creations of a deaf titan on the instruments of a world he had long left behind. But this is, as we agreed, an extreme example. Ever hear the early sonatas on a fortepiano? The textures and the conception lock together beautifully. Same with the Mozart piano trios. The rounded, flutey tone of the modern grand is all out of context in these works. They are written for, and require, the proper texture to do justice to the conception. I submit to you that the difference is so profound, that performances on modern instruments in this case should be regarded as transcriptions.

(-) But what about musicianship! I was at the Marlboro Music Festival once and I heard these works performed with a trio under Rudolph Serkin. Such spontaneity and grace. Your proper textures ceased to matter. Like Glen Gould playing Bach. I was listening to his last *Goldberg Variations* before he died. I was transported from all the ills of Earth. I've heard some of your authentic performances. Careful, anemic sounding and bloodless. They stank of the midnight oil.

(+) They were courageous first attempts at getting back to the composer's time, to ...

(-) But you see, there *is* no getting back there. These works either survive in the world or they don't. It's the natural selection of greatness. And I submit to you—that those works that are so reliant upon proper textures and authentic performance practices to prolong their lives are not worth saving.

(+) Well, that takes care of the entire Middle Ages and almost all the Renaissance. Or would you have us use the Chicago Symphony to accompany the *Play of Daniel?*

(-) Where do you draw the line?

(+) I don't. It's a continuum. A performance is successful to the degree that it conforms to the spirit and the letter of the composer's inspiration and direction.

(-) But you're a composer!

(+) Right.

(-) You hear music in your head. Right?

(+) Right.

(-) Does it always come fully orchestrated? I mean, do the muses yell down "Too high, use a piccolo instead of a flute, you idiot!"? Or else "you know that trill isn't practical on the viola!"?

(+) Ah, no they don't.

(-) See, your inspiration isn't tied down to your earthly tools. If it were, you'd be a pretty trite composer.

(+) A composer's inspiration includes the proper transmission of the message to his audience. It's not to be ignored. Anyway, what about the Middle Ages and the Renaissance?

(-) If the performance is faithful to the spirit of the work, then it's a performance we should delight in.

(+) But a better one is possible.

(-) Not just then, no.

(+) Better than nothing, definitely.

(-) We're really getting nowhere. It looks like we agree on only this then: that the use of original instruments and authentic performance practices are important only to the extent that we are interested in their use. Agreed?

(+) No… I don't like that.

(-) You know what it is? I don't really like the way that authentic performances sound. Whiney strings with no life-giving vibrato, breathy flutes, tiny ensembles with their too-brisk tempos…

(+) I love those timbres and customs, but I certainly wouldn't describe them as you have. If you love this music, you've got a duty to hear it as it's meant to be heard. You'll grow to love it. To prefer it even. All those beautiful Baroque choral works like Bach's *St. Matthew's Passion* and Handel's *Messiah* that you listen to by guys like Klemperer and Beecham, you'll see them for what they really are—giant Romantic transcriptions of overblown and bloated proportions.

(-) If you ever heard those bloated performances, you'd see what your anemic ones are missing.

(+) I've heard them. They're monumental and glorious to the max; but it's not Bach and Handel.

(-) You're impossible.

(+) I think the only thing we agree on is this: a bad authentic performance is just as bad as a bad modern one. Agreed?

(-) Yes, agreed. Probably even worse!

℘

STAYING CURRENT

How much can the classical music scene change after a thousand years? Quite a bit, actually. Probably faster now than it ever did.

It's an *industry*. Yes, a revered 'art form' *blah blah blah*, but it's the industry attached to it that keeps it humming. There's the recording industry, the concert promotions industry, the composers, the performers, the publishing industry, the concert and recital presentation industry, the artist agencies, the music reproduction hardware industry, etc.

Of course, you don't have to keep current. You can just get some reference material, or even strike out blind and just buy stuff that seems compelling. But staying up with things is a keen part of appreciating the classical music scene. The old record store, the temples to high art that were ubiquitous a generation ago, was a great gathering place for the tribe. The connoisseurs, the snobs, the sages and the newbies, all would gather to discuss, argue and fight, occasionaly even buy things. It was glorious. Now it's gone. Now we do this, like we do too many things—virtually.

There are websites, natch, and a few remaining print magazines with their attendant websites that have sprung up to fill the gap. If you peruse these below, or just a few at regular intervals, you won't miss much that happens on the classics scene.

There are also some sites mentioned below that are not about what's going on in the industry so much, but just gathering places that seek to emulate, on a nationwide scale, what we used to have in the local store. You know— *conversation*. Forums exist where people talk classical music in all its dimensions all day and night. That might be for you. But like all such sites, watch out for 'flame wars' because classical music lovers are just as passionate and obnoxious as anyone else.

Print Magazines
A few still abide.

Musical Opinion; *www.musicalopinion.com*
Britain's Oldest Classical Music Magazine.

Quarterly print mag; rates €32 per annum, €52 US if paying by check, student rates (UK only) €16

Their website is mostly a web presence offering info on content and subscription information.

They describe themselves as follows:

"The first *Musical Opinion* was published on October 8th, 1877 and critically reviewed Brahms' new *Second Symphony* and in 1879 his *Violin Concerto*. In 1921 Musical Opinion launched its highly regarded sister magazine *The Organ*. The October 1936 issue carried an interview with Rachmaninoff and championed the young William Walton as Britain's most exciting young composer! New music, Composers, Concerts, Operas, Festivals, Dance, CDs, DVDs, Books, Operas, Opera Houses and Concert Halls are all examined in knowledgeable detail."

Opera News; *www.operanews.com*

Monthly print and web magazine; Print $130 per year; Web version $80 per year

There are free feature articles and news about the current opera scene, but for the goodies you need to whip out the credit card.

They describe themselves as follows:

"OPERA NEWS, currently the largest-circulation classical-music magazine in North America, began publication in May 1936. It is the only magazine in the U.S. that covers opera nationally every month. Editorial content includes profiles of up-and-coming singers as well as established artists of the present and past; features on the art form's history, as well as new works and productions; performance, CD and DVD reviews; and opinion pieces on the current opera scene. OPERANEWS.COM, the magazine's web presence from 1993, regularly includes online-exclusive features, Q&As, audio surveys, blogs, photo galleries, recording excerpts and reviews of performances, CDs and DVDs. ... OPERA NEWS's frequency has changed several times over the years. The first issues of OPERA NEWS were published weekly during the opera season in New York. During Frank Merkling's tenure, in July 1972, the magazine began publishing on a year-round schedule. OPERA NEWS has been a monthly periodical since July 1998, when Rudolph S. Rauch was editor. OPERA NEWS is an editorially independent publication, and the opinions expressed in the magazine do not represent the views of the Metropolitan Opera Guild or the Metropolitan Opera. The magazine's "In Review" section carries reports by local correspondents on opera performances throughout North America and Europe; the annual festival issues (May and June) and season preview (September), as well as the monthly Noteworthy & Now department, provide performance information for a wide variety of opera companies and festivals."

Fanfare Magazine; *www.fanfarearchive.com*
Bi-monthly print and web magazine; Web only $60 per year; Web & print $95 per year; other rates for places and subscription lengths available
The website is archival. Reviews and features since 1977 are to be found here, if you are a subscriber.
Wikipedia describes them as follows:
"Fanfare is an American bimonthly magazine devoted to reviewing recorded music in all playback formats. It mainly covers classical music, but since inception, has also featured a jazz column in every issue. Fanfare was founded on 1 September 1977 "as a labor of love" by elementary-school teacher turned editor named Joel Bruce Flegler (born 1941). He is still the publisher. The magazine now runs to over 600 pages in a 6" x 9" format with about 80% of the editorial copy devoted to record reviews, and a front section with a substantial number of interviews and feature articles. It avoids equipment and pop music coverage and manages to include reviews of many more classical releases than is typical for other magazines in this genre. Fanfare's editorial contributors have a range of expertise from the Medieval to Contemporary work. Describing itself as 'the magazine for serious record collectors,' its reviews cover not only the quality of live performance, but also that of sound and recording."
There is some controversy about Fanfare's review policy. There are claims of better editorial treatment if you buy an ad. This is not an unusual arrangement. It's a dodgy situation that you are encouraged to investigate online.

BBC Music Magazine; *www.Classical-Music.com*
13 issues per year; website has lots for free. Good, useful stuff. $100 per year.
Wikipedia describes them as follows:
"The first issue appeared in June 1992. BBC Worldwide, the commercial subsidiary of the BBC was the original owner and publisher together with the Warner Music Enterprises during its initial phase. Immediate Media Company has been the publisher since 2012. BBC Music Magazine has also an edition in North America which was first published in March 1993. The magazine reflects the broadcast output of BBC Radio 3 being devoted primarily to Classical Music, though with sections on jazz and world music. Each edition

comes together with an audio CD, often including BBC recordings of full-length works. The magazine's circulation is 37,530. Profits 'are returned to the BBC' The magazine features articles on subjects such as the favorite conductor of professional conductors. For its October 2009 edition, the magazine asked 10 composers to discuss the latest trends in Western Classical music in the 21st century."

They feature interviews with notable artists, latest news and opinions from around the music world, also review over 100 recordings every issue. These reviewers, unlike most, are well-paid for their efforts. It's a class act. More youthfully-oriented than Gramophone.

Gramophone Magazine; *www.gramophone.co.uk*

13 issues per year; website has lots of good useful stuff for free. The print mag is $90; Digital edition is $115; Both are $130.

Wikipedia describes them as follows:

"Gramophone is a magazine published monthly in London devoted to Classical Music, particularly to reviews of recordings. It was founded in 1923 by the Scottish author Compton Mackenzie. It was acquired by Haymarket in 1999. In 2013 the Mark Allen Group became the publisher. The magazine presents the Gramophone Awards each year to the classical recordings which it considers the finest in a variety of categories. In the title bar of its website Gramophone claims to be: 'The world's authority on Classical Music since 1923.' This used to appear on the front cover of every issue; recent editions have changed the wording to 'The world's best Classical Music reviews.'"

Like the BBC magazine, they feature interviews with notable artists, latest news and opinions from around the music world; also review over 100 recordings every issue and well-paid reviewers. A bit more high-brow than the BBC mag, and more stodgy in that inimitable Brit way.

Internet-only Websites

This is a snapshot in 2024 of a fast-changing scene. There are others, but these highlighted below are your best bet at this writing.

Allmusic; *www.allmusic.com*

Free, internet only. They are currently owned by Tivo.

My alma-mater. I was Content Director of Classical Music from its inception through the publication of *The All-Music Guide to Classical Music*. The classical part of the site has been integrated into the pop site, and when you visit allmusic.com, there is no hint of classical data on the homepage. There is, however, a searchbox. Most of the data on composers, their works and their recordings can still be accessed this way and it is quite comprehensive. Indeed, many classical reference sites have licensed this data to use as their own. The vast body of essays and lists are no longer available. Pity. The classical part of the site, for all its former comprehensiveness, is now a corporate afterthought.

American Record Guide; *www.americanrecordguide.com*
No longer a print-mag; 400 new reviews per issue; $48 per year
Their website is just a web presence offering info on content and subscription information. "Anyone can see most of this website without logging in. There is no need for passwords and such. Log-in is required for the cumulative index and for the current issue. Only current subscribers can log in. Follow directions. Past issues cannot be read here, but you can order them without logging in."
They describe themselves as follows:
"Founded in 1935; American Record Guide is America's oldest Classical Music review magazine. In 1992 it absorbed the editorial side of Musical America, so it also covers important concerts, orchestras and musicians on the American scene. We cover only Classical Music. There are up to 500 reviews in every issue, written by a freelance staff of over 80 writers and music critics. Many issues have an 'Overview,' an extensive survey of recordings of one composer or one area of the repertoire, such as 'Guitar Music.' 'Independence' is a guiding principle: in an industry dominated by advertising, ARG remains free of advertiser influence, which results in few ads and no puff pieces for record labels or artists."

Bachtrack; *https://bachtrack.com/*
Classical music website that keeps you up-to-date on the scene internationally. Nice idea nicely laid out.
From the site:
"Bachtrack was founded in January 2008 and is the largest site for live classical music. In 2020 we created a substantial section of the site to focus on video listings, both live streamed and on demand, so those unable to get to live events could also enjoy fabulous performances online. Over 900 events are in that section. We list over 30,000 events each year in classical concerts, opera and dance and publish around 200 reviews every month from our team of around 150 reviewers based all around the world. We also interview leading

singers and instrumentalists together with some of the stars of the future and preview festivals, competitions, and new seasons."

Classical Music Sentinel; *www.classicalmusicsentinel.com/*
Free; internet only
Dedicated exclusively to reviews of classical CDs. Free.
Here's what they say about themselves:
"Classical Music Sentinel is a music review website that is dedicated to providing recommendations of the best and latest in classical music recordings on the market today. Everything from baroque, chamber music and the renaissance, to orchestral works, opera and contemporary music, can be found here. Our goal is to present reviews in a concise and candid but knowledgeable manner in order to assist classical music enthusiasts in making their next recording purchase. Our rating system is simple -- There isn't any. Every title listed on this site is very good and definitely worth having. We are always on the lookout for the best recordings."

Classics Today; *www.ClassicsToday.com*
Daily web magazine; there's a lot there for free. Subscription to special features and archives $49 per year.
They describe themselves as follows:
"ClassicsToday.com is the world's first and only Classical Music DAILY. Taking advantage of the latest electronic publishing technology, ClassicsToday.com is proud to offer what the audience for Classical Music has long been waiting for: comprehensive review coverage of new recordings that's both accurate and completely up-to-date. Unlike conventional magazines, with their limited space and huge lead-times between release dates and review publication, ClassicsToday.com updates its news and reviews each day. There's no waiting for months and months to see if a recording by your favorite artist or composer will ever get reviewed. Our staff of internationally respected critics and music journalists is constantly at work, listening to and writing about each month's new releases. We hope that you'll take the time to browse around our site and get to know us. ClassicsToday.com prides itself on offering trenchant reviews backed by a clear, 1-10 rating system of both performance and sound. In addition to the new reviews posted each day, we also highlight a select group of the month's best recordings: those that receive our 10/10 rating, as well as a specially selected Disc of the Month. Special feature articles include coverage of major reissues, artist interviews, comparative discographies, and thoughtful essays about recordings of special merit."

Living the Classical Life; *www.livingtheclassicallife.com*
Interviews. free, but consider donation option. It's that good.
Great idea, beautifully executed. One of the great music sites on the web.
"We are a 501(c)(3) nonprofit organization dedicated to bringing back into Classical Music the human dimension lost in an ever more commercialized and dehumanized music business. Living the Classical Life is an ongoing series of filmed interviews as well as intimate, one-of-a-kind performances hosted by Zsolt Bognár. Its goal is to educate viewers so that they can experience music again as speaking directly from the heart to the heart. The episodes focus on the inner world of Classical Musicians and the essence of music itself. Performers at various stages of their careers generously share what Living the Classical Life is about—its passions, fears, obstacles, and its rewards. The intense, very personal exchange between host Zsolt Bognár and his guests is itself a real-time model for Living the Classical Life. Each episode has its own individual trajectory and its own intellectual, emotional, and visual flavor, created by Elyria Pictures, NYC, our highly professional, artistic, and passionately engaged team. Any viewer, whether music critic, opera fan, or occasional concertgoer, will enjoy these new, exciting insights into the heart of Classical Music. In a first encounter with a seemingly daunting, closed world, the experience of its humanity is nothing short of transformative."

Musicweb International; *www.musicweb-international.com*
Free; internet only
From their website:
"Musicweb International was founded by Dr Len Mullenger in 1995, as a website for the William Alwyn Society, and hosted on the servers of the University of Coventry. From these humble beginnings, it has developed, purely on a volunteer basis, into the largest non-commercial classical music resource on the web.

"Every weekday we post new classical CD and DVD reviews (usually 10) - there are more than 54,000 in the archive. A free weekly summary is available by e-mail.

"Unlike at least one of our peers, MusicWeb is not a subscription site.

"To keep it free, please support us by purchasing discs from our partners Amazon, Presto Classical & ArkivMusic, via the sales links on the review pages.
Musicweb also offers a range of labels for sale directly."

Operabase; *www.operabase.com*
Free, except for professional services likely not relevant to you
From their website:
"Operabase has documented operatic activity worldwide since 1996, with over 430,000 performances on file. It records the work of artists in over 900 theatres and publishes season information to opera-goers in 23 languages.

The majority of Operabase's information is provided free of charge. The public area contains access to the current, last and announced future seasons. The information can be searched in different, flexible ways :

- search by artist, title of the work, composer, city, company, dates or a combination of these criteria
- fields with autocompletion fields which allows to find names without knowing the exact spelling
- search in different languages for city and country names
- geographic information is used to create mouse-sensitve maps and listings of performances in neighbouring cities"

Planet Hugill ; *www.planethugill.com*
Free; internet only
Hugill is a respected journalist and his site is meaty and interesting.
From his website:
"Planet Hugill is written by Robert Hugill, singer, composer, journalist, lover of opera and all things Handel. Planet Hugill contains regular reviews of concerts, CDs and operas by Robert, our contributors, Anthony Evans and Tony Cooper and guest posters, along with concert previews, classical music news, interviews and feature articles on subjects as diverse as Handel opera, Bizet's Carmen and English opera in the 1950's."

Slipped Disc; *www.slippedisc.com*
Free, internet only. Dozens of posting per week.
Site is run by music-obsessed gadfly Norman Lebrecht. Norman's opinions are often controversial and his annoyance factor to many is high. He boils over easily, and some may fault his judgment from time to time, but if something happens in the classical music world of importance, he's likely to be on that thing like chrome on a trailer hitch. He is regarded, even among his detractors, as a very important player on the scene. He can take a punch as well as he gives one. He's obsessed with his own Judaism and occasionally veers completely off the topic of music in his zeal for the subject. It's annoying but

can be ignored like the foam you skim off of a glass of beer. It takes a lot to get Norman to censor comments, even ones that target him personally. I ought to know.

As the industry's decline proceeds nonstop (will it stop?) there are just as many articles in a week as there always were, but way too much minutia and obits of historically inconsequential minor-leaguers recently passed. This is a worrying trend.

Here it is from the horse's mouth:

"Welcome to Slipped Disc, the world's most-read cultural website. *[If he does say so himself.]* You have joined a readership of more than one million visitors a month. Slipped Disc was founded on www.artsjournal.com in 2007 by the author and broadcaster Norman Lebrecht with the aim of providing swift and reliable inside information on the most fascinating of art forms. In response to investor interest, it upgraded to this present site in May 2014. Slipped Disc is an interactive site that receives a constant flow of information from its readers around the world. If something happens in music, you are likely to read it here first. We welcome readers' comments and vigorous debate in the space below each item."

He talks big, but it ain't braggin' if you can do it.

Forums

Flame on, brothers and sisters…

Talk Classical; *www.talkclassical.com*
"A community covering every aspect of Classical Music!"

The Reddit Classical Music Forum; *www.reddit.com/r/classicalmusic/*
Of course, they have one. Hundreds of thousands of subscribers.

"Before posting, consider whether one of our sister subreddits may be more appropriate for your submission. For instance, music identification requests could be posted to /r/tipofmytongue, your own compositions to /r/composer, movie soundtracks to /r/moviemusic and video game soundtracks to /r/gamemusic. Memes belong in /r/classicalmemes."

CMM Classical Music Forum;
www.tapatalk.com/groups/classicalmusicmayhem/index.php
Free to view all posts and discussions

"Classical Music Mayhem!! is the forum for all matters relating to Classical Music. Cutting past traditional hyperbole to promote genuine excellence in composition, recordings and live performances. With specialism [sic] in authentic ('period') instruments and performance practice."

If you pony up $2.99 a month you get features. Here are a just few:

- No Ads;
- Stay Anonymous - Anonymously dislike other posts and view other user's profiles.
- Show Original Content - Because Google and other ad providers do not allow ads on pages with adult or inappropriate content, including certain swear words, that content is filtered. Since VIP+ members are not served ads, word filters can be disabled so you can view original content without restrictions. …
- Bigger Attachments and More attachments per post - VIP+ members can upload up to 20 files per post and 50MB per file (compared to 10 files/post and 20MB/file for standard users)

GMG Classical Music Forum;
www.good-music-guide.com/community/index.php

"Join over 800 other members in an informal discussion of all things to do with classical music. Join the most active classical music forum on the net. Want a piece of music identified? Need recommendations for further listening? Whether your taste is middle-of-the-road or esoteric classical, you are sure to find a wealth of information on our forum."

The Classical Music Guide Forums; *www.classicalmusicguide.com*
Half a million topics and counting.

Classical Forums; *www.classicalforums.com*
Forums, articles and blogs.

Special Mention
Internet sites of note

All of Bach; *https://www.bachvereniging.nl/en/allofbach*
They are aiming for just what the title says, ALL of Bach, and they have an excellent start. They are attacking all genres at once with amazing video performances of everything from solo harpsichord preludes to complete Passions. All luscious top-notch HD video, multi-camera productions, and all performances are top-notch. If you like Bach you will spend much quality time here.

Not Another Music History Cliché
notanothermusichistorycliche.blogspot.com
Linda Shaver-Gleason was her name, and debunking nonsense was her game. Until recently. She was a young musicologist with great intelligence and wit. This is a great blog.
From her blog:
"If you consider yourself a classical music lover, chances are you know a lot of stories about composers: Bach had a bunch of children. Beethoven went deaf. Schumann went crazy. Spend enough time reading concert reviews, and any composer's name sets off an array of associated phrases in your brain: Mozart = child prodigy, classical, perfection, crude humor, makes you smarter. The stories surrounding classical music are as familiar and as old as the pieces themselves--or so you might think.

However, not all of these stories are accurate. Some of them were invented years after the fact, then repeated so many times that people came to accept them as truth. Some are not exactly untrue, but they're reductive. Some are actively harmful. Yet people who write about classical music continue to recycle the same phrases and factoids because that's what their readers expect.

… That brings us to the purpose of this blog. Here, I'll be collecting published articles that resort to lazy clichés and debunked anecdotes when writing about classical music. I'll point out what's wrong, and I'll propose alternatives. Moreover, I'll do so without using jargon or resorting to abstract academic theories. My aim is to reach that broader audience who loves classical music but didn't major in it in college, the same audience that these articles are trying to speak to."

YouTube; *https://www.youtube.com/*

Countless videos and hundreds of video channels of art music from top-pros in state-of-the-art production to unlistenable grandchildren's recitals in poor video. All the audio is compressed but satisfactory for research and general entertainment.

Check out:

https://www.youtube.com/user/smalin

Introducing the *Music Animation Machine,* animated graphical scores by Stephen Malinowski. Nothing like it, and a good teaching aid for kids and adults to learn about form. Try it.

CR

ON THE CONCERT EXPERIENCE

U nless you live in a musical household, concerts and recitals are where music happens. Actual music. Not recordings. Music. But the concert experience is multi-faceted, and many of the variables which affect our appreciation are unconscious and even unrelated to the music itself.

Much of our feeling regarding a concert performance is related to our expectations of the event. When the average concertgoer drops $150 on a superstar event, one expects the best that the world has to offer and judges accordingly. This is the big-league, and our sense of appreciation is, consciously or not, tempered by this factor. A little-publicized, free recital is not *supposed* to sound 'big-league,' and when it does, we are delighted well beyond our expectations. If it's lousy, well—we got what we paid for.

Related to our expectations of an event is the sense of occasion which envelopes it. In 1989 Leonard Bernstein conducted the *Ode to Joy* from Beethoven's *Ninth Symphony* near the Berlin Wall to celebrate its crumbling. Was it a good performance? The short answer is: "Who cares?" Could one in attendance ever separate the overwhelming emotional ambience in that situation from how good the performance was? Knowing the musicians involved, the performance was at least competent, but would not the sense of occasion and the pure visceral drama of the moment elevate even a fair performance to the level of never-to-be-forgotten?

Concerts and recitals stand out in one's mind as memories awesome and horrendous. I witnessed Sergiu Celibidache lead the Munich Philharmonic in what this listener can only recall as a sacramental ritual of the Bruckner *Fourth Symphony*. A shining domestic example of this vital sense of occasion was provided for me by pianist Brian Connelly, who played Olivier Messiaen's *Twenty Visions of the Christ Child*. This marathon performance of an emerging classic of piano literature took tremendous courage and ambition on the part of that young man, and his success was unqualified.

The opposite end of that spectrum is the routine performance, imported or domestic, which reduces the art to a passionless punch of the timecard and, oddly, is often to be found in the alleged 'superstar' category of performers who travel the world playing the same pieces of music long after the honest freshness of the music has evaporated for them. I was the classical music writer for the *Ann Arbor News* for a decade, and some nights it was just too obvious that the performers were quite aware that Ann Arbor is not New York City or London and played likewise. It's sometimes called 'phoning it in,' and it's more common than it ought to be.

What about the concert itself? First, obviously it must have good music in it. It is surprising how many do not. Programming is a high art in itself. 'Rehearsal time is expensive, so what does the orchestra already know?' 'That Modern piece will take hours to get right—we can't afford it.' 'If we must do Modern let's do some Minimalism—they can almost sight-read that stuff.' This is the sort of behind-the-scenes sausage-making that eventually results in a concert series.

Often orchestras who are associated with major universities are obliged to program Professor X's new endless and unlistenable orchestra piece. This is one reason why Contemporary music fails so frequently in the concert hall. There is too often a political reason why much of it is programmed, rather than a musical one. Concert producers face a terrible quandary: fewer big subscription ticket patrons care for Contemporary music, but without new blood the orchestra and classical concerts become a museum, not a living and vital experience. That's pretty much what we have now—a museum.

A concert full of lowest common denominator 'chestnuts' is just as annoying to music lovers as one filled with obscurities. It is the balance of tradition and innovation which gives maximum pleasure. The proper amount of each is a subject for debate, but both must be present to ensure a healthy and satisfying experience as well as contributing to the health and longevity of the orchestra.

In the 18th century people flocked to the concert stage and opera house because it was the happening music of the day! It's what the cool people did on the weekend. No dusty relics here, and no sanctimony (unless it was connected to Royalty). People drank, ate, talked, laughed, made-out and occasionally paid attention to what was happening on stage. If they liked what they heard and saw, they would clap and cheer and celebrate the performers with all-night reveling; if they didn't, they would boo loudly, yell insults and lob a few ripe tomatoes your way and then laugh their asses off.

Now this might sound shocking and ill-mannered to the modern patron, but these events have gradually degenerated into the solemn deadly ritual that has become the modern concert experience and it is not healthy nor viable for much longer. We are worshipping the past at the expense of the lifeblood of the present. That will make the classical music scene irrelevant. Perhaps a happy medium between the unbuttoned past and the hidebound present is in order. Because if the situation is not rectified the museum will become a morgue.

A program that is too short can leave people feeling short-changed, but one that is too long can cause pleasant moments earlier in the concert to be forgotten, and the feeling of relief supplants any pleasure one may feel at concert's end. Concerts in Beethoven's day could be four hours long, and in an unheated church in the winter. Would anyone go to such a concert today? The attention span of the average person—far less than it ever was—could never endure such a scenario.

The ordering of pieces on a program is as important to our spirits as the ordering of courses in a banquet to our stomachs. Dessert ought to come *last*, and there should be at least one main dish. Musica Antiqua Koln is surely one of the greatest Baroque ensembles ever assembled, but it offered me an evening of appetizers, and in place of a main course gave us some plastic fruit in the form of a "newly discovered" J. S. Bach piece *that was obviously not by Bach*. On the other hand, the Fischer Duo and Friends, a local group, recently presented an all-Shostakovich program of wide variety, good placement and perfect proportions, making the evening's offerings seem far greater than the sum of its parts.

Of course, good performers are essential to a satisfying concert experience. A technique equal to the demands of the music is the usual situation, but transcendental technique—a condition in which the audience's attention is never drawn to the technical aspect—is quite rare. Only then can the music really speak its spirit without encumbrance. If you are hearing the performer before you are hearing the music, then the rendering is faulty.

Charisma accompanies the best performers. This trait has little, often nothing, to do with physical comeliness. It is always confident, and usually serene. It is an inscrutable attitude of success before-the-fact. A performer with charisma will suspend the critical facility in his or her listeners and render them trusting as children, and they'll never know it's happening.

Artur Rubinstein once remarked that many conservatory graduates are such accomplished virtuosos that they routinely perform technical feats that he would never even attempt. "But when they come out on stage," Rubinstein said, "they may as well be soda-jerks."

Charisma is undefinable, for if it could be formulated, then everyone could have it. But everyone can't, for in its nature it is like a gift. When combined with transcendental technique, the result is a performer of importance and wide influence.

This performer wields a sharp and deadly double-edged sword. When there is submission to the service of a great composer's intention, the result is the living re-creation of the composer's inspiration. This occasion is not trivial, it's as close as many will ever get in this lifetime to what used to be called a 'religious experience.'

But no performer is greater than great music—no matter who the performer is, no matter how famous they are, and no matter how noble and influential the tradition from which they spring.

When the composer's tradition is ignored by such an influential re-creator as Itzhak Perlman, not only the composer, but his adoring audience suffers a disservice. For many look to a great interpreter to light the way to the understanding of a great composer. An enormous amount of superb music benefits at the hands of Itzhak Perlman, for example, but like all of us, he fails outside of his sphere. When I heard him in recital, I was hearing Perlman most of the time, not the composer.

The impish James Galway, for instance, did an Irish routine, making Mozart flute concertos sound like they're being played by a leprechaun. It used to be part of his schtick before he became accepted as the obviously superb musician that he grew to become. By then, the 'act' was no longer needed.

As a seasoned listener, I don't want to hear Mozart played by a leprechaun; or Beethoven from a tradition that post-dates the composer by almost a century, ignoring basic tenants of the Classical style.

Some years ago, percussionist Evelyn Glennie was a hot item. She's attractive, and she's deaf. The angle of the article was the notion that Glennie has made an international career *despite* her deafness. This is an erroneous, but politically-correct interpretation. Glennie has an international career *because* of her deafness. A fine percussionist she surely is, but she is no better than many other top percussionists who lack a spotlit career because they can hear just fine and lack her knock-out beauty. (Do you recall the feature on CNN some years ago about the blind painter? The paintings sold like hotcakes, but is that because they are better than the paintings produced by artists who can see?)

All this is not to detract from Glennie's obvious virtues as a musician, but to put her fame in perspective. The classical music world is no different from any other industry. It has proved helpful to a career to stand out from the crowd in a way unrelated to your discipline if you want the whole world to sit up and take notice, whether by extraordinary beauty, bizarre idiosyncrasy, or handicap.

In a concert the senses merge. Good concert producers know that it takes more than good music and musicians to make a show special. Though a presenter can't help what your mood is like before you arrive, or what the weather might be, the savvy producer will take responsibility for mood and environment as soon as you enter the hall of music.

A staff that's friendly and efficient, and a performance area that's comfortable and pleasing to the eye ought to be the concert-goer's first impressions while settling down to enjoy a show. The cold, the rain, and a sour mood can all be forgotten in these first few minutes of preparation.

That's because the venue in which music unfolds itself becomes a musical instrument of great significance on its own. The craft of good acoustical architecture and design is a black art. Many millions of dollars have been sent down the drain in the past century or two in the building of glorious new concert halls that are acoustical nightmares. Some have been abandoned, some replaced, but usually they are reluctantly put to use.

A small choir singing in a dead space—a room with insufficient reverberation—loses so much of its intended effect that the concert will likely fail on this ground alone. A ringing ambience is written into the score of most choir music. Likewise, an over-reverberant acoustic plays havoc with a large orchestra, blurring the lines and obscuring the details.

Actual presence at a live music-making event is not related in essence to the necessarily sterile world of recorded music. Its many components bring all our senses into play, whether we consciously realize it or not. People-watching is a hoot at concerts, I find. Even the smell of the place, the feel of the seats. The visual aspect of a concert can be truly mesmerizing. The conductors, the soloists (especially singers) can radiate so much charisma that it almost burns. In a concert or recital one can observe the music actually being created—the muscles of the body as they manipulate the instrument, the expressions on the faces of the musicians as they bring the sounds to life in your very presence. *This* is Music.

Live music-making is a delicious gamble, for though we know what we expect, we never really know what we're going to get.

CR

HOARDER, COLLECTOR, CURATOR

Hoarders *are neurotics*. Why do they hoard? Because they have lost track, indeed, if they were ever on it, of what it means to value a thing or an idea in their heart.

Hoarders come in two flavors.

I had an acquaintance, call him Bob, who hoarded CDs and LPs. Also old open reel recordings. Also 78s. He was a single, wealthy guy, and he listened to classical music whenever he had the chance. His equipment was state-of-the-art. His *discarded* equipment, all fantasy top-of-the-line stuff, lay inert in various piles and stacks, taking up entire rooms about his mansion. But he *was* a keen listener and astute observer of the art music scene. So, he wasn't a full-blown nutjob hoarding for the sake of hoarding, but he *was* a hoarder.

Bob bought *everything*. This is not hyperbole. He bought every new release at his local store at which I worked back in the day, and what we wouldn't stock he had special ordered. He had, however, little idea of what discs he owned or where exactly they could be found in his home—shelf, floor, table, wherever. Of his tens of thousands of CDs, most were unopened and there were hundreds of duplicates. Instead of checking if he already had something, he would just buy it again "just to be on the safe side," he told me.

Bob would buy discs by composers he loathed and performers for whom he would vent nothing but bile and insult. I never met a more perfect example of what I hope none of you become.

Bob was a rarity, so of no great cultural concern. But the vulgarity that infected him has appeared lately as a massive cultural force and it disturbs me. Bob's malady has morphed into the present day's technology and a new generation, a second flavor, of hoarder. Instead of hoarding *material*, they are hoarding *digital audio files* on their phones and PCs. The files come compressed, and the promise to the present generation is that they can "have tens of thousands of their favorite songs" on one device.

How many favorite songs do *you* have? I am filled with envy at anyone who actually has tens of thousands of favorite songs. It puts me in mind of Facebook addicts who boast of having 2,000 'friends.' If you even have *one* actual friend, you can count yourself lucky. I wish Facebook would adopt as its slogan a quip from Confucius who said, "He who has many friends has no friends."

There's another big difference between the two hoarder mindsets. The former was a rare neurotic; the latter is distressingly common, and the result of 'music' becoming so cheap and ubiquitous that it's all pretty much a throwaway proposition. Fifty years ago, kids gave up a good chunk of their newspaper-delivery money to buy a couple Beatles albums which they treated like gold and some still own and cherish. No need for that these days. Go online to Piratebay or YouTube and *steal it*. It's just a stream of ones and zeros, what the hell. Or download it for near-free from Google, Apple and others who pay composers *a fraction of a penny* per download for their efforts. The files are compressed but the quality sorts well with your crappy earphones, so who cares?

Music recordings have been trivialized to the point that there is nothing about them other than utility. And research shows that most recordings on these devices have never been, and indeed *never shall be*, played, never mind actually *listened* to.

Hoarding is mindless. It is a form of gluttony. It's spiritually corrosive. It trivializes what should be a noble experience. Resist the urge. Apply some intelligence in your collecting habit.

Collectors *seek comprehensiveness in their area of specialization.* Why do collectors behave this way? Because they want to build and maintain a comprehensive library for study and the pride of ownership, or perhaps to pass on to another generation or educational institution when they are gone.

Most collectors specialize in a particular area of the art because no one likes everything. The opera collector may have 30 recordings of Puccini's Tosca but not a scrap of chamber or keyboard music. They don't need to be 'objective'; they need to be completists in their chosen area of study.

Collectors distinguish themselves from the hoarder mainly because they know what they have. Usually, a collector will have a database on their PC as reference. Some just keep a spreadsheet file on Excel, others spring for one of many software solutions that offer fill-in-the-blank convenience in a pre-formatted inventory package for recordings.

LP and CD collectors who seek a comprehensive library have usually already amassed sometimes thousands of material recordings and have resisted turning these into digital files, because they themselves have a life. No matter how you do it, it's a ton of work and takes a lot of time. You can pay someone or some company to do this but be prepared to dig way deeper than you imagined paying for the task.

Many with smaller collections have converted their LPs and CDs to musicfiles and sold the CDs and LPs. I had a friend who converted his entire library to digital files but put all his LPs and CDs in storage. Why? I do not know. As an investment? Can't bear to part with it all? He was never clear, but looked annoyed when I asked him

The collectors I have known differ from hoarders in another important way: they know where things are and are usually quite meticulous in their library habits. Some file by era, some alphabetically by composer. But what about collections and other miscellany? There is no obvious way to do this and most collectors have their own system.

They might lend you a disc or LP (less likely) that you're interested in but don't count on it. One generous collector I knew would make me a copy of anything I wanted to hear. It was his way of being generous while jealously safeguarding his collection.

Curators *aim for concision.* Why do they curate instead of collect? Economy, often, and not just about money. Also about space. Also as an exercise in efficiency. Curators usually take pride in the knowledge and logical rigor that is required to maximize the essence and minimize the bulk. Curators aim for the best of the best in the most efficient way possible. Collectors want it all; Curators agonize in order to pare down to essentials. Curators operate under the delusion that they are objective enough to be the judge of what 'essential' actually means.

I labor under this delusion. (I know—you're shocked.) I am a curator of the strictest sort. I don't feel I'm 'better' than a collector but doing it this way sorts with my nature. I like the Brucker symphonies, for example, but unlike my collector friend Jim who has every recording of the Bruckner symphonies he can obtain (his library is all about the Romantic-era, and he can intelligently discuss every one of his Bruckner recordings), I have one of each of the nine numbered symphonies by the Bavarian master. If I encounter recordings I like much better than what I have, I'll replace it with the new favorite.

This philosophy can be difficult to implement. Getting a 'definitive' recording of, say, the Bruckner *Seventh Symphony* is like getting a definitive photo of Mt. Everest. It's not really possible. That's why Jim and those like him have so many. But I seek the 'best' example of the music I admire, and it is a pleasant contest to whip my collection into shape as a lean, mean, classical recording machine. Jim finds my approach inconceivable, even indefensible, but I enjoy the challenge and the result.

Okay, what really sets Jim off, is the fact that I didn't even bother to purchase the best individual symphonies—I bought my favorite boxed set! (Stanislaw Skrowaczewski and the Saarbrücken Radio Symphony on Oehms Classics. Awesome.) I am fine with this, but I can see why Jim, and the many others like him, would disapprove of my solution. But the indispensable Bruckner symphonies? I got 'em covered. That's just how I roll.

Likewise, I have boxed sets ripped to lossless musicfiles for the Mahler and Beethoven symphonies, because I want them all. I have several Haydn and Mozart symphonies but not complete sets. Why? If I were a collector, I probably would want all of them; as a curator, I only want a selection. Not all Haydn (104!!) or Mozart (46 or so) symphonies are especially compelling to me, and *I don't need what I don't want.*

I have converted all my material recordings to musicfiles on my PC to the FLAC format. That was an eye-crossing, saliva-drooling timesuck of Homeric proportions but I'm glad I did it. And these files, many hundreds of gigabytes in total, are backed up on a portable hard drive at my home and also in the cloud. I use Microsoft OneDrive but there are many acceptable cloud backup solutions. *Pick one.* Make sure you are backed up locally and on the internet. That's a lot of work to lose and it happens every day.

Let me put it more baldly—*if you collect electronically and do not back up you shall lose your collection.* It's due to hardware failure mostly. But one encounter with a ransomware virus like that which recently infected a friend's un-backedup PC and you're toast.

CR

ANALOGUE & DIGITAL

The good ones sound fine, the bad ones sound awful. What am I referring to here, LPs, CDs or musicfiles? All three. Neither digital nor analogue technology is any guarantee of a great production, or even a good one. Today's engineers are never done learning how to best cope with the demands of recording and playback.

Perhaps the most noticeable aspect of an all-digital production is the almost total lack of noise. This is no biggie to anyone born after 1975 or so, but to those who grew up in an earlier time, or who listen to recordings from an earlier era, the lack of noise is remarkable. There is no hiss, no pops, no scratches, all replaced by a deathly quiet (if your equipment is quiet). It is a most pleasurable aspect. In the cases where an older analogue recording is remastered and transferred to CD, there will be no consciously audible playback noise—only the noise from the original master, and much of that can be automagically eliminated in the digital remastering process.

The *dynamic range* of many recordings is also greatly increased in the CD format. This is the measure of the range of volume between the quietest passages and the loudest passages. In a live performance of a full orchestra, the dynamic range may extend from near inaudibility up to and including the threshold of pain. LPs are, as a rule, unable to reproduce this range as well as the digital format can. This does not mean that all your CDs will reproduce at concert volume, only that many are able to do this if the production is of highest quality and your hardware permits it.

Some feel that digital technology, at least in its present form, is unsuitable for music reproduction. They site reasons of sampling rate insufficiency, unmusical filtering philosophies, super- and sub-sonic interferences, and poor analogue output stage design, specifically the circuitry involved in turning the digital signal back into an analogue signal so that the music can sound through the vibrating cones of speakers or headphones.

Though digital recording is a 'connect the dots' proposition, the basic theory behind its successful operation cannot be disputed. As the music is fed through microphones into the digital recorder, it takes fast snapshots of the sonic action. These are called *samples*, and though the original waveform can then be approximately reconstructed with a minimum of samples, these samples are fitted to pre-existing values. This is a radical departure from the old days of analogue recording, when the idea was to try to fit the technology to the infinite scope and variety of the music, not vice versa. For example, current digital standards accept that our conscious and unconscious hearing spectrum ends at about 20,000 cycles per second. Everything above that is filtered out. That is *theoretically* sound. (But we don't just hear with our ears, we hear also with our bodies. Also, we may not consciously hear above 20K Hz but we may still sense these signals.)

Instead of pursuing and preserving the maximum amount of music unleashed in a performance, digital technology seeks the opposite. It says, in effect, "let's chop the performance up into a certain number of tiny pieces and fit the true values to the pre-defined limits of our system." This may be convenient, quiet and profitable, but it may not be the last word in musicality.

Ideally, I think that recordings ought to be listened to in the formats in which they were recorded. But the ideal is just too annoying a prospect for me and most others. The mixing of the two formats has created interesting circumstances, the first common as dirt, but the second I think is a pure anomaly that is difficult to justify, and it comes with a big warning.

- *A to D: Analogue recordings remastered and digitized for CD and musicfile distribution.* This is very common. Most classical music of note was recorded in analogue before the 1980s and listening to them converted to digital format on CDs or from a device is satisfactory to all but a minority of audiophiles. This remastering and digitizing process makes all recordings made before the '80s available to be played on CD or stored as musicfiles. The best part of the digital reprocessing of analogue originals is often in the *remastering*. That means unwanted noise can often be eliminated from the original production. No more tape hiss. Frequency adjustments can be made to mask defects in the original recording, if any. The ambience of the original recording can be adjusted. *This can and is often overdone.* A hissy, noisy but realistic and vibrant analogue original can easily be turned into a sterile, lifeless and icy cold corpse of the source material. It's not at all uncommon. But a good hand at the tiller can make an old recording sound new and fresh. How does the digitized file compare to a pristine LP on the turntable over a good stereo? The debate rages, never to be put to rest.
  - ○ ***Big warning here:*** *All analogue recordings that end up on LPs are not necessarily analogue LPs.* That's because it's far easier to remaster an old analogue master tape recording by converting it into the digital realm in order to do the remas-

tering, and then press an LP using the new digital file as the source. This is unethical at worst but the purveyors of this sort of thing believe that if you're dumb enough to not know the difference you deserve what you get. Plus, they can use the new digital remaster to release the recording on CD and musicfile formats. Study and make sure that the 180-gram vinyl recording of the Chicago Symphony from 1959 that you paid $30 for is analogue right the way down the chain, and never pays a visit, *no matter how briefly*, to the digital realm. Else you're just wasting money.

- *D to A: Digital recordings pressed onto an LP*. When digital recordings are transferred to the analogue realm and played back on an LP, I have to wonder why people find this acceptable. Because it's so cool to play records! is all I can come up with. Much of the current LP inventory is made up of digital recordings placed onto the analogue playback medium of the LP. I don't see what is to be gained here, other than making playback more cumbersome and finicky. If it began life in the digital domain, there, I believe, it ought to remain till it gets to your ears.

I *like* digitized recordings because with a good digital recording I can get an 'X-ray' of a favorite piece of music, so cleanly etched are the details of a good digital recording. At best we get a beautiful reproduction, at worst a detailed autopsy. I like CDs and musicfiles also because I am not fastidious, and deeply appreciate the convenience of the format (unless compression is involved, which can easily eliminate 90% of the original signal for convenient storage and the ability to email songs to an interested recipient). This is the factor that digital design was to highlight. Secretly, CDs were never intended to be a high-fidelity medium, except in the well-coordinated media blitz that accompanied their burst upon the scene.

I *don't like* digitized recordings because orchestras too often sound like the Electronic Philharmonic and can lack warmth. Voices can be glassy. Words like icy, dry, shrill, glairy, electric and unsubstantial come to mind. I don't always sense a solid, earth-based foundation in the playback, even in the recording studio where I use a digital sampling rate two-and-one-half-times the CD standard. I find too, that when digital technology is imperfectly implemented it can filter the emotion from a performance. You can sample a waveform, but not a feeling.

Lately, people have told me that I am not really hearing these differences that I claim to hear. Have you ever had anyone tell you that what happened to you didn't really happen? But I have not 'reasoned' this out. These aren't thoughts, they're impressions, feelings, gut responses. They're true to me but they won't do *you* any good at all. Listen to all the formats. You may like them or not. What you will hear will depend upon a dozen things, such as: the quality of the player and its attendant components; the ambience and structure of the listening room; your age; your mood; the music auditioned; what audio system you're used to; and we're not nearly done. The opinions of the most highly-acclaimed ears of the century should be meaningless next to the truthful testimony of your senses.

The final test, whether you are being held captive by an audio showroom shyster, or relaxing with a knowledgeable and wealthy friend in her amazing listening room is: what do your ears tell you? *Don't let anyone not using your ears tell you what you are hearing.*

It should also be noted that the pursuit of audio perfection is an endeavor unrelated to the appreciation of music. This is because we listen *through* equipment, not *to* it. Our imaginations can unconsciously fill in details far more beautifully than the unheard nuance may actually have been. There is no measuring apparatus for this.

And never, ever forget—*a recording of music is not music.*

CR

RECORDING MEDIA: LP, CD, MUSICFILES

No audio reproduced in a home environment will ever sound as good as music performed in a live concert hall or in a studio.

CD

How do you feel about fetish objects? Clinically speaking, that is what the LP, CD and DVD offer us—something to hold in our hand. These are *things*—objects with pictures and print, and they hold recordings of music.

CDs are small. That's good for storage. But that's bad for art and annotations.

An obvious plus for this format is the possibility of an 80-minute playing time without having to 'flip the record.' But a soundfile can be many hours longer, and a list of them can theoretically play forever!

CDs are approximately 1.4 jillion times easier to care for than LPs and they wear better than LPs *for the most part*. There is a definite caveat here that most people are not generally aware of. Some of the first CDs manufactured some 30 years ago are starting to deteriorate! The format is not "Perfect Sound Forever" as the admen promised us a few decades ago. They will likely deteriorate and are therefore unsuitable for archival storage unless you only plan to store for a few short decades.

Keep greasy thumb-prints off your CDs, and for all their near-indestructibleness, tempt not the gods. For instance, when you feel a need to clean them, get out your soft cloth and wipe the surface of the CD *radially*, and not in an arc around the disc. This is because the information is stored in such a way that an accidental straight scratch is not as catastrophic as a scratch which follows the 'groove,' and, thanks to sophisticated error-correction, will probably not even be consciously audible.

If you want to keep things pristine, CD baggies are available and can keep your jewel boxes, which scuff up very easily, crystal clear for years. Or just buy more jewel boxes when the old ones crack or cloud up. They're about a buck each, half that if you buy 50.

LP

Let's consider the perceived advantages of the Long-Playing vinyl record format. I say "perceived" because now, even after 30 years, the analogue vs. digital debate will not cease. Some people are convinced that pre-digital LP technology is the closest humans have come to capturing the true nuance of musical performance in a mass-produced format. Others are certain that such a view is absurd.

Sonics aside, the large surface area of a disc jacket allows extensive annotations regarding repertory, artists and the like. I miss those. The art of producing a nice album cover with attractive cover art and expert annotations was a wonderful thing back in the day, and it's nice to see that many LP producers are keeping the artform alive. CDs and DVDs are just too tiny to do this job as well. Downloads and streaming? Maybe you'll get some art and notes you must view electronically, but probably not.

LPs can be a pain to store. They take up more room than CDs (or, obviously, musicfiles) and if they are stored improperly, they will mildew. Yuk. If they get too hot, they melt. If you put a jacketed LP down on a flat surface then something—cup of hot tea, an ice-cream sandwich, an anvil, *whatever*—will appear on top of it and damage it.

You're only going to get 30-minutes max on one side of an LP. Don't underestimate the annoyance factor in having to interrupt your carefully-engineered repose to flip a record. And near that 30-minute mark 'innergroove distortion' raises its ugly head if the company actually tried to cram 30-minutes of music on one side.

But the main disadvantage of LPs (other than the nature of analogue sound itself, which some find inferior) is, paradoxically, what so many find attractive about the medium: It can be a struggle. You need to work for it, and then revel in what your labor has brought forth. LPs demand much greater care in handling and constant attention to cleaning, lest they rapidly and severely deteriorate. CDs and digital files are not plagued with the inevitability of scratches, skips and pops that are all too easy to inflict upon tender vinyl by even the slightest mishandling. (If you tend to be sloppy, LPs may just flat-out not be for you.) Nor are CDs or musicfiles vulnerable to the onslaught of dust and dirt as are LPs. However, with a bit of care—discussions of cleaning methods and maintenance supplies are easy to find online—these serious problems can be greatly diminished. Don't fall prey to the snakeoil salesmen, though. There are plenty of dubious products for the unwary. Investigate, It's part of the fun of LPs.

Some Essential Tips:

Handle discs by the edges or by the labels. Never touch the grooves or try to blow dust from them, saliva in the grooves being very noisy when dried.

The more serious you become about collecting fine records, the more incensed you will be with the recording industry's inane custom of using paper sleeves on old mid-price and budget recordings. Occasionally these cheap and destructive expedients will even turn up on full-priced discs. These all-paper sleeves are quite capable of causing irreparable damage to any record unfortunate enough to be held captive in one. Paper sleeves also increase the amount of static on a record. Protective inner-sleeves should be purchased separately and substituted for the cheap paper product. Also, if you really want to be protective of your collection, you may buy plastic outer sleeves quite cheaply and replace the original shrink-wrap the record was sold in. (The shrink wrap should be removed immediately after purchase since it continues to shrink.) An economical replacement for the shrink-wrap is a common food storage bag; these are available in just the right size.

If static is a problem with your records, do not buy spray-on, rub-on, or any other kind of goop that promises to "take care of static for the life of the record." Often these products do what they say, but they may also gum up the grooves, leave a residue on the stylus and damage the vinyl. Don't believe the claims—I found out the hard way. For static problems, use an anti-static mat with your turntable, or a Zerostat-type device—a gun that literally neutralizes static. Very low humidity such as occurs in the heated homes of listeners in the cold months is a prime cause of static build-up. For this situation a humidifier works wonders (also for your skin, mucus-membranes, and any musical instruments you have in the house).

Record geeks of the highest order will have a record-cleaning machine. They are usually as large as a turntable and expensive. A more compact option is a record washing system—inset the disc vertically and manually spin it clean. There are vinyl record vacuums, and the good old record cleaning brush. A very acceptable record-cleaning system is the Spin-Clean system, which cleans both sides of your records at once, but many swear by the Nitty Gritty 1.0 Vacuum Record Cleaning System.

The Nitty Gritty company sells a wide assortment of record cleaners ranging in price from $529 to the Mini-Pro 2 at $1,579. This solution is not for sissies or lazy listeners. It is likely the best cleaning system available.

Oh—and never use pure alcohol to clean a record. It will adversely react with the vinyl and decompose it.

MUSICFILES—Digital Audio Formats

Just the facts, ma'am, just the facts. Here we have a string of 1s and 0s you never see or touch. Nothing to hold, nothing to read, nothing to look at. No art, no lyrics, no liner notes.

For zillions of avid listeners that's just fine. If you go this route, you'll have one major decision you must make, because if you don't, the industry will make it for you, and they are less concerned with your critical faculties than they are with their bottom line. Whether you are streaming your music from a service like Spotify, Pandora or the like (see the feature on Streaming), or accumulating musicfiles from Apple, Amazon, etc. and storing them locally in your library, you sometimes have a choice of file format. The closer you get to 'CD-quality' (and beyond) the more you'll pay.

Popular Lossless Compressed Audio Formats

Lossless compression is something of a counterintuitive miracle: it reduces file size without any loss in quality between the original source file and the resulting file. You won't get the 90% reduction in file size as you would with a standard MP3, more like 50%, but you will have all the bits and bytes of the original file reconstituted to your ears' delight.

FLAC

FLAC stands for Free Lossless Audio Codec. Easily the most popular lossless format.

FLAC typically compresses an original source file by up to 60% without losing a single bit of data. FLAC is an open source and royalty-free format so there is no constraint on its use.

The average Apple fan cannot use this format in any Apple operating system. See below.

ALAC

ALAC stands for Apple Lossless Audio Codec. ALAC is sometimes referred to as Apple Lossless.

It's less efficient than FLAC when it comes to compression, so why bother with it? Because most non-geek Apple users don't have a choice. Apple Music, the old iTunes and iOS both support ALAC and do not support FLAC. More adventurous Apple users can always install a third-party music-player that will play most anything. If you download FLAC files for your library or if you want to rip CDs to your Mac in FLAC format, I suggest you play and rip them through a player such as VLC. It's a free download.

WMA

WMA stands for Windows Media Audio. This is their lossless version, not the lossy one as described below. Stay away from this format. It is poorly supported by many player codecs.

Popular Lossy Compressed Audio Formats

Lossy compression loses data during the compression process. In the context of audio, that means sacrificing quality and fidelity for file size. But this has been so cleverly accomplished, that most people, in most cases, cannot hear the difference.

Or rather, they *think* they cannot hear the difference. Remember that we are talking about classical music *recordings*. Not music; *recordings* of music. When we hear a recording and accept it as music, we have automatically been dumbed-down. You are listening to an audio-only extract of a concert which, when the signal is processed ad nauseum and reproduced on the average stereo, is a poor facsimile at best of the audio one gets in concert. And it is completely missing the concert experience and the effect the music has on your body. For most people this is not a conscious experience, but it is nonetheless powerful.

Lossy compression eliminates much of the signal from the original recording, which is already, as explained above, compromised. For classical music, how can this be a good thing? Compression is a second level of dumbing down. We might 'think' we can't hear the difference, but so much of the original sonic experience has been stripped away (no matter how cleverly engineered the process) that I submit that 'most people' simply have no problem with being dumbed-down.

MP3

MP3 is the dowager queen of audio codecs. Because it's so great? Nah. It's old and familiar, supported widely, and it delivers on its promise. It stands for MPEG-1 Audio Layer 3.

So, what is its promise? It's to cut out all the sound data that exists beyond the 'hearing range' and ability of most normal people and to reduce the quality of sounds that aren't as easy to hear, and then to compress all the remaining audio data that has been deemed essential, as efficiently as possible. A standard 128 kbps MP3 file reduces filesize about a staggering 90%. This was a game-saver in the early 90s, when diskspace was expensive, internet connections were slower, and portable devices didn't have a whole lot of storage space. And it's true that most people claim they cannot hear the difference. I can. Many can. But not most. This is because most people's 'critical listening skills' are not very critical; also, because most people listen to music on not very good equipment or on portable devices with cheesy headphones.

Nearly every digital device in the world with audio playback can read and play MP3 files, whether we're talking about PCs, Macs, Androids, iPhones, Smart TVs or whatever else. When you need universal compliance, MP3 will never let you down.

MP3s, like AAC below, is measured based on its bitrate. Common bitrates include 64, 128, 192 and 256 kbps (thousand bits per second).

AAC

AAC stands for Advanced Audio Coding. It was developed as a superior successor to MP3, and though sound quality is demonstrably better than MP3 at the same bitrate, it hasn't overtaken MP3 as the most popular for everyday music and recording.

Though most consumers have ignored the format, savvy media companies have not. AAC is the standard audio format used by YouTube, Android, iOS, iTunes, Nintendo portables and PlayStations.

Perhaps most importantly, Apple has adopted AAC as its file format for audio. All songs sold at the iTunes Store, and all songs from Apple Music, are in the AAC format and encoded at 256 kbps, which affords better resolution but a larger filesize than standard MP3 files (usually offered at 128 kbps).

OGG (Vorbis)

OGG stands for, well… Ogg. This is a container, not a codec. That means it can hold all kinds of compression formats but is most commonly used to hold Vorbis files—which is why these audio files are usually called Ogg Vorbis files.

Vorbis is open source software. Not proprietary. This means a lot to a large class of music and computer geeks who disdain having to rely upon profit being the motive for the quality and availability of their tools. Also, at the same file size, Vorbis makes better-sounding files than MP3 and some may discern this.

Support for Ogg is not universal but seems to get more widely adopted as a viable option every year.

WMA

WMA stands for Windows Media Audio. It's a proprietary format created by Microsoft. Stay away. Support for the decoding of WMA files is not nearly universal.

WMA tried to outdo MP3 in efficiency, and theoretically it does, but the results, I believe, are inaudible to all but a savant.

High Resolution Audio Formats

The LP encouraged everybody to replace their 78s. Stereo prompted all to replace their old monophonic records. 'Original Instruments' and 'Authentic Performance Practices' encouraged everybody to replace their Classical-era-and-before LPs. CDs encouraged everybody to replace their records. Electronic storage encouraged everybody to sell their CDs and download recordings to store on their devices. Audio streaming encouraged everyone to say to hell with all that stuff and just rent whatever you want when you want it and never worry about storing anything anywhere. All these were gifts to the industry which kept it humming along famously.

Now what?

Record labels have always salivated at the opportunity to re-sell you their catalog in some new, 'improved' format. Their latest update comes in the form of high-resolution digital audio—music delivered at better-than-CD quality, intended to come as close as possible to the fidelity of a record's original masters. Hi-res audio refers to music files that have a higher sampling frequency and/or bit depth than CD, which is specified at 16bit/44.1kHz.

Some websites claim that they are offering streaming or downloads that are hi-res, but their definition is not relevant to this discussion. They are merely talking about offering uncompressed audio files—FLAC or ALAC—in standard CD specs. Properly, hi-resolution audio refers to specs that *exceed* CD standards.

Sampling frequency (or sample rate) refers to the number of times samples of the signal are taken per second during the analogue-to-digital recording or conversion process. And the more bits there are, the more accurately that signal can be measured, so going 16bit to 24bit can allegedly deliver a noticeable leap in quality. Hi-res audio files usually use a sampling frequency of 96kHz or 192kHz at 24bit. You can also have 88.2kHz and 176.4kHz files too.

Hi-res audio does come with a few downsides though: file size, for one. A hi-res file can typically be tens of megabytes in size, and a few tracks can quickly eat up the storage on your device. Storage is cheap and getting cheaper, so it's easier to maintain higher-capacity devices. That said, the size of the files can still make hi-res audio cumbersome to stream over your wi-fi or mobile network.

A couple easy points to know here. First, many recordings are made at the standard 16bit/44.1kHz. No amount of re-diddling with those numbers will improve on the sound. The original is what it is. But, ironically, just because a recording is an old analogue one doesn't mean it can't be converted digitally into high-resolution. It can, and this will be a huge part of the catalogue if hi-res really catches on.

You won't be able to buy a physical medium, like a CD, that will have hi-res audio on it. Higher-resolution audio is a matter of files either downloaded or streamed over broadband internet connections, and the playing devices are basically audio computers. But some of these 'computers' are phones. Many high-end phones can now store and play hi-res files. The problem with any computer, big desktop or otherwise, properly outputting a hi-res audio file is mainly in the DAC (Digital-to-Analogue-Converter) chip. The one you have is probably not up to the task.

The DAC is a chip that reads all the 1s and 0s that comprise your digital audio files, converting them to analog audio signals that can be played back through a speaker. The more sophisticated the DAC, the cleaner the analog audio signal should sound. Many built-in DACs make compromises for size and cost (and top out at 16-bit), so upgrading to an external DAC is often the first step to getting the most out of hi-res audio files. They can range from $40 mobile units for your phone or laptop, all the way up to home units that cost several thousand dollars.

Now to the punchline: *Is it worth it? Can you hear the difference?* Well... I don't know, can you?

I'm not being glib. Like the 'compressed vs. uncompressed' argument, *you cannot let someone else decide this for you.* There is no doubt that there are those who can hear the diff, but they are listening with a good DAC on even modest equipment. Conversely, there are many people who truly love listening to recordings who cannot tell the difference between a low-res MP3 and the highest of hi-res files available, no matter what kind of setup they are listening through. And even if you can hear the difference, is the hassle of disc space economy, DAC replacement and the expense of obtaining files in the new format worth the bother?

You will pay dearly to obtain the goods. At this writing I cannot recommend any of the very few sites that offer hi-res downloads. The scene is in such flux now that there are still no accepted standards in place for all to adopt to make this a viable routine choice.

So Which Format Should You Use?

✓ If you're *ripping* an LP or CD to a musicfile and want faithful audio representation, use lossless audio compression, FLAC for most of us and ALAC for the benighted Apple-lover who is tied to the Apple Music scene. Serious listeners *always* go for FLAC/ALEC over MP3. Note that you'll need more storage space for these, but storage is cheap.

✓ If you absolutely need to conserve disk space, you are compelled to use lossy audio compression. It's said that most people can't hear the difference between lossy and lossless compression. I don't believe this. If they could compare a standard MP3 file with the same file in lossless format *on very high-quality audio equipment*, I think the average listener would note the difference.

✓ That said, on the other end of the spectrum, if you use a typical portable playback device, especially with standard-type earbuds, it really doesn't much matter what format you are listening to.

CR

A FEW RECOMMENDED RECORDINGS

Recommending recordings is a dodgy business. It's the stuff of massive arguments, but I feel I must throw a few out there that I hope represent a good selection with which most aficionados would have to agree. Nice thing about the digital age is that, not only will fewer things 'go out of print,' but items long unavailable will come back to the catalogue, either in the form of LPs as meat for that growing body of enthusiasts, or as musicfiles because there is no distribution cost. If you see something long out of print that you must have come back into availability on one of these formats, don't wait for the CD or LP because you may wait forever.

What is changing in most genres is that, with the advent of digital, there is no need to keep the same works together on an 'album' because the concept of the album is evaporating. Just want two of the cuts from the new *Itchy and the Lepers* release but not the rest? Well, you can usually do that. But with classical, there is still the idea of the production, and preserving the concept of a project. CDs are still the way most classics get out into the world, though digital distribution is growing. Streaming is another issue, but we'll talk about that later. This is about building a library.

The selections below are from available CDs, many of which can also be downloaded digitally. Try to avoid MP3 files. I have tried to select items that are not just good but easily available and likely to stay available as long as people buy classical music.

I have included some recommended music from the Modern and Contemporary eras, even though they may not stand the test of time and fail to be included in the repertory of classical music. I got a good feeling about these pieces.

 C႙

Gregorian Chant
Any recordings featuring the monks of Saint-Pierre de Solesmes
Various labels

Music of the Gothic Era
The Early Music Consort of London, dir. David Munrow
DG

Music of the Middle Ages
Studio der Fruhen Musik—Early Music Quartet, dir. Thomas Binkley
Telefunken

Hildegard von Bingen: *A Feather on the Breath of God*
Emma Kirkby; Gothic Voices, cond. Christopher Page
Harmonia Mundi

Guillaume de Machaut: *Messe de Nostre Dame*
Taverner Consort & Choir, dir. Andrew Parrott
EMI

Guillaume Dufay: *Missa L'homme Armé, etc,*
Oxford Camerata, dir. Summerly
Naxos

Johannes Ockeghem: *Missa pro defunctis, Missa prolationum*
Musica Ficta Vocal Ensemble Copenhagen, dir. Bo Holten
Naxos

Josquin Des Prez: *Inviolata, integra, et casta es Maria à 5, other motets*
Pomerium, dir. Alan Black
Archiv

Thomas Tallis: *Spem in alium, other motets, Mass*
Oxford Camerata, dir. Jeremy Summerly
Naxos

Giovanni Palestrina, Tomás Luis Victoria: *Masses & Motets*
Westminster Cathedral Choir, dir. Martin Baker
Hyperion

Orlando de Lassus: *Lagrime di San Pietro*
Ensemble Vocal Européen Choir, dir. Philippe Herreweghe
Harmonia Mundi

William Byrd: *Masses For 3, 4 & 5 Voices*
Pro Arte Singer, dir. Paul Hillier
Harmonia Mundi

William Byrd: *Consort & Keyboard Music*
Tessa Bonner, Timothy Roberts
Red Byrd, Rose Consort of Viols
Naxos

Giovanni Gabrieli: *Sonate e Canzoni*
Jan-Willem Jansen, Charles Toet, Liuwe Tamminga,
Concerto Palatino, dir. Bruce Dickey
Harmonia Mundi

Claudio Monteverdi: *L'Orfeo*
Lynne Dawson, Anthony Rolfe Johnson, Anne Sofie von Otter, John
Tomlinson
English Baroque Soloists, Monteverdi Choir, His Majestys Sagbutts and
Cornetts, cond. John Eliot Gardiner
Archiv

Claudio Monteverdi: *Vespro Della Beata Vergine*
James Bowman, Robert Tear, John Shirley-Quirk, Felicity Palmer
Monteverdi Choir, Philip Jones Brass Ensemble, Monteverdi Orchestra, cond.
John Eliot Gardiner
Decca

Michael Praetorius: *Terpsichore* (excerpts)
New London Consort, cond. Philip Pickett
L'oiseau Lyre)

All at Once Well Met - *English Madrigals*
King's Singers
EMI

Giacomo Carissimi: *Jepthe, 2 oratorios*
Monteverdi Choir & Soloists, His Magesties Sagbutts & Cornetts, Members
of the English Baroque Soloists, etc., cond. John Eliot Gardiner
Erato

Archangelo Corelli: *Concerti Grossi Op. 6*
Ensemble 415, cond. Chiara Banchini
Harmonia Mundi

Henry Purcell: *Dido & Aeneas, Ode*
George Mosley, Carolyn Watkinson
English Baroque Soloists, Monteverdi Choir, cond. John Eliot Gardiner
Philips

Henry Purcell: *Fantazias & In Nomines*
Fretwork
Erato

François Couperin: *Tic Toc Choc, etc*
Alexandre Tharaud, harpsichord
Harmonia Mundi

Antonio Vivaldi: *Le Four Seasons; Concertos, RV 454 & 332*
Il Giardino Armonico, cond. Giovanni Antonini
Teldec

Antonio Vivaldi: *Gloria, etc*
Sarah Fox, Deborah Norman, Nico de Gier, Michael Chance
Academy of Ancient Music, Cambridge King's College Choir, cond. Stephen Cleobury
Warner Classics

Jean-Philippe Rameau: *Pièces de Clavecin*
Trio Sonnerie
Virgin Classics Veritas

Jean-Philippe Rameau: *Les Indes Galantes*
Jaël Azzaretti, Patricia Petitbon, Nicolas Cavallier, Valerie Gabail
Les Arts Florissants, cond. William Christie
Opus Arte

J.S. Bach: *Goldberg Variations*
Glenn Gould, piano
Sony Classical *(either of two versions, separated by an entire career)*

J.S. Bach: *Mass in B minor*
Lynne Dawson, Jane Fairfield, Jean Knibbs, Patrizia Kwella
English Baroque Soloists, Monteverdi Choir, cond. John Eliot Gardiner
Archiv

J.S. Bach: *Brandenburg Concertos*
Musica Antiqua Cologne, cond. Reinhard Goebel
Archiv

George Frideric Handel: *Messiah*
Robert Brooks, Otta Jones, Henry Jenkinson, David Blackadder
Academy of Ancient Music, Oxford New College Choir, cond. Edward Higginbottom
Naxos

George Frideric Handel: *Concerto Grossi Op.6*
Academy of Ancient Music, cond. Andrew Manze
Harmonia Mundi

Dominico Scarlatti: *Harpsichord Sonatas*
Colin Tilney
L'oiseau Lyre

Giovanni Battista Pergolesi: *La Serva Padrona*
Performer: Michele Govi, Federica Zanello
Ensemble Regia Accademia, cond. Marco Dallara
Tactus

Franz Joseph Haydn: *Symphonies Vol. 7, #45, 46, 47, 51, 52, 64*
Academy of Ancient Music, cond. Christopher Hogwood
L'oiseau Lyre

Franz Joseph Haydn; *Sonatas for Piano #59-62*
Jénö Jandó, pianist
Naxos

Franz Joseph Haydn: *String Quartets, Op. 76, #4, 5 & 6*
Kodaly String Quartet
Naxos

Wolgang Amadeus Mozart: *Piano Concertos*
Malcolm Bilson
English Baroque Soloists, cond. John Eliot Gardiner
Archiv

Wolgang Amadeus Mozart: *Symphonies #39, 40*
Freiburg Baroque Orchestra, cond. René Jacobs
Harmonia Mundi

Wolgang Amadeus Mozart: *The Magic Flute*
Reinhard Hagen, Hans-Peter Blochwitz, Linda Kitchen, Rosa Mannion
Les Arts Florissants, cond. William Christie
Parlophone

Beethoven, Ludwig van: *Symphonies (9)*
Orchestre Révolutionnaire et Romantique, Monteverdi Choir, cond. John Eliot Gardiner
Archiv

Beethoven, Ludwig van: *Piano Sonatas #28 thru 32*
Maurizio Pollini
DG

Beethoven, Ludwig van: *The Late String Quartets*
Lasalle Quartet
DG

Beethoven, Ludwig van: *Piano Concertos #4 & 5*
Claudio Arrau
Dresden Staatskapelle, cond. Colin Davis
Philips

Rossini, Gioachino: *Il Barbiere Di Siviglia*
Luigi Roni, Stefania Malagú, Renato Cesari, Enzo Dara, Luigi Alva, Hermann
Prey, Teresa Berganza, Paolo Montarsolo
London Symphony Orchestra, Ambrosian Opera Chorus, cond. Claudio
Abbado
DG

Donizetti, Gaetano: *Lucia Di Lammermoor*
Joan Sutherland, Luciano Pavarotti, Ryland Davies, Nicolai Ghiaurov,
Huguette Tourangeau, Sherrill Milnes
Royal Opera House Covent Garden Orchestra, Royal Opera House Covent
Garden Chorus, cond. Richard Bonynge
Decca

Schubert, Franz: *Symphony #9*
North German Radio Symphony Orchestra, cond. Günter Wand
RCA

Schubert, Franz: *Piano Sonatas Op.120, 143, Impromptus*
Sviatoslav Richter
Musical Concepts

Bellini, Vincenzo: *Norma*
Ebe Stignani, Mario Del Monaco, Athos Cesarini, Maria Callas
Italian Radio Chorus Rome, Italian Radio Symphony, cond. Tullio Serafin
Myto Records

Berlioz, Hector: *Symphonie Fantastique, 3 Overtures*
Royal Philharmonic Orchestra, cond. Charles Mackerras, Yuri Simonov,
Alexander Gibson
Musical Concepts

Mendelssohn, Felix: *String Symphonies (complete)*
Hanover Band, cond. Roy Goodman
RCA

Mendelssohn, Felix: *Piano Concertos #1 & 2*
Martin Helmchen
Royal Flemish Philharmonic, cond. Philippe Herreweghe
Pentatone

Schumann, Robert: *Symphonies #1 & 4*
Wiener Philharmoniker, Ricardo Muti
Philips

Schumann, Robert: *Symphonic Etudes for Piano, 3 pieces*
Sviatoslav Richter
Musical Concepts

Chopin, Frederic: *Nocturnes*
Artur Rubinstein
RCA

Chopin, Frederic: *Etudes*
Andrei Gavrilov
EMI

Liszt, Franz: *Sonata in B minor, Liebestraume*
Jorge Bolet
London

Verdi, Giuseppe: *Aida*
Nicolai Ghiaurov, Placido Domingo, Piero Cappuccilli, Luigi Roni, Fiorenza
Cossotto, Montserrat Caballé
Royal Opera House Covent Garden Chorus, New Philharmonia Orchestra,
Trumpeters of the Royal Military School of Music, cond. Riccardo Muti
Warner Classics

Wagner, Richard: *Tristan and Isolde*
Dietrich Fischer-Dieskau, René Kollo, Kurt Moll, Werner Götz, Margaret
Price, Anton Dermota, Brigitte Fassbaender, Eberhard Büchner, Wolfgang
Hellmich
Leipzig Radio Chorus, Dresden Staatskapelle, cond. Carlos Kleiber
DG

Bruckner, Anton: *Symphony #7*
Saarbrücken Radio Symphony Orchestra, cond. Stanislaw Skrowaczewski
Oehms

Brahms, Johannes: *Violin Concerto, Double Concerto*
Performer: Gil Shaham, Jian Wang
Berlin Philharmonic Orchestra, cond. Claudio Abbado
DG

Brahms, Johannes: *Fantasien Op. 116, etc*
Wilhelm Kempff, pianist
DG

Bizet, Georges: *Carmen*
Angela Gheorghiu, Roberto Alagna, Inva Mula-Tchako, Thomas Hampson, Elisabeth Vidal, Isabelle Cals, Ludovic Tézier, Nicolas Cavallier, Nicolas Rivenq, Yann Beuron
Toulouse Capitole Orchestra, Les Elements Chamber Choir, La Lauzeta, cond. Michel Plasson
EMI

Mussorgsky, Modest: *Pictures at an Exhibition (Ravel orchestration)*
Ukraine National Symphony Orchestra, cond. Theodore Kuchar
Naxos

Tchaikovsky, Peter Ilyich: *The Sleeping Beauty*
National Philharmonic Orchestra, cond. Richard Bonynge
London

Tchaikovsky, Peter Ilyich: *Symphony #4, 5, 6*
Leningrad Phil., cond. Evgeny Mravinsky
DG

Dvorak, Antonin: *Symphony #8, 9*
Budapest Festival Orchestra, cond. Iván Fischer
Philips

Dvorak, Antonin: *Serenades (2)*
London Philharmonic Orchestra, cond. Christopher Hogwood
London

Grieg, Edvard: *Concerto for Piano, Peer Gynt*
Jean-Efflam Bavouzet
Bergen Philharmonic Orchestra, cond. Edward Gardner
Chandos

Fauré, Gabriel: *Requiem, Pavane, Pelléas et Mélisande Suite*
Elly Ameling, Bernard Kruysen, Daniel Chorzempa, Jill Gomez
Rotterdam Philharmonic Orchestra, Netherlands Radio Chorus, cond. Jean Fournet, David Zinman
Philips

Elgar, Edward: *Cello Concerto, Enigma Variations*
Jacqueline Du Pré
London Philharmonic Orchestra, Philadelphia Orchestra, cond. Daniel Barenboim
Sony

Puccini, Giacomo: *Tosca*
Tito Gobbi, Maria Callas, Giuseppe Di Stefano, Franco Calabrese
Milan Teatro alla Scala Orchestra, Milan Teatro alla Scala Chorus, cond. Victor De Sabata
Regis

Mahler, Gustav: *Symphony #2*
Isabel Bayrakdarian, Lorraine Hunt Lieberson
San Francisco Symphony Orchestra, San Francisco Symphony Chorus, cond. Michael Tilson Thomas
San Francisco Symphony label

Mahler, Gustav: *Symphony #9*
Berlin Philharmonic Orchestra, cond. Herbert von Karajan
DG

Debussy, Claude: *La mer, Prélude à l'après-midi d'un faune, Images, Nocturnes*
Boston Symphony Orchestra, cond. Charles Munch
RCA

Debussy, Claude: *Piano Works*
Pascal Rogé
London

Strauss, Richard: *Salome*
Klaus Lang, Cheryl Studer, Leonie Rysanek, Horst Hiestermann, Clemens Bieber, Bryn Terfel, Marianne Rorholm, Uwe Peper, Karl-Ernst Mercker, Warren Mok, Aimée Willis, Peter Maus, Manfred Röhrl, Friedrich Molsberger, Ralf Lukas, William Murray, Bengt Rundgren
Berlin Deutsche Oper Orchestra, cond. Giuseppe Sinopoli
DG

Strauss, Richard: *Also sprach Zarathustra, Ein Heldenleben*
Chicago Symphony Orchestra, cond. Fritz Reiner
RCA

Sibelius, Jean: *Symphonies #2, 5*
Minnesota Orchestra, cond. Osmo Vänskä
Bis

Vaughan Williams, Ralph: *The Lark Ascending; Fantasia on a Theme of Thomas Tallis; Symphony #5*
Iona Brown, Trevor Connah, Stephen Shingles, Kenneth Heath
cond. Neville Marriner, Roger Norrington
Decca

Rachmaninoff, Sergei: *Piano Concertos #2, 3*
Lilya Zilberstein
Berlin Philharmonic Orchestra, cond. Claudio Abbado

Rachmaninoff, Sergei: *Symphony #2, Vocalise*
St. Petersburg Philharmonic Orchestra, cond. Yuri Temirkanov
RCA

Schoenberg, Arnold: *Verklärte Nacht, Chamber Symphonies*
Orpheus Chamber Orchestra
DG

Ives, Charles: *The Concord Sonata*
John Kirkpatrick, pianist
Sony

Holst, Gustav: *The Planets*
Royal Liverpool Philharmonic Orchestra, Royal Liverpool Philharmonic
Choir Women, cond. Charles Mackerras
Virgin Classics

Ravel, Maurice: *La Valse, Boléro, etc ,*
Cleveland Orchestra, cond. Christoph von Dohnányi
Teldec

Ravel, Maurice: *Beautiful Starry Night - Thibaudet Plays Ravel*
Jean-Yves Thibaudet
Decca

Bartók, Béla: *Concerto for Orchestra, Music for Strings, Percussion & Celesta*
Montreal Symphony Orchestra, cond. Charles Dutoit
Decca

Stravinsky, Igor: *Le sacre du printemps, Pétrouchka, Firebird, Apollo*
Orchestra/Ensemble: City of Birmingham Symphony Orchestra, cond.
Simon Rattle
Warner Classics

Webern, Anton: *Symphony, Six Pieces, etc.*
Philharmonia, cond. Robert Craft
Naxos

Berg, Alban: *Violin Concerto, 3 Orchestral Pieces*
Gidon Kremer, violin
Bavarian Radio Symphony Orchestra, cond. Colin Davis
Philips

Prokoviev, Sergei: *Piano Concertos #1, 3; Sonatas 2, 3*
Gary Graffman, piano
Cleveland Orchestra, cond. George Szell

Prokoviev, Sergei: *Symphonies #1, 5*
Philharmonia, cond. Rudolf Barshai
Musical Concepts

Orff, Carl: *Carmina Burana*
Gundula Janowitz, Gerhard Stolze, Dietrich Fischer-Dieskau
Schöneberg Boys Choir, Berlin Deutsche Oper Chorus, Berlin Deutsche Oper
Orchestra, cond. Eugen Jochum
DG

Gershwin, George: *Porgy and Bess*
Andrew Smith , Hartwell Mace , Mervin Wallace
Houston Grand Opera Orchestra , Houston Grand Opera Chorus,
cond. John DeMain
Sony

Copland, Aaron: *Appalachian Spring, Rodeo, etc.*
New York Philharmonic, cond. Leonard Bernstein
Sony

Partch, Harry: *The World of Harry Partch*
Daphne of the Dunes; *8 Hitchhiker Inscriptions from a Highway Railing at Barstow,
California;* Plectra and Percussion Dances: from Castor and Pollux
Various performers, cond. Danlee Mitchell
Sony

Scelsi, Giacinto: *Quattro Pezzi su una nota sola; Uaxuctum; La nascita del Verbo*
Vienna Radio Symphony Orchestra, cond. Peter Rundel, Johannes Kalitzke
Mode

Shostakovich, Dmitri: *Symphony #5, 9*
Kirov Theater Orchestra, Valery Gergiev
Philips

Shostakovich, Dmitri: *String Quartets #2, 3, 7, 8 & 12*
Borodin Quartet
Erato

Messiaen, Olivier: *Turangalila Symphony*
Tristan Murail, Paul Crossley
Philharmonia Orchestra, Esa-Pekka Salonen
Sony

Barber, Samuel: *Concerto for Violin, Concerto for Piano, Adagio*
Isaac Stern, John Browning
New York Philharmonic, Cleveland, and Philadelphia Orchestras, cond.
George Szell, Leonard Bernstein, Eugene Ormandy

Cage, John: *Sonatas & Interludes for Prepared Piano*
Aleck Karis
Bridge

Britten, Benjamin: *Peter Grimes*
Peter Pears, David Kelly, Lauris Elms, Claire Watson, James Pease, Geraint
Evans, Iris Kells, Jean Watson, Raymond Nilsson, John Lanigan, Marion
Studholme, Owen Brannigan, Marcus Norman
Royal Opera House Covent Garden Orchestra, Royal Opera House Covent
Garden Chorus, cond. Benjamin Britten

Britten, Benjamin: *Prelude & Fugue, Simple Symphony*
London Chamber Orchestra, cond. Christopher Warren-Green
Erato

Xenakis, Iannis: *Metastasis, Pithoprakta, Eonta*
Orchestra/Ensemble: ORTF Philharmonic Orchestra, Paris Contemporary
Music Instrumental Ensemble, cond. Jean-Louis Le Roux, Konstantin
Simonovic
Chant Du Monde

Ligeti, György: *Atmospheres, Lux aeterna, etc.*
Ensemble InterContemporain, North German Radio Chorus Hamburg, Vienna Philharmonic Orchestra, cond. Pierre Boulez, Helmut Franz, Claudio Abbado
DG

Feldman, Morton: *Rothko Chapel, Why Patterns?*
California EAR Unit (Performer), UC Berkeley Chamber Chorus
New Albion

Stockhausen, Karlheinz: *Stimmung*
Penelope Walmsley-Clark, Nancy Long, Suzanne Flowers, Rogers Covey-Crump, Gregory Rose, Paul Hillier
Singcircle, cond. Gregory Rose
Hyperion

Crumb, George: *Ancient Voices of Children, Music for a Summer Evening*
Michael Dash, Jan DeGaetani, Richard Fitz, Gilbert Kalish
Contemporary Chamber Ensemble, cond. Arthur Weisberg
Nonesuch

Takemitzu, Toru: *A Flock Descends into the Pentagonal Garden, etc.*
Bournemouth Symphony Orchestra, cond. Marin Alsop
Naxos

Penderecki, Krzysztof: *Anaklasis, Threnody for the Victims of Hiroshima, Capriccio, etc.*
Polish Radio Symphony Orchestra, Cracow Philharmonic Chorus, London Symphony Orchestra, cond. Krzysztof Penderecki
EMI

Riley, Terry: *In C*
Ars Nova Copenhagen, Percurama Percussion Ensemble, cond. Paul Hillier
Dacapo

Pärt, Arvo: *Tabula Rasa, Fratres, Cantus in Memory of Benjamin Britten*
Gidon Kremer, Keith Jarrett, Tatiana Grindenko, Alfred Schnittke
Stuttgart State Orchestra, Twelve Cellists of the Berlin Philharmonic, Lithuanian Chamber Orchestra, cond. Dennis Russell Davies, Saulius Sondeckis
ECM

Reich, Steve: *Music for 18 Musicians*
Steve Reich Ensemble, cond. Steve Reich
Nonesuch

Glass, Philip: *String Quartets #2 – 5*
Kronos Quartet
Nonesuch

Glass, Philip: *Akhnaten*
Milagro Vargas, Melinda Liebermann, Tero Hannula, Helmut Holzapfel
Stuttgart State Opera Chorus, Stuttgart State Opera Orchestra, Dennis Russell Davies
CBS

Monk, Meredith: *Dolmen Music*
Meredith Monk, Collin Walcott, Steve Lockwood, Paul Langland
ECM

Adams, John: *Chamber Symphony, Shaker Loops, Phrygian Gates*
Ensemble Modern, cond. Sian Edwards
RCA

Adams, John: *A Flowering Tree*
Eric Owens, Jessica Rivera, Russell Thomas
London Symphony Orchestra, Schola Cantorum De Venezuela, cond. John Adams
Nonesuch

Eno, Brian: *Music for Airports*
Virgin / Astralwerks

Rihm, Wolfgang: *Gesungene Zeit; Lichtes Spiel; Coll'Arco*
Tianwa Yang, Rheinland-Pfalz State Philharmonic Orchestr, cond. Darrell Ang
Naxos

Saariaho, Kaija: *Notes on Light, Orion, Mirage*
Paris Orchestra; cond. Christoph Eschenbach
Ondine

Adès, Thomas: *Asyla*
City of Birmingham Symphony; Simon Rattle
Warner Classics

CR

GETTING THE GOODS

My grandson asked me the other day, "Grampa, what's a record store?"

How would he know? Records, at least for a 10 year-old and his peers are… what now? I explained how back when dinosaurs roamed the earth there were flat black discs about yea big with grooves on both sides called 'records,' and you placed the disc onto a spinning platter and dropped a diamond sliver (or sapphire if you were a cheapskate) into the groove and that's how people got their music. I think he thought grampa was pulling his leg, and not just about the dinosaurs.

These temples to art and conversation that dotted our landscape, like the records themselves, are mostly gone now. So, what is the best way to get your music?

Local Purchase

If there still is a functioning CD/record store in your area, and you enjoy going there, enjoy it while it lasts because the future does not look good. Patronize the hell out of it.

Go to the Library

In our culture the good ol' library is how we steal media and are allowed to not feel bad about it. I never understood this. In your average public library in your average big town, it's easy to borrow and rip an entire, really nice classical recording collection. I'm not moralizing. I've made many visits of my own. I just don't understand why I'm not supposed to feel bad about it. Same applies to borrowing the CDs from your friends or having them copy musicfiles for you from their collection. There's no real taboo about it. Is there?

Stealing It

Stealing is a very popular way to get music. Shall we now consider 'file-sharing' sites such as Piratebay and 1337x 'The Library of the Internet'? Bear in mind that the innocent download from YouTube is no different than going to a pirate file-sharing site. Both are stealing. Why is this bothersome? Ignore

303

the major record companies who have been short-changing artists, dumbing-down and degrading the culture for decades now. But do consider that when you steal, the composer and musicians get screwed out of whatever pittance is coming to them. You know, same as getting it at the library.

It's your call.

Buy LPs, CDs & Musicfiles on the Web

As of this writing I recommend these sites, in no particular order. There are and will be others, and the game changes quickly.

Arkiv Music; *arkivmusic.com*
CD, DVD, LPs
I have used and I recommend this service. Their bios and work lists of composers seems truly massive and impressive, but it is all my old data from All Media Guide, which was most impressive at the time, but has not been updated for years. I hope they get people on this. Soon, it will start to be very noticeable.

From their website:

"ArkivMusic specializes in the efficient delivery of the broadest selection of classical music titles in the U.S., direct to the consumer. There are currently over 120,000 CD, DVD, SACD, and Blu-ray Disc titles in the ArkivMusic database, shipping from over 20 distribution centers around the country. This distribution network allows ArkivMusic to have more titles in stock every day than any other online retailer, assuring the most expeditious delivery and largest selection of classical music. In addition, ArkivMusic has more than 10,000 titles in its ArkivCD reissue program. These are recordings that have previously been out of print or otherwise unavailable."

Discogs; *discogs.com*
LP, CD
This is the favorite site for many to purchase LPs. Discogs now has 13 million releases, 7 million artists, and more than 60 million things for sale from 150,000 sellers. Think e-bay but more reliable.

From their website:

"We're on a mission to build the biggest and most comprehensive music database and marketplace. Imagine a site with discographies of all labels, all artists, all cross-referenced, and an international marketplace built off of that database. It's for the love of music, and we're getting closer every day.

The Database

The heart of Discogs is a user-built database of music. More than 587,000 people have contributed some piece of knowledge, to build up a catalog of more than 14,093,171 recordings and 7,591,780 artists. We're far from done and you can contribute too! Discogs also offers the ability to catalog your music collection, wantlist, and share your ratings and reviews.

The Marketplace

The Discogs Marketplace connects buyers and sellers across the globe. With more than 61 million items available and thousands of sellers, this is the premier spot from new releases too hard to find gems. Because the Marketplace is built on top of the accurate Discogs database, it is easy for sellers to list their inventory and buyers are able to specify the exact version they want.

The Story

Originally created as a hobby project in 2000 by Kevin Lewandowski, Discogs has grown to become a definitive resource for Vinyl and CD recordings."

Esprit International Limited;
https://eil.com/shop/genre/Genre_List.asp?Genre=CLS&GenreName=Classical
a UK outfit that sells CDs, DVDs and LPs.
From their website:

"Click on the Classical artist of your choice to Buy New, Rare, Collectible, Used and Hard to Find CDs, CD Albums, Vinyl Albums, Vinyl records, Rare CD Sigles [sic], Picture Discs, Rare Vinyl, 12" singles, 10" singles, 7" singles, Limited Editions, Promos, Promotional items, Imports and Music Memorabilia from the 1960s, 1970s, 1980s, 1990s and 2000s along with Full Discography's [sic]"

Amazon; *amazon.com*
CD, DVD, MP3-only downloads
Search function isn't the best, but good prices on many items.

eClassical; *eclassical.com*
downloads only, FLAC and MP3; charge by the second; some 24-bit recordings

"We thought the music business needed a new pricing model. In any of today's common music websites, customers pay per track, regardless of how long the track is, up to a limit - then they pay double, triple or more, depending on some rules that make sense to those who decide on the pricing, but that leave customers quite confused and unsure of what they get for their money. Or often, it is a fixed album price, regardless if it is 39 minutes or 82. Hmm…

It's the same with postage. I know it's not only me that gets irritated when one has to pay double postage just because the letter weighs 21 grammes, 1 gram over the 20 gram limit. So, for this 1 gram one pays the postage for a further 29 grammes, since the next limit is 50 grammes.

At eClassical we have decided to rethink the whole pricing system, and so from now on, you pay for precisely what you buy, not more, not less. This is done by charging per second, and the charge is set at a level where a normal album will not be more expensive than before, rather very often the contrary. The per second price in US$ is 0.2-0.3 cent/sec, which works out at 8.40-12.60 for a 70-minute album. In 24-bit these numbers are 0.3-0.55 cents/sec or 12.60-23.10 for a 70-minute album.

So you can forget about tracks and track durations, or albums and their durations. You can just buy whatever you want to have, from any album, and, the way this works out, you get what you pay for!"

Pristine Classical; *pristineclassical.com*

FLAC and MP3, also CDs, also high-quality streaming; Also sells *The Pristine Audio Digital Music Collection*

From their website:

"PristineClassical.com was launched in 2005. We specialize in bringing classic historic recordings back to life using cutting edge digital technology and making them available as high quality downloads and on compact disc. 12,000+ unique, remastered classics; 2,500+ composers, ensembles, and artists; 1,000 exclusive Pristine Streaming tracks. Listen in either 320kbps MP3 or high-quality FLAC."

This interesting company offers what they call *The Pristine Audio Digital Music Collection* (about $1120).

"Delivered to you on a 1TB (1000 GB) plug-and-play high quality pocket-sized 2.5-in high speed USB 3 external hard drive. Simply plug into your PC, Mac or compatible digital music player and you've got the lot - all our Pristine album releases (well over 800 at the time of writing) as 16-bit and, where applicable, audiophile 24-bit FLAC formats - plus all our Pristine Exclusives (in

MP3 format). This includes mono and Ambient Stereo versions where applicable - it really is everything. The drive is DRM-free - copy it to your own system, make CDs from it, use it as you wish. It's big on the inside but it's small enough on the outside to slip into your pocket.

"KEEP UP TO DATE BY SUBSCRIBING - Purchasers of the Digital Music Collection are eligible for our updates service. For just €20/month (plus €5 shipping) you'll get a DVD (or two!) through the post every month with all our latest releases, as well as free unlimited download access to our entire site so you don't have to wait for the postman and full access to Pristine Streaming. This special subscription option will be enabled in your Account Subscriptions section after you've purchased a Pristine Audio Digital Music Collection."

An awesome project. We should wish them well.

HDTracks; *hdtracks.com*
Downloads of FLAC and AIFF (many hi-res), MP3
From their website:
"HDtracks is the premiere online music store for audiophiles who demand the best sounding music. It is our purpose to provide the largest online library of studio-quality high-resolution music downloads complete with liner notes. We believe a great recording is not only the tracks of sound, but also the creative collaboration of composers, producers, musicians, recording engineers, annotation writers, and visual artists. We feel strongly that not only everyone involved in the creative process is recognized for their work, but that music consumers be able to learn about the people involved in the production of the music and therefore participate in a deeper understanding of the music. HDtracks provides audiophiles who demand the highest quality recordings with an online experience not available anywhere else. We offer 'high definition' audio in FLAC format, ... We also offer AIFF formats and only the highest quality MP3 formats at 320k for some of the albums in our catalog."

Classical Archives; *classicalarchives.com*
MP3; $80 per year
Bills itself as "The Largest Classical Music Site in the World." Interesting site. You can listen to anything they have, but MP3-only downloads is a minus.

Streaming

'Streaming' is the display of a form of multimedia—text, images, audio, video or animation—to a viewer via the internet. *This is the most popular way for the majority of people to experience their music.* But classical aficionados? Not so much. Yet. At least for audio-only. Video is a different story.

Seems like everybody has a big screen and a fast connection, and it's a rare classical or opera, even ballet performance of high-caliber these days that is not video recorded in hi-def. It's another revenue stream for orchestras, though it may be cutting into live ticket sales, the logic being why bother with the hassle and expense of going to the game when you can watch it on TV.

Streaming is different from downloading in that what is being streamed can be watched or listened to as it arrives on a computer or other device but is not saved there. Watching television or listening to a radio program or a podcast on the internet are common examples of 'streamed media.' Spotify, Pandora, Google Play, Amazon and Apple Music are prime examples of top-tier streamers at present.

Streaming has revolutionized the way the world listens to music, but it has failed to revolutionize classical music. (It shall. It's inevitable.) One reason is that I suspect classical listeners are more prone to collecting than listeners of other genres. Another reason has to do with *metadata.*

Metadata refers to the descriptions for files that are embedded into any song or piece. For a pop song, that includes artist, song name and the album, which has become the standard formula artists must follow when submitting a track to digital music services. Things tend to get a little more complicated with classical tracks. The composer, piece title and album name are important, but so are things like the conductor, the ensemble or the soloists performing. Often these data are ignored or implemented poorly. Also, the number of tracks in a work has caused difficulties in implementation. Consider the *Goldberg Variations* by Bach. Is that 34 separate 'songs' at a dollar each? Yikes! On some services, a symphony is considered four separate 'songs.' The better sites have claimed to solve these problems.

For classical music folks there are different sorts of streaming.

- *Internet radio station*—you get what they choose to play. You're essentially 'listening to the radio.' Do you have a favorite classical music station? Go to the website and press the LISTEN NOW button. Ta Da! You're streaming. Sometimes the stations, such as CBC, will offer alternative streams of music from specific genres.

- *Genre-specific streaming*—some websites, such as Classical Radio (classicalradio.com) or Your Classical (yourclassical.org) and Naxos (naxos.com; $20 per year) let you choose among streams of music representing one of sometimes dozens of different genres and sub-genres of classical music. They offer their wares in typical compressed format, but Classical Radio will give you better-quality compressed music for a nominal subscription fee.

- *Recording-specific streaming*—these two sites have large libraries and good search engines that allow you to zero in and listen to any specific recording of whatever specific work suits your fancy at the moment. They will also stream in a specific genre. These sites offer lossless FLAC files as their format. At this writing, Idagio and Primephonic are the leaders in their field.

- *Video streaming*—concerts, opera, ballet, recitals, interviews, even master classes are making strong inroads into enthusiasts' viewing rooms. Almost all major orchestras and many chamber music organizations offer this service, both the live streaming of concerts and usually a rich collection of archival material available on-demand. Almost all charge a fee for the privilege. This is the future.

Audio and Video Classical Streaming Service

Idagio; *idagio.com*

Idagio offers a free account option, compressed at 192Mbps. The free tier plays occasional ads between tracks. It's radio play only, no video offered. For $10-per-month you get on-demand audio streaming and true lossless quality. Highest level is $16.67 per month and offers on-demand audio streaming and true lossless quality, and includes all upcoming and archived video concert performances. These are top-tier concerts and recitals from around the world.

From their website:

"Chosen by Time as one of the best inventions of 2019, IDAGIO is the world's leading streaming service for classical music. It offers video and audio streaming to music lovers in over 160 countries worldwide. Its acclaimed audio streaming service is uniquely tailored to the demands of classical music, featuring optimized meta-data and complemented by curation by music-lovers for music-lovers.

IDAGIO's Global Concert Concert Hall, launched in 2020, offers access to live and pre-recorded concerts from around the world. Artists and ensembles that have appeared in the Global Concert Hall include: Yo-Yo Ma, Emanuel Ax, Julia Bullock, Miloš Karadaglić, Mirga Gražinytė-Tyla, Zubin Mehta, The King's Singers, Vienna Philharmonic, Orchestra dell'Accademia Nazionale di Santa Cecilia, Philharmonia Orchestra and many more.

All artists on IDAGIO benefit from IDAGIO's Fair Pay Model: up to 80% of net profits from the Global Concert Hall go directly to the performers; audio stream revenue is calculated not by stream but by the second, making for a much fairer remuneration model.

A word about two giants: Apple Music and Spotify. Right now, they use high levels of compression and are not easy to navigate. Lossless options are on the near horizon for Spotify, but classical offerings will likely be a back-burner scenario, and confidence is not high for ease-of-use for the classical user. Apple has already introduced it's 'lossless' service but there are issues. You can't really stream the audio without some type of signal processing going on that makes the music different from the lossless version on CD and on other lossless services. Some suspect 'digital watermarking' which is a form of tracking and copyright protection. In addition, it's not possible to get a consistent lossless stream for much of the music Apple claims is 'lossless.' I do not recommend either service for classical music. Also, Apple has purchased Idagio's only real competitor, Primephonic. Expectations for Apple to make it into an awesome classical streaming service, considering Apple's history, are not high.

Video Classical Streaming Services

marquee.tv

marquee.tv

$100 per year.

From their website:

"Marquee TV is a streaming service that allows our members to watch a wide variety of award-winning and critically acclaimed dance, opera, music, and theater performances on internet-connected devices. In our ongoing efforts to support the performing arts, live and special events are also available for an additional fee. There are no advertisements, so your four-hour opera isn't extended to five!

- 7-day free trial for new subscribers
- Unlimited HD Streaming

- Enjoy on web, Apple TV, iOS, Android, Android TV, Fire TV and Roku
- Download & watch on the go on mobile devices
- Up to 3 simultaneous streams"

medici.tv
medici.tv
$105 for the first year; $149 per year, after that.
From their website:
"The world's leading classical music channel, medici.tv has offered access to the best of classical music to viewers worldwide since 2008.

More than 150 live events are broadcast each year, in partnership with the world's most prestigious venues, opera houses, festivals and competitions...

medici.tv's library features over 2,000 programs (3,000 original works), including: concerts and archived historical concerts; operas; ballets; documentaries, artist portraits and educational programs; master classes.

... medici.tv is available in English and French on all screens: PC, Mac, mobiles, tablets (iOs and Android) and television via AirPlay or Chromecast."

They are a little cagey about sound quality, but there are few complains.
From their website:
"We offer 5 different video stream qualities - low bitrate to high definition - in order to ensure all types of connections, from 3G to fiber. The video bitrate is adaptative: by default, it is best that can be accepted by the user's connection. In this way, the user benefits from the best service he can expect. The audio bitrate remains constant, so the audio quality is always at its very best. All our videos are encoded in mp4, H. 264 codec for video and AAC for audio."

Here follows a non-exhaustive listing of video streaming services of opera, ballet, and classical music. If you have a favorite orchestra or arts group not on this list, go to their website and see if they are set up for streaming. If they aren't now, it's likely that they will be soon. Some are pricey, some are free. Thanks to the excellent Playbill *Magazine (playbill.com) for some of these listings.*

OPERA
Met Opera
New York's Metropolitan Opera offers On Demand subscription plans at $14.99/month and $149.99/year for its library of over 600 performances, viewable on iOS devices, Apple TV, Android Roku and Samsung Smart TV. Additionally, a different recorded performance is being streamed for free on the Metropolitan Opera's website every night.

Vienna State Opera
Offering over 40 productions, the Vienna State Opera charges $16 for live/new performances and $6 for archived performances.

OperaVision
Live/Demand
OperaVision represents 30 opera companies from 18 countries in Europe, including upcoming operas for free.

PBS - Great Performances and Live at Lincoln Center
(or your local PBS station)
PBS offers an assortment of operas, concerts and dance performances under the Great Performances and Live at Lincoln Center banners. The search feature of the PBS site can help unearth video treasures. PBS's flagship NYC affiliate Channel 13 also offers video content.

Arte
The French/German cultural channel, Arte has a site for their live and On Demand streams of concerts and opera.

Culture Box
French TV's site archives broadcasts of opera and classical events for a limited time.

Staatsoper.TV (Bayerische Staatsoper)
Free live streams of opera and ballet from Staatsoper Unter den Linden, the home of the Berlin State Opera.

Royal Opera House
The Royal Opera House is offering free streams of recorded performances every week.

CLASSICAL MUSIC
Berlin Philharmonic
With over 40 live concerts in the season. It has also recently developed an archive of filmed performances.

New York Philharmonic
The New York Philharmonic "Watch and Listen" has recorded concerts but also artist Interviews and "Behind-the-Scenes" features.

The Royal Concertgebouw Orchestra
The Netherlands' Royal Concertgebouw orchestra recently opened their own "Watch & Listen" site with a large selection of concerts recorded at the famed concert hall.

Detroit Symphony Orchestra
Free live concert streaming, but access to their library, with several videos, requires an orchestra donation.

Gothenburg Symphony
The Swedish symphony orchestra streams almost all concerts live for free—seven or eight events monthly. A rich archive is available and particularly interesting are videos of encores by solo stars.

Bergen Philharmonic Orchestra
There are several concerts available for viewing On Demand and every month or so one performance is streamed live.

Carnegie Hall
"Carnegie Hall Fridays" will stream performances most Fridays.

DANCE
New York City Ballet
Free streams of recorded performances are offered.

San Francisco Ballet
Free streams of recorded performances.

CR

A Note about
Music Reproduction Hardware

An in-depth discussion of audio equipment is outside the scope of this book, but a few observations on the topic may be in order.

An astonishing thing happened to me some years ago. I owned a miserable old car that sported an FM/cassette deck. It was supposed to be stereo, but since I kicked my foot through the speaker in my door, I had to put the mono switch on so that I could hear the whole signal through the other door speaker. There was this Saturday-afternoon-old-opera-record type show on, and since I had to wait for my wife anyway, I thought it would be amusing to listen to it.

It was. They were playing old acoustic recordings from the first decade of the 1900s. First, they played an aria by some Romantic Italian guy, sung by this baritone. For some reason that I can't explain, I felt like he was standing next to me, and that everything that was important in his performance I felt with great precision. He sounded alive. This was from 1908, but the purely musical experience of that moment completely transcended any consideration of the equipment through which I was obliged to listen.

It seems paradoxical, particularly if you've just blown a wad on some nice new audiophile equipment, that the equipment might not matter as much as we'd hoped, or that musical enjoyment doesn't always improve with the 'specs' of your system. The necrophiliac tendencies of the audiophile too often means attending autopsies rather than enjoying music.

When faced with a choice between a great performance and a lesser one, no matter how good it's supposed to sound by the fashionable ears of the day, you are foolish to choose fashion.

But do I want to listen to my recordings through one mono speaker in my old Datsun? No thanks. Generally, I like to be comfortable and I enjoy good sound, though I also keep it in perspective. Odd how composers and musicians are rarely obsessed about obtaining top-line audio components for themselves. None of the audiophiles I know are musicians. Not a one. Nonmusicians with plenty of discretionary income are generally the ones who strive to duplicate the reality of the studio or a live performance; the initiated know that this is impossible and generally don't bother trying that hard. It's the difference between being in a savage battle and watching a war movie on TV. In the comfort of your viewing room, you can be certain that, no matter how 'realistic' the presentation, none of those bullets whizzing by have your name on it. Musicians know that a *recording* of music will never be music, any more than a painting of a landscape will be an actual landscape.

All that said, what equipment does one require these days to enjoy classical music? We need the music first. If it's on a CD, we need a CD player. Let's consider this example.

The audio hardware world is like anything else. It is designed to take as much money as you can afford to spend, but still not quite accept what you have settled for, and instead to long for what is just out of reach. To listen to CDs, you can use the disc player in your PC. Newer PCs sometimes come without, so you can buy an external USB CD/DVD player for $20. Or, if you listen via your home stereo equipment, you can spend between $30 and $75,000 for a player. It's the same story for every piece of audio equipment. Even interconnects—you know those pieces of wire that run from your CD-player to your pre-amp or amp? You can shell out anywhere between $4 and $400 for a three-foot length. Or maybe some nice $45,000 speaker cables. Not speakers. *Cables.* The system is designed to relieve you of your money to the degree of your wealth, gullibility, and/or sheer insanity.

No matter how much you spend you will never replicate a live musical performance in your listening space. There are simply too many forces at play in the creation and *witnessing* of a good musical performance to make that a possibility.

With this in mind, a sane approach, regardless of how much discretionary income you have, is to study the scene, read owners' comments, talk to folks, and most ideal, bring some source material you know and like with you to audition a few components at the local audio store. Keep in mind that the audition room at the audio store is *not* your listening room, and that whatever component you are auditioning is being played through cleverly-matched and incredibly expensive equipment. Also, note that a common error is to buy speakers and amps that are too big and powerful for your listening space.

Also look at used equipment, but some savvy is called for here. They are sold in audio shops and on the internet. You need to know what you're buying so read reviews of the product on the web before you do anything rash. Just about every piece of decent audio equipment ever made has had many owners and many published opinions are to be found. New does not equal good, but neither does old.

Don't be rushed into anything. Enjoy the process.

○੩

A GLOSSARY: FORMATS & FORMS

Large-Scale Formats

Ambient Music—a piece for instruments, electronics, natural sounds and/or voices, meant to provide a sonic background. Successful examples may be listened to carefully or almost completely ignored to equally good effect.

Ballet—music, almost always orchestral or instrumental, sometimes electronic, used to accompany a dance.

Concerto—the usual meaning is of a solo instrument interacting (sometimes singing together, sometimes in conflict) with a larger ensemble or orchestra. Since the Baroque era these have usually been in three movements—slow/fast/slow—with ample display of virtuosity on the soloist's part, often allowing for sections of improvisation (called a **Cadenza**). There is much variation here. There are double and triple concertos featuring two or three solo instruments, also concertos for orchestra which spotlight entire sections throughout the work.

Concerto Grosso—a form of (usually) Baroque music in which the musical material is passed between a small group of soloists (the *concertino*) and full orchestra (the *ripieno*). There are two forms of the concerto grosso, the *concerto da chiesa* (Church concert) which usually had more slow sections and fast sections that were not as frivolous as, the *concerto da camera* (chamber concert) which was often a suite of dance pieces.

Divertimento—always light-hearted, usually 18th century music for small ensemble. No specific format, but usually multi-movement.

Madrigal—a secular text or poem sung by a multi-part choir in the vernacular, as opposed to sacred texts sung in Latin, which is the **Motet**. Usually, but not always, unaccompanied by instruments.

Mass—a musical setting, purely vocal or vocal and/or choral with instruments, of some of the main portions of the Catholic Mass service. They usually include at the core the Kyrie, Gloria, Credo, Sanctus and Agnus Dei. Other sections may be included, with or without instrumental interludes.

Motet—a setting in Latin from the Bible or other authorized texts of the Catholic Church sung by a multi-part choir. Usually, but not always, unaccompanied by instruments.

Cantata—Usually sacred but sometimes secular texts set in Latin or the vernacular, in multiple sections sung by one or more soloists and/or chorus with instrumental accompaniment.

Opera—staged musical play of a secular nature (a sacred music drama is called an **Oratorio**), comic or tragic, completely sung throughout, accompanied by instruments, and in the vernacular. There are usually multiple vocalists acting their parts and a chorus is usually included. The form has been with us, thriving, since about 1600.

Oratorio—a sacred opera, in Latin or the vernacular. Often presented in concert rather than fully staged.

Organum—a Gregorian chant melody with at least one added voice to enhance the texture, developed in the Middle Ages and pretty much dying therein. This added voice is often identical to the main voice, entering later. Organum was originally improvised; while one singer performed a notated melody (the *vox principalis*), another singer, singing 'by ear,' provided the unnotated second melody (the *vox organalis*). Over time, composers began to write added parts that were not just simple transpositions, thus creating harmonies of true polyphony. Eventually more vocal parts were added, creating the **Motet**.

Partita—mostly Baroque (appearing less frequently in later eras), essentially a suite composed of dance forms, but often less frivolous in nature than a dance suite. Usually composed for a single instrument, often keyboard.

Requiem—a Mass or service, sacred or secular, for the dead.

Serenade—strictly speaking, a musical greeting performed for a lover, friend, person of rank or another person to be honored. The classic usage would be from a lover to his lady love through a window. The custom of serenading in this manner began in the Medieval era. Music performed followed no one particular form, except that it was typically sung by one person accompanying himself on a portable instrument, most likely a guitar, lute or other plucked instrument. Later composers would write serenades for larger ensembles, even the entire orchestra and in multiple movements. They are, in any case, typically serene, light pieces of music.

Sinfonia concertante—an orchestral work, normally in several movements, in which solo instruments, generally two or more, contend with the full orchestra. It emerged as a musical form during the Classical period as an evolution of the Baroque **Concerto Grosso**. The sinfonia concertante itself evolved into the double and triple concertos of the Romantic period.

Sonata—literally, sonata means a piece played on an instrument rather than sung. The term is vague. It can refer to a 2-minute piece for harpsichord by Scarlatti, or a half-hour multi-movement piece from the Romantic era written for solo instrument with piano accompaniment. Don't conflate *sonata* with sonata form, sometimes called **Sonata-Allegro Form**. More on that below in *Forms*.

String Quartet—the most important of the chamber music formats. (Others include the string trio, piano trio, sonatas for solo instrument and piano, woodwind quintets—pretty much every combo imaginable, but the string quartet holds a special place due to some ineffable archetypal quality that composers have become enchanted by.) Haydn is most responsible for the cultivation of the format, wring more than 80 fine examples that are still played today. The string quartet is almost exclusively comprised of two violins, viola and cello. Classical versions are in four movements, though in time this became more flexible.

The Classical era was about *balance*. Here follows an excellent illustration of the difference between balance and symmetry, courtesy of Haydn himself.

When he was first experimenting with his new-fangled string quartet idea, the formula he used was: fast/slow/fast/slow/fast. Perfect balance, right? Wrong. Symmetry is not balance. It is not mindless schematics. So, he was dissatisfied and reworked the scheme and eventually settled on this:

I. Fast. (Sonata-allegro form)
II. Slow
III. Minuet and Trio
IV. Fast. (Rondo or Sonata-allegro form)

Now *that* is balance. *That* is Classical.

Suite—a multi-movement work for solo instrument, instrumental ensemble or orchestra often comprised of dance forms.

Symphony—a work for orchestra usually in four movements, often in the format of fast/slow/minuet-or-scherzo-usually-in-triple-meter/finale. There are many exceptions and variations. The Classical and Romantic eras were the heyday for the format, which had lost its grip from the Modern era though they are still written today.

Tone Poem—a work for orchestra, usually in one movement, that suggest a story, or a sound painting of a thing or idea, as opposed to abstract music. An important format in the Romantic era, embraced by composers of almost every Western nation.

Trio Sonata—a genre typically consisting of three or four movements with two contrasting melody instruments and a bass or accompaniment section consisting of cello and harpsichord. (Wait! Isn't that four people? Yes, but there are only three parts, hence the designation trio—the two solo instruments and the **Continuo**, or accompaniment.) Originating in the early 17th century, the trio sonata was a favorite chamber ensemble combination in the Baroque.

CR

Forms *(what large-scale formats are made from, though they may stand alone)*

Allemande—French word for 'German dance.' Often used as the first movement of a Baroque dance suite. A succinct description is impossible as it has gone through so many reworkings and alterations over the centuries of its use and meant different things to different composers.

Aria—a self-contained piece for one voice, usually with, but sometimes without instrumental or orchestral accompaniment. Normally part of a larger work, usually an opera but also oratorio or cantata. Originally used to refer to any expressive melody, usually, but not always, performed by a singer.

Bagatelle—literally means a short unpretentious instrumental composition. Usually for a piano but there are bagatelles for almost everything. Beethoven's three sets are the most famed.

Ballade—can refer to one of two forms. Since the late 18th century, ballade refers to a setting of a literary ballad, a narrative poem, in the musical tradition of the **Lied** (see below). It also refers to a one-movement instrumental piece with lyrical and dramatic narrative qualities reminiscent of such a song setting, especially a piano ballad. Those by Chopin and Brahms are best known.

Cadenza—a usually elaborate flourish or showy passage introduced, often extemporaneously, just before the end of a movement in a **Concerto**. Before Beethoven, the burden of creating the content of a cadenza was often the soloist's own. This is his or her big chance to strut their stuff, both in the music they come up with (which should have some thematic connection to the music of the movement the cadenza is in) and the virtuosity they call forth in their execution. Some of today's greatest soloists improvise their cadenzas on-the-spot; some work them out beforehand; others use cadenzas written out by others. Beethoven, sick of bad cadenzas, wrote his own into the works, which always seemed to me to be contrary to the spirit of a cadenza and a bad move historically. Most composer thereafter followed suit. But the best performers often still roll their own.

Canon—a contrapuntal (counterpoint-based) compositional technique that employs a melody with one or more exact imitations of the melody which enter after a given duration (e.g., quarter rest, one measure, etc.). The initial melody is called the leader (or *dux*), while the imitative melody, which is played in a different voice, is called the follower (or *comes*). The simplest form of canon is called a round. *Row, Row, Row Your Boat* and *Frère Jacques* are popular examples. For this simplest of contrapuntal forms, there are all sorts of variations and transformations to apply to the form and still adhere to the main definition. These transformations can be found under the **Fugue** section.

Caprice—or *capriccio* is a piece of music usually free in form and of a lively character, typically fast, intense and often virtuosic in nature.

Carol—usually refers to a festive or holiday song, generally religious but not necessarily connected with Church worship, and often with a popular character. It may be sung as a one-part song or harmonized. Today the carol is represented almost exclusively by the Christmas carol but despite their present association with religion, it has not always been so.

Chaconne—popular in the Baroque era, it was used as a vehicle for variation on a repeated short harmonic progression, often involving a short repetitive bass-line (*ground bass*) which offered a basis for variation, decoration, figuration and melodic invention. In this it closely resembles the **Passacaglia**.

Chanson—usually means a French art song of the Middle Ages and the Renaissance, but the idea and essence of this sort of song—more serious and artsy that a mere pop offering—still abides today.

Courante—a triple meter dance from the late Renaissance and the Baroque era. In a Baroque dance suite an Italian or French courante is typically paired with a preceding **Allemande**, making it the second movement of the suite or the third if there is a **Prelude**.

Étude—designed to highlight a particular technical aspect for the performer to master, usually a rather short piece and of considerable difficulty. Began in the early 19th century with the rapidly growing popularity of the piano. Of the vast number of études from that era some are still (unfortunately) used as teaching material (particularly pieces by Czerny and Clementi—not of the first rank, so why would one bother?), and a few by major composers such as Chopin, Liszt and Debussy (yes, yes and yes). These have righteously achieved a place in today's concert repertory.

Fantasia—it means 'fantasy.' No definition. No rules.

Fugue—The fugue is the pinnacle of Baroque-era formal development. To truly appreciate the music of the High Baroque without some understanding of fugue is not possible. We may be seduced on the level of 'just liking how it sounds,' but the conscious understanding of what is taking place formally adds an essential dimension to true appreciation.

The focus of the fugue is its *subject*. Like any essay, it must be 'about' something. A fugue is about its subject. A fugue opens by the simple statement of the subject by a single instrumental or vocal line, no harmony or accompaniment, just a single line which we shall call a voice. A fugue can contain any number of voices though the three-voice and four-voice fugues are the most common.

A fugue subject can consist of any number of notes in any rhythm; it may be a simple melody or a very severe plastic theme that is simply easy to work with and open to many possible operations, which will be described below.

After the first voice has stated the subject, the second voice enters. It must enter with the exact statement of the same subject. This second voice usually enters in a different key, and usually that key is the *dominant* of the first voice's key (which is called the tonic). For example, if the fugue began in C major (the tonic), the second statement would be in G major (the dominant). Any time after the second voice has completed its statement of the subject a third voice may enter the picture. When it does, it must state the same subject upon entering. Usually the third voice enters in the original key, but an octave higher or lower. In our example, that would again be C major. After this third voice states the subject then a fourth voice may enter, again of course—with the exact quotation of the subject, and usually in the dominant key, like the second voice (G major in our example).

Of course, while the voices are entering with the subject, the voices which have already stated the subject are not silent. There are a great many possibilities for what they will be up to. Sometimes they simply give harmony to the subject's entrance in another voice. Sometimes they become a bass line. Sometimes they're silent. Sometimes they will introduce a *counter-subject* while waiting for all the voices to enter with the subject. This counter-subject may see some reappearances and development later in the piece.

When all the operative voices are in play (that is, when the last voice has entered with the subject statement), then this signals the end of the first part or *exposition* of the fugue. The exposition can be compared to the opening section of an essay, wherein the subject is stated, and some of its future ramifications are implied. No development or explanation has been offered, no data to support the case, and no conclusion offered. The case has just been stated. That's all. Some fugues end here. They are called short-fugues or *fughettas*.

After the exposition, a development section may ensue. Here, the subject may undergo several operations. In one or another of the voices the subject may be changed to a minor key from the original major key (or vice versa, of course). The subject may be broken up into fragments, and these fragments may be developed. Besides these, there are a small number of other transformations which may take place.

- *Augmentation*—This is the doubling (rarely, trebling) of the note values in any statement of the subject. Half notes become whole notes, quarters become halves, etc. This makes the subject twice as long, because twice as slow.

- *Diminution* (its opposite)—This is the halving (rarely more) of the note values in any statement of the subject. Whole notes become half notes, halves become quarters, etc. This makes the subject half as long, because twice as fast.

- *Inversion*—This is the turning upside down of the subject, as in a mirror lying along the bottom of the staff and reflecting the subject. Notes that went up now go down by the same interval. Notes that went down now go up, by the same amount or interval. Note that the original rhythm is preserved.

- *Retrograde*—This is the statement of the subject back-to-front. Note that the original rhythm is not preserved because it is stated backwards.

- *Mensuration* or *Prolation*—this refers to one or more of the subsequent voices entering in some rhythmic value other than half (which would make it a fugue voice in *diminution*) or double (which would make it a fugue voice in *augmentation*). It can be any ratio. These are tricky to pull off.

One can combine the above operations. There are, for example, retrograde inverted fugues in augmentation. (Incidentally, the normal, upright, forward, original rhythm form of the subject is called the *rectus* form.)

This leaves one final feature to be discussed. The *stretto*. The stretto is the overlapping of the statements of the subject. That is, before one voice finishes the statement of the subject, another voice enters with a statement of the subject. In a double-stretto, a voice will enter with the subject, but before it finishes the statement, two voices will have entered at different times with the overlapping subject statement.

Some of the above operations are implied in any chosen subject. Some are not as well suited. A good composer can look at a theme and quickly sum up the possibilities implicit therein. The composer must be careful not to overwork a subject, or to be too obvious with his treatment. That is why the working out of a fugue subject into a piece of music is called 'solving' the fugue or offering a 'solution' to the subject.

Though not a brief explanation, the above offers only the barest outline of the infinite possibilities inherent in the powerful form of the fugue—the apotheosis of Baroque-era musical thought.

Galliard—a lively dance in triple time for two people, including complicated turns and steps. Popular all over Europe in the 16th century and used in conjunction with the **Pavane** in many Renaissance instrumental and keyboard compositions, and later as a dance in Baroque suites.

Gavotte—medium-paced French dance, popular in the 18th century, never in triple time, beginning on the third beat of the bar.

Gigue—a lively Baroque dance derived from the Irish jig. It was imported into France in the mid-17th century and usually appears at the end of a suite. A gigue is usually in 3/8, 6/8 or 12/8 time.

Ground Bass—also *bass ostinato*. A usually short motif in the bass that is constantly repeated as the other parts of the music vary. Provides the basis underlying variations as the motif repeats.

Impromptu—a free-form composition with the character of an improvisation, as if prompted by the spirit of the moment, usually for a solo piano. Chopin and Schubert have masterful examples.

Intermezzo—an intermission piece, often inserted between acts of a play or opera scenes, often to allow for scene changes.

325

Lied—a setting of a German poem as a song, especially of the Romantic period, typically for solo voice with piano accompaniment.

March—a piece of music with a strong regular rhythm in 4/4 time which, in origin, was expressly written for marching to and most frequently performed by a military band, though there are marches for most instruments and ensembles, including many for the piano. In mood, marches range from the death march to the brisk military marches of John Philip Sousa and the martial hymns of the late 19ᵗʰ century.

Mazurka—a Polish folk dance in triple meter, usually at a lively tempo, and with strong accents often alternating on the second or third beat. Chopin wrote many masterworks in the genre for piano.

Minuet—a slow, stately ballroom dance to be danced as a couple, in 3/4 time. Dominated aristocratic European ballrooms especially in the 18ᵗʰ century.

Nocturne—piece of music inspired by, or evocative of, the night. Solo piano versions are best known. John Field invented the form, Chopin perfected it.

Passacaglia—like the **Chaconne**, with which it is often conflated, this was popular in the Baroque era, often used as a vehicle for variation on a short repetitive bass-line (*ground bass*) which offered a basis for variation, decoration, figuration and melodic invention. So, it's very much like the *chaconne*, but the passacaglia is usually considered to be of a more solemn character than the chaconne. The only real difference between the two seems to be that in the chaconne the theme is always kept in the bass, while in the passacaglia it could appear in any part, often so disguised and embroidered amid ever varying contrapuntal devices as to become hardly recognizable.

Passepied—a lively dance, sort of a fast waltz, originating on Brittany and adopted around 1650 by French and English aristocrats, who, during the century of its popularity, frequently danced it dressed as shepherds and shepherdesses. For some reason. Used as a movement in Baroque dance suites.

Pavane—a stately, processional dance, sometimes performed in church on solemn occasions, in slow 2/4 or 4/4 meter, popular in the Renaissance and often performed in elaborate clothing. Outside of church, it was often followed by its afterdance, the **Galliard**. This pair of dances was a popular format in Renaissance instrumental and keyboard music and is considered a forerunner of the instrumental dance suite in the Baroque era. Later, the pavane would stand on its own in notable works by Ravel and Fauré.

Polonaise—a stately processional dance of Polish origin in triple time, performed by couples who walk around the dance hall; the music is in triple meter and moderate tempo. Often used from the 17th to 19th century to inaugurate court balls and other royal functions.

Prelude—a short piece of music, the form of which may vary. The prelude may be thought of as a preface. During the Baroque era it often served as an introduction to a succeeding movement or movements of a work that were longer and more complex, often as in *Prelude & Fugue*, or placed at the head of a dance suite. During the Romanic era, it was often a stand-alone piece of music, usually for the piano. Stylistically, the prelude is usually improvisatory in nature. (A good instrumental player, a guitarist, for example, would not just tune his instrument on stage, he would do some 'preluding,' in which he would tune and check his instrument but do it in a way that appeared to be an interesting improvisation.)

Rhapsody—a single movement piece with no definite structure. In that sense rhapsodies can be considered like fantasias, as both types of pieces display features of improvised music. Rhapsodies, however, tend to be more episodic and flighty, often making extreme contrasts in terms of tonality and mood.

Ricercar—an often elaborate instrumental composition in fugal or canonic style, typically of the 16th to 18th centuries. A flimsy term, however, as it was also used for works in free fantasy as well as highly contrapuntal works.

Recitative—musical declamation of the kind usual in the narrative and dialogue parts of opera, oratorio and cantata, sung in the rhythm of ordinary speech with many words on the same note. Since operas are by nature thoroughly composed, as in—music all the way through—recitative is used instead of speaking. Speaking is reserved for musical theatre such as we call the *musical* here in America and the Germans call the *singspiel. The Magic Flute* of Mozart is a singspiel, not an opera.

Rondo—an instrumental form characterized by the initial section and subsequent restatement of that section, the various statements of which are separated by contrasting material. Let me put it another way: A-B-A-C-A-B-A, for example. The A section of the work returns (sometimes altered but recognizable) but in this case different material is inserted before each return of the A section. It was a very popular form during the Classical period, often used as the last movement in a concerto or a sonata. Free-standing rondos were also popular concert pieces. It's a fun form that is not intellectually taxing.

Sarabande—a slow, stately dance in triple time. It went through many permutations, starting off as a rather vulgar dance to castanets done by amorous couples. It was actually banned in some places. But by the time it hit the courts of France in the early 1600s it became the slow, serious processional dance in 3/2 time that we find in instrumental and keyboard suites in the 18th-century. It was often the third movement in these suites.

Scherzo—it means 'joke.' It replaced the minuet as the third movement in four-movement symphonies around the time of Beethoven. Still usually in triple time, it is more robust (but still playful) than the courtly, wimpy (and old-fashioned) **Minuet.**

Sinfonia—in the 17th and 18th centuries an orchestral piece in one movement used as an introduction, interlude, or postlude to an opera, oratorio, cantata or suite. When used in the more modern eras it refers to a small orchestral work.

Sonata-Allegro—(or *sonata form*, or *first-movement form*) is a musical structure consisting of three main sections: an *exposition*, a *development* and a *recapitulation*. It has been used widely since the early Classical period as the form of choice for most first movements of multi-movement works such as symphonies and sonatas, and often final movements as well. It is so important that, like the *fugue*, it demands some elucidation.

- It may begin with an *introduction*, which is, in general, slower than the main movement. Haydn was famous for this in his later symphonies. In terms of structure, introductions are a little prelude to the main musical argument.

- The first required section is the *exposition.* The exposition presents the primary thematic material for the movement: one or two themes or theme groups, often in contrasting styles and in opposing keys, connected by a modulating transition.

- The exposition is followed by the *development* where the harmonic and textural implications of the thematic material are explored.

- The development then transitions back to the *recapitulation* where the thematic material returns in the main key of the piece.

- The movement may conclude with a *coda,* a little tail, beyond the closing of the recapitulation.

Toccata—is a virtuoso piece of music, typically for a keyboard or plucked string instrument, featuring fast-moving, lightly fingered or otherwise virtuosic passages or sections, with or without imitative or fugal interludes, generally emphasizing the performer's dexterity.

Waltz—as a dance it is characterized by a step, slide and step in 3/4 time. With its turning and embracing couples, the dance shocked polite society. It became the ballroom dance par excellence of the 19th-century and maintained its popularity in the 20th. There are many waltzes written for piano and for orchestra.

CR

THE FATE OF CLASSICAL MUSIC

When American pianist Van Cliburn won the *International Tchaikovsky Competition* in Moscow in 1958, the event rocked the world. Cliburn's performance of Tchaikovsky's *Piano Concerto No. 1* and Rachmaninoff's *Piano Concerto No. 3* earned him a standing ovation lasting eight minutes. After the ovation, Van Cliburn made a brief speech in Russian and then resumed his seat at the piano and began to play his own piano arrangement of the much-beloved song *Moscow Nights,* which further endeared him to the Russians. When it was time to announce the winner, the judges felt obliged to ask permission of the Soviet leader Nikita Khrushchev to give the first prize to an American.

"Is he the best?" Khrushchev asked.

"Yes."

"Then give him the prize!"

Cliburn returned home to a ticker-tape parade in New York City, the only time the honor has been accorded a classical musician.

A ticker-tape parade. For a classical musician. In New York City. This is literally *unimaginable* today.

'Classical Music' as we have known it here in the West for a hundred years or so—is on life support. That is not a bad development. That's a *good* development. Things either change or die, and a big change is in order.

The old structures are dying out. To put it in a nutshell: *there used to be a special kind of aura around the classical music scene. That aura is gone.*

The traditional bedrock of the classical scene—the symphony orchestra—is in decline and has in a way run its course. And those who are outraged at that statement may at least allow that it is surely not in its heyday. The same holds true with instrumental soloists. Gone are the days of 'legendary violinists' and 'giants of the keyboard.' Technical perfection is now routine and some of these incredible virtuosi possess charisma, but that doesn't mean they have character, intelligence or sagacity, and the savvy that it takes to differentiate a great artist from mere flash is an uncommon trait among listeners. The result is the perception of a certain 'sameness' about the players. A hilly landscape devoid of Himalayan peaks.

Many orchestras and classical performance organizations are in poor financial shape. They are simply not supportable by ticket sales. People just don't want to pay for what it all actually costs. We're losing these outfits faster than we are creating new ones.

Does that mean that soon we won't be hearing Beethoven and Brahms symphonies anymore? Of course not. It's just that you may have to drive farther to hear them, and the tickets may cost more.

Orchestras function mostly as museums now. Back in the Classical era, even throughout most of the 19th century, the concert hall was where new music was presented to eager audiences. I don't want to underplay the museum aspect, it's desirable, but if it's not more than that, it's doomed. It would be nice to say that the new music being programmed is attracting new listeners in droves, but it's simply not true, which reinforces the 'museum' aspect to keep these giant organizations afloat.

So why don't modern audiences like new music for orchestra? Because what is being presented is not as compelling to audiences as it used to be in earlier ages. I suspect that a lot of potentially interesting music is not given a chance because the composer must be a member of the club to be allowed admission, and many of these men and women may be writing listenable music but are not members of the club, and their orchestra music goes unplayed. There is way too much reliance on academic composers—the true card-carrying members of the club—but who have driven audiences from the concert hall more effectively than a cholera outbreak.

A popular exception to this has been Minimalism. But one reason why Minimalism was so successful and often programmed is because the need to rehearse the music is minimized. In other words, it's cheap to do. It's also easy on the ears—not much is demanded of the listener, and with today's record-setting short attention span audiences, that's just swell. Many complex works of intricate beauty are not programmed because lazy ears wander away, and for the bean-counters it takes orchestras too much time to get it right. Money is too tight.

An astute reader chimed in with a few good points. "We really need to stop insisting that orchestras are a critical indicator of the artistic health of classical music, as they are simply economically out of reach for too many communities, while chamber music still endures in festivals and tours that touch upon destinations where orchestras will never exist. Living composers have clearly adjusted the scope of their work to accommodate smaller forces, also offering the musicians a fresh assortment of styles and technical challenges."

I think these are great points, although I feel that the orchestra is a bellwether indicator of the status of the art form in general. I hope, as I so often do, that I am being too hard in my evaluation.

A new threat that hangs over the industry like the Sword of Damocles is the wretched curse of equity and political correctness. Put more women on the program! (Umm… does it matter which ones? It doesn't appear to.) Hire more Black orchestra musicians! (Instead of blind auditions?) Our new conductor has *got* to be a woman! No… a gay woman! Wait… in a wheelchair!!!

This nonsense is killing the art faster than another Covid scam. The moment quality takes a back seat to conforming to the PC Narrative the cancer takes hold.

At the start of this book I mentioned how very difficult it is, when pressed, to say exactly what classical music is. The reason that classical music is hard to define is that it's quite simply undefinable. Many aficionados would like to think of it as basically 'art music,' or 'serious music,' but this implies an incredible cultural bigotry at work, which only in the past decade has become terribly obvious. America is changing, the West is changing, the *world* is changing, and there is more to the idea of 'art music' than the traditional Western orchestra and its offshoot ensembles and soloists. New influences are coming to us and into all the genres from all over the world. And the 800-pound gorilla in the room is electronics and Artificial Intelligence (AI). It is sweeping through and even creating many genres on its own and may one day become the major influence on the sort of music concept we call 'classical.'

AI is in its infancy as regards the 'art' world, but it shall surely put most composers of video game music and film music out of business. AI already does an adequate job in those two arenas and the money saved is just too tempting not to put AI to use there. What about art music written as pure music? I have not heard anything remotely compelling in the sense of great music but that doesn't mean it won't happen. The whole question scares the bejesus out of me.

So who are the certified gatekeepers these days who get to say what 'art music' is and what it shall become?

Nobody, that's who.

So when the term 'classical music' falls apart under examination and the idea of an objective 'art music' goes up in smoke, what is left?

You are. *You* decide. It's part of humanity growing up.

All the Arts are still pretty much in the doldrums, praying for a stiff wind to fill the sails again. There needs to be a new impulse and until we get it, the arts in the West will continue to stagnate. It's not just music. The visual arts, even physics and philosophy have been stuck in the same rut for many decades. And what is literature doing that it hasn't done since e.e. cummings and James Joyce? How many ways can a sculptor hammer on a block of marble to make the sort of thing that has never been made before?

But recovery will not start with a stiff wind; it will be a wafting breeze, and I believe it may be happening right now. The latest generation is offering a hopeful glimpse into a new age. Catastrophe may necessarily precede it.

In music, what has not been done? From Gregorian Chant to electronic noises and chance music, what have we not tried? The era of Minimalism, a form nearly half a century old, is passing and being replaced by an anything-goes aesthetic that uses any method, tool and philosophy ever conjured throughout the centuries in any combination in order to create a compelling concert experience. We have gathered 1000 years of arrows for the quiver, to be used *ad libitum*. In the right hands, interesting music is starting to be created again. And these new artists seem to share a common trait: *To hell with schools and systems and shalls and shall-nots*. For that is the poison that has made so much of new music unlistenable for so many decades.

Technology will play a large part, for technology is coming that will be indistinguishable from magic. The art of combining the arts, the art of the *installation,* is about to enter a new stage. Four-dimensional spaces that feature an artistic area to meander through while the soundscape changes depending upon where you are, just as an example. Hard to pull off this sort of thing now, but that's the sort of thing on the horizon.

That's some good news. But the news isn't *all* good.

How the culture is evolving is the bad news. We've entered a time when what is biggest is considered best; instead of classics, we have best-sellers; instead of genius, technique; instead of real thought, mere information; instead of inner value, glittering externality; instead of sages, smart asses.

Let's examine the future audience. Consider the vast dumbing-down of America's youth and the mis-education of the young. They are not taught *how* to think, they are told *what* to think, and they are being taught this by 'educators' who are themselves not thinking very well. The ones who know what I am talking about are too terrified and intimidated to resist and they feel powerless to challenge the system. There are great teachers out there and *many* exceptions to this observation, but they are no longer the rule.

Children aren't taught the arts or philosophy. They're being trained sociologically, but how well are they being educated? This mis-education is being done quite systematically in order to raise the kind of people who are easy to manage and manipulate. Ever wonder why there are no required high school classes to the effect of 'How to manage money and not be a victim of a system that is designed to exploit you and bleed you dry'? The narrative that drives modern education is contrary to the formation of adults with life skills, courage and curiosity or with any refinement of aesthetic.

It's much easier and cheaper to just dumb them down. Why go through the trouble and expense of hearing live music when you can download an mp3? It's not as good, of course, but it's pretty good, I guess. Why spring for a decent sound system that at least *tries* to create the illusion of fidelity when these earbuds on my phone are… well… they're pretty good, I guess?

Does this sound off-topic? It isn't. The future of classical music is not divorced from the future of any high art. And the appreciation of high art is an activity of the *soul*, a spiritual activity. I did not say a *religious* activity. High art moves the soul, and the soul is being discounted and devalued as the insidious diseases of materialism and commercialism tighten their already brutal grip on the Western world. It's evident in the confusion and the anguish of the youth, the tantrum-inducing addiction to 'screen-time' in children, in the wastrel mindset of the digital hoarder, the drug addiction rate among children and adults to illegal *and legal* drugs, and a skyrocketing suicide rate.

Nothing 'material,' nothing you can grab and hold on to, can touch this deficit in the souls of so many contemporary Western men and women. This isn't 'off-topic'—we're talking about Art, what ought to be the most sacred form of expression and appreciation that mankind can muster. It's our umbilical cord to the Divine. And its near-future is bleak.

It's going to get worse before it gets better. It will be a dark time, but we will have to endure it as best we may in order to come out the other side. We'll have to learn our lessons and become weary and sick to our core of the soul-killing materialism that is bringing us low, and the banality and tedium of how we have been expressing ourselves in what we have been calling Art for the past many decades.

Can this be done in peace, or must there be a catastrophe? This is the 800-pound gorilla in *that* room. Still, I can feel the breeze. A new impulse is brewing in the Arts. But it requires a worthy audience large enough to sustain the art, and I'm not sure when, or even if, we will have one.

Sincere happy listening.

CRISOCRISO

Photo credits:

ORGAN SWELL: Photographer: Fabian Zohren, Aachen, Germany (edited by norro) - Photo of Fabian Zohren, Aachen, Germany, his own photo

RAUSCHPFEIFES: rauschpfeifes Sopranino (shorter) and soprano (longer) rauschpfeifes. Photograph taken by Mattmm on 7 May 2006.

SACKBUT: Multimann - Self-published work by Multimann

THEORBO: Given by Cezar MAteus (the author of the instrument) expressly for Wiki

https://creativecommons.org/licenses/by-sa/3.0/legalcode

Many thanks to Wikipedia for its many photos and some excellent insights into many artistic topics.

ABOUT GERALD BRENNAN

I was born on September 2, 1953, in Jessup, PA. At age two I moved to Dearborn, MI, where I lived with my family until my late teens. The eldest of six children, I went to Catholic school, and when my brain started working at about age 15, I left the Church, my youthful mind appalled by its many dogmas. Nor did the priests and nuns wish to indulge my curious nature. When we had philosophical questions, the answer was usually along the lines of "Shut up." It was in high school that I began to write down the music in my head.

Wandering in the desert for many years, I drank heavily, experimented with drugs, and studied music, science and philosophy. Though I never had any formal music education, living in Ann Arbor put many wonderful resources at my disposal, including many fine Steinway grands sprinkled merrily throughout the University of Michigan campus back in the day when there didn't need to be a lock on every door.

I became a good pianist in the following years, as well as composer. I had many musical adventures—breaking a Steinway grand playing Liszt at the University of Michigan music school, playing Liszt's American Steinway at the Smithsonian Museum in an impromptu recital that drew quite a wondrous crowd. I improvised madly (after all, this was Liszt's piano), and the crone that ran the joint nearly had a stroke as she screamed at me to STOP STOP!!! STOP!!! as I was summarily ejected from the premises. That was a real nice piano, incidentally. I may go on to fill a book with like tales, but not here.

I became a National Public Radio affiliate producer with WUOM, WVGR and WFUM out of the U-M. I produced hundreds of weekly programs in my decade there—including *The Musical Theatre, New Music, New Releases, From the Monophonic Era, Music of Our World, Excursions* and *Nocturne*. One of the highlights of my career as broadcaster included a carefully-engineered presentation of all nine symphonies of Beethoven, played *simultaneously*. In those days, it took two assistants, five turntables, four CD players, a few stopwatches and multiple attempts to get all that onto tape. The night it was premiered some listeners called the cops, who stormed the studios looking for Classical Music felons. There were many dozens of phone calls. Half the callers thought I was the coolest DJ ever; the other half wanted me dead, as soon as possible and as painfully as that could be accomplished. Now *that's* good radio.

In 1980 I organized the Ann Arbor-based Sinewave Studios for the development and propagation of new art music. I produced about 20 concerts and conducted the North American premier of Karlheinz Stockhausen's *Für kommende Zeiten* at the Detroit Institute of Art. I never asked Stockhausen's permission to do so and never paid him any royalties. I feel bad about that now that I am a creator who likes his own royalty money, but at the time it never occurred to me to pay him. Never even entered my head. You know when it *did* enter my head? *Years later when I was talking to him.* I considered, for the first time, as the words were coming out of my mouth, that I had never asked permission to do the premiere and never gave him a nickel. To his credit, he let it pass. This was contrary to his reputation, and I have always been grateful to him for that.

My writing career started in 1984 when I wrote and self-published a booklet on starting a classical record collection. Borders Books agreed to carry it, and it finally made its way into the paws of a publisher. They asked me to expand it into a sure enough book and thus was born *Classical Records, Starting Your Collection.* After it was published, I took it to the Ann Arbor News and asked them if they needed a music reviewer. Turned out they did, and so, all while I had the radio gig, I was reviewing the best acts in the world that came through town. It got old though, and when we radio producers all lost our jobs, I also quit reviewing. I found it to be spiritually corrosive to have to say negative things about other people's performances, even if they richly deserved it. That said, it did help feed me, my wife and my two kids.

Before all that I worked in record stores, including the famous Liberty Music. I also sold pianos, moved pianos, sold sheet music, managed U-M's record and sheet music store, and wrote for various national music journals.

In 1998, I was headhunted by a visionary fellow named Michael Erlewine, who decided that it would be a good idea to get hold of every album in the world and put every bit of information about it into a database. Eventually the idea included taking a photo of the album and doing sound samples. They started with a core of a few music geeks and began by going through their own collections. The company Erlewine founded was called All Media Guide (www.allmusic.com), which became the world's largest repository of product data and editorial information about music.

Erlewine asked me to assume the post of Director of Content of Classical Music at AMG, to create a department that would be devoted to Classical Music. I jumped at it, and in four years my amazing staff and I, along with scores of excellent writers, amassed the data, created the classical website, and produced the giant reference book, *AMG Guide to Classical Music,* which I edited and saw published in 2005. My mission was accomplished; my staff was a well-oiled machine and easily the best and happiest of all AMG's departments. Then 'investor fatigue' set in among the shareholders and AMG was appointed a slick new president who knew little about what we did or why but was hired to sell the company at a good price to whomever, and *fast*. He disliked me and my open resistance to his schemes and I was fired. I had no hard feelings. I had completed my mission and it was time to go.

Now I write music and books, make recordings and give the rare recital.

Books include this one, also *Prince of Pines*, a dystopian male-adventure novel set in Michigan's Upper Peninsula; *The Complete Short Stories;* the recent *The Angel Jophiel*, a fantasy novel about the Classical Music world and an angel sent to Earth to help rejuvenate the dying Arts, and *Song of Blood and Ashes*, a vampire tale set in contemporary Ireland and Ann Arbor. Also, *Views & Reviews Chronicles from the twilight of the Golden Age of Classical Music*. This book contains the original unedited versions of my previews, reviews, and interviews of the finest classical music soloists, ensembles, and orchestras in the world during what may well be looked back upon as the final flowering of Classical Music in the West. Also available is a quasi-autobio called *There was this guy once…*

Musically, I've to-date got 90 songs published in three *SongBooks*, many chamber and orchestral pieces, piano works, a full-length Broadway-style musical called *Penelope*, choral works, and a large orchestral piece known as *Sinfonia Matrix,* which requires some 80-octillion years to be heard in its entirety. Therefore, performance versions are extracted depending upon available forces, duration required and occasion.

Available CDs include *Mythos* (piano pieces based upon Greek myth characters, recorded in recital and in-studio), *Five Fantasy Nocturnes* for piano, *Campfire—The Burning Psaltery* (a phantasmagorical piece for an innocent 12-string psaltery), *7 Solo Songs from Penelope*, and several CDs from the *SongBooks* recorded in studio and at home, by me and various performers.

Also available on CD is the electronically-based *Ambient Music Series*, which includes *Ambient Counterpoint, Grand Starbells, Monochrome Frescos, The Singing Moon,* and *Whisperings of Angels*.

Not-actually-available is the CD of *Beethoven's Nine Symphonies Played Simultaneously*. This is a digital recreation of the earlier radio project, this time featuring John Eliot Gardiner conducting all nine at once in a carefully tailored orgy of magnificent aural splendor. Like nothing you ever heard or will hear again. Why not available for sale? Because it is also the most magnificent copyright violation of all time—nine in the space of one! See, I don't fancy ending up in Classical Music Prison. I'm a good-lookin' old guy and there's some mean hombres in there, especially the violists.

All items detailed above are published by DreamStreet Press and available on Amazon or through DreamStreetPress.com.

Other Books by Gerald Brennan

Jophiel

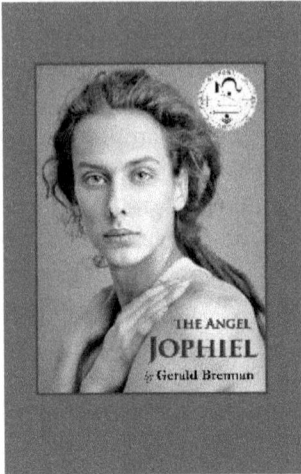

Jophiel, Angel of the Beauty of the Divine Presence, incarnates in a mid-western town to a lovely woman and her outlaw husband in this tale set in near-future America.

Prince of Pines

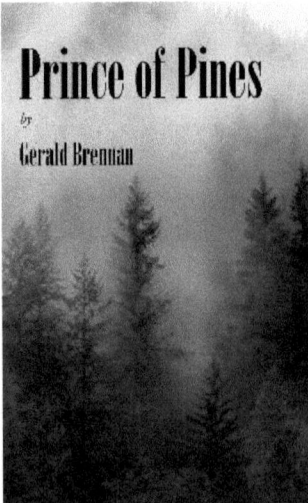

Pure unapologetic dystopian male-adventure, intelligent and well-crafted, with plenty of guns and good women.

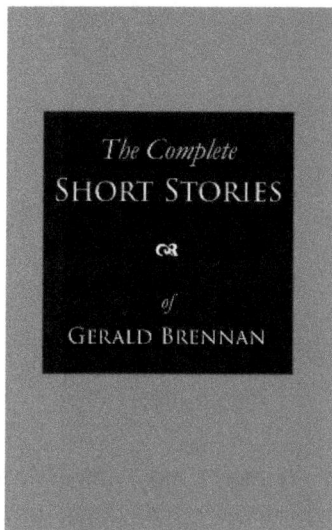

Contemporary tales in many different genres.

SONG OF BLOOD & ASHES

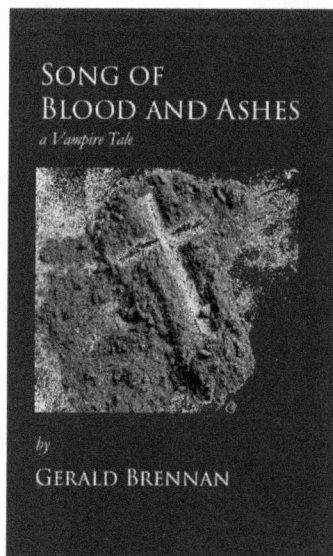

An ancient Vampire finally creates a protégé after centuries of searching. Blinded by her beauty and innocence, his choice was unwise. She loves a 'mortal' who does not reciprocate her affection. Her depraved appetites provoke a most horrifying catastrophe.

343

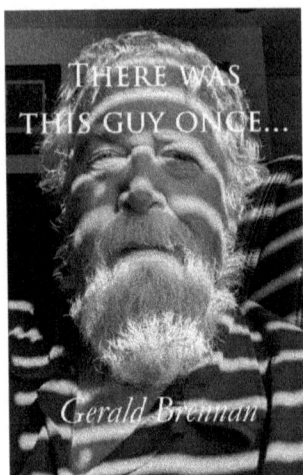

There is no plot but many characters. Not exactly autobiography, but a case could be made. This is a book about the people, influences, hopes, fears, and favorite things about my life as a composer, novelist, journalist, performing musician, and person.

VIEWS & REVIEWS

This book contains the original unedited versions of Gerald Brennan's previews, reviews, and interviews of the finest classical music soloists, ensembles, and orchestras in the world during what may well be looked back upon as the final flowering of Classical Music in the West.

www.ingramcontent.com/pod-product-compliance
Lightning Source LLC
Chambersburg PA
CBHW060039100426
42742CB00014B/2638